The Cycle of Coalition

How does coalition governance shape voters' perceptions of government parties and how does this, in turn, influence party behaviors? Analyzing cross-national surveys, election results, experiments, legislative amendments, media reports, and parliamentary speeches, Fortunato finds that coalition compromise can damage parties' reputations for competence as well as their policy brands in the eyes of voters. This incentivizes cabinet partners to take stands against one another throughout the legislative process in order to protect themselves from potential electoral losses. The Cycle of Coalition has broad implications for our understanding of electoral outcomes, partisan choices in campaigns, government formation, and the policy-making process, voters' behaviors at the ballot box, and the overall effectiveness of governance.

David Fortunato is Associate Professor in the School of Global Policy and Strategy, University of California, San Diego. His research has been published in the *American Political Science Review, American Journal of Political Science*, and *Journal of Politics*, among others.

The Cycle of Coalition

How Parties and Voters Interact under Coalition Governance

DAVID FORTUNATO

University of California, San Diego

CAMBRIDGE
UNIVERSITY PRESS

University Printing House, Cambridge CB2 8BS, United Kingdom

One Liberty Plaza, 20th Floor, New York, NY 10006, USA

477 Williamstown Road, Port Melbourne, VIC 3207, Australia

314–321, 3rd Floor, Plot 3, Splendor Forum, Jasola District Centre, New Delhi – 110025, India

79 Anson Road, #06–04/06, Singapore 079906

Cambridge University Press is part of the University of Cambridge.

It furthers the University's mission by disseminating knowledge in the pursuit of education, learning, and research at the highest international levels of excellence.

www.cambridge.org
Information on this title: www.cambridge.org/9781108834803
DOI: 10.1017/9781108877053

© David Fortunato 2021

First published 2021

A catalogue record for this publication is available from the British Library.

Library of Congress Cataloging-in-Publication Data
Names: Fortunato, David, 1981– author.
Title: The cycle of coalition : how parties and voters interact under coalition governance / David Fortunato.
Description: New York : Cambridge University Press, 2020. | Series: Political economy of institutions and decisions | Includes bibliographical references and index.
Identifiers: LCCN 2020031752 | ISBN 9781108834803 (hardback) | ISBN 9781108877053 (ebook)
Subjects: LCSH: Coalition governments – Great Britain – History – 20th century. | Coalition governments – Great Britain – History – 21st century. | Voting – Great Britain – History – 20th century. | Voting – Great Britain – History – 21st century. | Political parties – Great Britain – History – 20th century. | Political parties – Great Britain – History – 21st century. | Liberal Democrats (Great Britain) | Great Britain – Politics and government – History – 20th century. | Great Britain – Politics and government – History – 21st century.
Classification: LCC JN231 .F677 2020 | DDC 324.0941–dc23
LC record available at https://lccn.loc.gov/2020031752

ISBN 9781108834803 Hardback

Contents

Figures

Tables

Acknowledgments

About two years into graduate school at Rice University, I approached Lanny Martin, the director of graduate studies, about changing my major from American to comparative politics. "Of course," Lanny said, "you'll like comparative. The water's warm and the drinks are cold," and just then Lanny was interrupted by Mark Jones, who had stopped by to ask about something or another. After Mark apologized for interrupting, Lanny told him not to sweat it and that I was asking to change my major. "You're better off with us," Mark said, "the water's warm."

Shortly thereafter, Lanny invited me to write a paper with him that we would present at the European Consortium of Political Research in Potsdam (he actually told me it was Berlin – I cannot blame him). The plan was to travel to the conference, present the paper, then continue on to Prague to begin some archival work for his CAREER grant project, on which I was apparently now employed. This was a very good time to be me. The conference was great. I fumbled about with the display equipment before my presentation (still my favorite part of conferences), met people whose work I admired, who were exceptionally nice to me, and also met other graduate students with similar interests who still tolerate me.

Randy Stevenson joined Lanny and me on the trip. The train ride was several hours, and Randy and I spent most of it chatting while Lanny worked. This was the first time I really interacted with Randy outside of the classroom and we hit it off. At some point, we got to chatting about the upcoming parliamentary elections in Germany and had a pleasant disagreement about what would happen and why. That pleasant disagreement became a manuscript that Randy and I wrote together and also planted the seeds of my dissertation project – a series of papers on how coalition governance shapes the way voters relate to parties and how parties respond in turn. This book grew out of that dissertation and is, therefore, a product of limitless generosity and patience on the part of others, particularly Lanny and Randy, who supervised the project, but there are several more.

Georg Vanberg served as a de facto committee member, reading just about everything I wrote and giving me fantastic feedback. As a bonus, that feedback has typically been delivered over beers and that can really soften the blow of a very smart person pointing out how, in detail, you have made an avoidable error, and also ratchet up the effect of a very smart person pointing out that you may have done something correctly.

Royce Carroll and Rick Wilson were my first supervisors in graduate school and their fingerprints are all over my work. Not only were they directly helpful and influential, but they are also the model of good disciplinary citizenship. Monika Nalepa was my first comparative politics instructor in graduate school, saved me from a lifetime of area studies, and has been generous with her time ever since. Songying Fang and Keith Hamm read everything I ever asked them to read, even after I had finished school, and always gave great feedback. Bob Stein is a goddamned riot. At this point, I cannot remember if we actually talked about this project, but his door was always open, he was endlessly supportive and good for at least twenty minutes of unmitigated hilarity – a boon to anybody needing to clear their head before getting back on their grind.

I spent my fourth year of graduate school at the University of Mannheim, working primarily with Thomas König and Oli Proksch. That's really where this project came together, and chats with them were extraordinarily helpful – they are brilliant scholars and good friends. The other friends who I made there gave me great advice as well over the years: Mariyana Angelova, Hanna Bäck, Pierre Boyer, Catherine de Vries, Marc Debus, Zoli Fazekas, Zac Greene, Thomas Gschwend, James Lo, Will Lowe, Sebi Popa, Jae-Jae Spoon, and Federico Vegetti among others.

This project has also benefitted quite a bit from conference participants and discussants, in particular, Bing Powell, who discussed a very early version of the manuscript that would become the fourth and fifth chapters of this book and gave me fantastic advice. Jim Adams, Ray Duch, Lawrence Ezrow, and Zeynep Somer-Topcu have also seen those papers at various stages and provided thoughtful feedback. Thomas Meyer and Heike Klüver gave me excellent advice several times on what would become the sixth chapter of this book, but especially at the Manifesto User Conference (which is a fantastic meeting) in 2015. Indridi Indridason, Chris Kam, and Diana O'Brien also gave that manuscript the scorching it deserved at a meeting of the Southern California Comparative Political Institutions group (another fantastic conference series), and Henry Kim tore it up for me at the 2010 APSA meeting. Fun aside: my mother took the train down to DC from New Haven to see me present at that conference. I gave a bad presentation, Henry rightfully shredded the paper, and an audience member rightfully re-shredded the paper on entirely new grounds. My mother was there for the whole bloody affair. I put a lot more effort into my presentations now.

Importantly, I have benefitted from having very smart and very generous colleagues who not only gave me feedback on my work but also protected me as long as possible from non-research obligations that could prevent me from being productive. The entire political science faculty at the University of California Merced was amazing to me: Courtenay Conrad, Tom Hansford, Haifeng Huang, Steve Nicholson, Emily Ritter, Alex Theodoridis, and particularly Matt Hibbing, who was my principal partner in crime and a great friend and collaborator, Nate Monroe, who was my mentor as well as friend and collaborator, and Jessica Trounstine (for me, that one friend who just kind of understands everything), who explained how academic books work and provided endless support and great conversation.

Likewise, my colleagues at Texas A&M University were extraordinarily supportive and helpful. In particular, Bill Clark, Paul Kellstedt, and Guy Whitten were my mentors and gave me everything I needed to be productive. Additionally, Andrea Aldrich, Timm Betz, Zè Cheibub, Scott Cook, Florian Hollenbach, Christine Lipsmeyer, Diana O'Brien (again!), Alex Pacek, Brittany Perry, Amy Pond, Carlisle Rainey, Misha Taylor-Robinson, and Ian Turner were fantastic resources for things academic and otherwise.

I received a lot of help gathering some of the data analyzed here, particularly the data on legislation and speeches. For this research assistance, I am very grateful to Niels Appeldorn, Jacob Gutierrez, Andrea Junqueira, Ericka Ledesma, Thiago Moreira, Christy Phillips, and especially Tessa Provins who has set painfully high expectations for all future PhD students. I am also grateful to Simon Weschle for sharing data and SFB

884 "The Political Economy of Reforms," the Hellman Fellowship, and the Ray A Rothrock '77 Fellowship for funding support.

Finally, Ben Bishin really introduced me to the "science" part of political science while I was an undergraduate at Miami. A few years later, he was instrumental in getting me into graduate school, supported me all the way through, and continues even now.

A Lesson Learned Too Late

The ailing Liberal Democrats limped into their 2011 annual conference needing to discuss a new strategy. In the year and a half since joining the Conservatives in the United Kingdom's first formal coalition government since World War II their popularity had been halved and it was time for a change.

> On becoming deputy prime minister last year, Nick Clegg implored the Lib Dems to "own" everything the coalition did. Only then would the party get any credit if the government, led by David Cameron, the Tory prime minister, proved successful. That strategy has in recent months given way to one of conspicuous "differentiation." Some of this is a calculated wooing of left-leaning voters who deserted the Lib Dems in protest at their collaboration with the Tories.
>
> (Economist 2011b, 67)

Clegg and the Liberal Democrats had spent the previous year learning what many of their continental counterparts had long known: cooperation with one's coalition partners is vital to the cabinet's ability to govern effectively, but this cooperation may often come at the cost of electoral capital. Votes are won on the promise of pursuing a core set of policies, not on the promise of cooperation with some (often as yet unnamed) partners in coalition. Voters choose parties, at least in part, with the understanding that they will adhere to their campaign promises. And, should those parties appear to shirk their charge – to trade away or otherwise undermine their stated policy goals in a series of bargains or logrolls with their coalition partners – their supporters will likely interpret these actions as evidence that the party had misrepresented its goals, that its goals have evolved, or, more immediately worrisome, as evidence of manifest incompetence (Bawn and Somer-Topcu 2012; Fortunato 2019a).

This was, of course, the fate of the Liberal Democrats. Clegg's party experienced a precipitous decline in popularity following the formation of the United Kingdom's first coalition government in over fifty years. Liberal Democrats' support in vote intention polls fell from 20 percent in May 2010 when the government formed, to just 7 percent by the following January (Wells 2018).[1] Popular narrative attributed these painful early losses to the Liberal Democrats' willingness to compromise on key issues they had clearly staked out in their electoral platform in order to secure a referendum on electoral system reform – the institution of the so-called "alternative vote" (or, ranked-choice ballot, instant-runoff ballot, etc.), which, it was widely believed, would open up the United Kingdom's electoral system and lead to pronounced, durable gains for smaller parties like the Liberal Democrats. The referendum on the alternative vote was held in May 2011 and failed by a two-to-one margin, which made the effect of this public tradeoff – the tanking of Liberal Democrats' popularity – all the more biting. Indeed, *The Economist* noted that "[the Liberal Democrats] have a wholly new problem now. Lots of voters hate them, and think they have sold out for a perch in a ministerial Jaguar" (2011a, 70).

After their popularity bottomed out, Clegg and the Liberal Democrats chose to embark upon a campaign of differentiation from their partners in government. As we see later in the book, however, despite the Liberal Democrats' resolution to differentiate from the Conservatives, they failed to avail themselves of the central fora for differentiation and whatever actions that they may have ultimately taken, if they did, indeed, take any systematic actions at all, were largely ineffective.

There were some instructive attempts, however. In January 2011, the Conservative Minister of Health, Andrew Lansley, introduced the *Health and Social Care Bill*, a policy proposal that would decentralize the distribution of authority within the United Kingdom's National Health Service (NHS), placing ultimate control of health-care administration into the hands of "clinical commissioning groups" – local organizations that would be delegated immense authority in the provision of health

---

[1] Portions of this paragraph paraphrase concluding remarks from an earlier article (Fortunato 2019a).

care under the proposal. The media described the bill as sufficiently liberal as to "let Andrew Lansley wash his hands of health service" (Boseley 2011, Main 7). That is, the bill would, in effect, take accountability for the NHS out of the cabinet's hands and sever the direct, electoral connection between voters and the administration of their health care. The bill was unpopular with voters *and* with the majority of Liberal Democratic members of parliament.[2] Thus, after the bill's submission, the Liberal Democrats embarked on an aggressive ten-month campaign of legislative scrutiny – twelve committee markups in the House of Commons and fifteen in the House of Lords – culminating in a series of amendments that reinstated ultimate accountability for the NHS to the cabinet. Although many of the bill's less popular provisions survived, the spectacle made an impact.

In reference to this campaign of scrutiny, Clegg (2011) said that "[i]n a coalition, we have two kinds of power: The power to hold our coalition partners back and the power to move the government forwards." And Clegg was correct. Possessing the votes required by the Tories to form a legislative majority, he ultimately had the power to constrain the Conservatives in all of their pursuits. Indeed, he could have simply made an open demand that Lansley and the Health Ministry walk back their proposal or he would withdraw the Liberal Democrats' support of the government – the kind of demand that theoretical models of policy bargaining often argue are routinely made (or, at least, the kind of demand that often lurks in shadow of policy negotiations, often influencing outcomes even if not often made explicit). But, of course, he did not make this demand.

The Liberal Democrats had to do *something*, however. The policy risk to letting the bill progress was profound, but even more serious was the risk to the reputation of the Liberal Democrats. If they had allowed the bill to proceed through parliament unmolested, then voters could reasonably infer that (a) the Liberal Democrats supported the proposal in its original form, or (b) that Liberal Democrats were simply too weak to make any changes to the legislation. In other words, if Clegg allowed the legislation to breeze through markup phase and be quickly passed into law, he would damage his party's policy brand, its reputation for strength and competence, or both. Thus, while the Liberal Democrats did not demand retraction, they would still openly challenge their coalition

---

[2] Although the Liberal Democrats formally supported decentralization of the NHS, this proposal was too extreme for their tastes.

partner's legislative proposal, making a show of marking it up in the legislature, but without immediately imperiling the government's existence. It was a show – an attempt to save face, and one that would ultimately leave the majority of the legislation *intact*, even if it delayed the proposal's passage for over a year.

This performance is an artifact of the "dilemma of coalition governance" (Martin and Vanberg 2011, 3–4). Parties in coalition must cooperate in order to govern effectively, and yet they are simultaneously locked in zero-sum competition to expand their vote share and maintain the support of their base. Cabinet participation is thus defined by the continual ebb and flow of cooperation and conflict. Partners in coalition must stay close enough to move forward with their agenda but still maintain sufficient distance to protect the distinctiveness of their brand; safeguard the integrity of their stances; convince their supporters that they have not been forgotten. As such, the defining characteristic of multi-party governance is the struggle of its participants to balance competing incentives: how can they extract the maximum benefit from their term in office without alienating their core supporters (Strøm 1990a)? How can the Liberal Democrats show their electorate that their vision for the country differs from the Conservatives' without destroying the government in the process?

Of course, Clegg and the Liberal Democrats were not able to solve this puzzle. After their popularity crashed in January 2011, it stayed a shambles, hovering in the high single digits until their drubbing in the 2015 election. As we will see later in the book, though Clegg resolved to differentiate from the Tories, the resolution came too late and, with the occasional exception like the one discussed earlier, real, *systematic* changes in the Liberal Democrats' messaging and behavior never really arrived.

Parties must be proactive and agile in protecting their brand. Indeed, in countries with more coalition experience, party leaders even try to temper their supporters' expectations in advance of actually forming a government. For example, at the onset of coalition bargaining in the days following the 2012 Dutch parliamentary elections, *The Economist* reported:

Both [Liberal leader] Mr Rutte and Diederik Samsom, Labour's new leader, have tried to prepare voters for compromise, pointing out that in a coalition country such as the Netherlands it is hard for parties to stick to all their election promises. (2012, 34)

Rutte and Samson already knew what Clegg learned only after it was too late: campaign platforms are promises made and voters have the expectation that promises made will be promises kept. But coalition governance, by its very nature, makes it extraordinarily difficult for parties to deliver on their platforms in whole, difficult for parties to deliver on their platforms in part, and even difficult for parties to convince their supporters that they are making their best effort. The tension that coalition creates between the need to please voters and the simple realities of multiparty governance that obscure the relationship between individual party preferences, or brands, and jointly delivered outcomes is the focus of the book. Over the next several chapters, we will learn how the trappings of coalition conspire to erode the support of its participants and how cabinet parties manufacture intracoalitional conflict in order to protect their brand. We will learn how voters perceive the process of multiparty policy making, how these perceptions influence their voting behavior, and how that behavior (or, expectations for that behavior) in turn informs the choices that parties make in the legislature.

This is the cycle of coalition. Parties act, voters react, and parties adapt. That is, the rules and norms of coalition governance create an environment in which compromise and cooperation are simply unavoidable political realities. And, even if we want to believe that perfectly informed, rational voters *should* accept that fact and applaud parties for moving policy from the status quo closer to their ideal point, this is not in keeping with reality. We will find that voters' natural reaction to compromise is disappointment and dissatisfaction. In part, this is because they can nearly always envision a counterfactual in which they are unequivocal policy winners, which is related to our natural instinct to be optimistic, as well as our natural, more competitive instinct to deprive the "other team" of victory. As a result, voters commonly associate compromise with incompetence and untrustworthiness and punish it at the polls. More troublingly, in the long term, compromise can ultimately muddy parties' carefully constructed policy brands, making it unclear to voters what it is, precisely, that parties stand for, imposing far longer-lasting penalties – just as Cox and McCubbins (2005) argue, a party's brand is its most valuable asset and maintaining the integrity of the brand is the chief motivating factor of Congressional parties when enforcing discipline and managing the legislative agenda. Just as Congressional parties must manage *internal* threats to brand consistency, so, too, must parliamentary parties engaged in coalition governance manage external threats to brand consistency.

Unfortunately for its member parties, the very formation of a coalition cabinet is an overt commitment to broad and wide-ranging policy compromise. Participants are publicly declaring their intention to negotiate and cooperate throughout the legislative period, often publishing the terms of their agreement for all to see. Each policy proposal is, therefore, a product of (often protracted) internal negotiation between coalition partners, and the process of translating these proposals into outcomes is defined by institutionalized executive and legislative constraints designed specifically to prevent one party from getting the policy it wants at the expense of its partners (Martin and Vanberg 2011).

And as difficult as the processes of coalition may already seem to make it for parties to signal their preferences or demonstrate to their supporters that they are fighting the good fight, it gets worse. Not only are party brands muddied by the processes of cabinet formation, policy negotiation, and institutionally enforced compromise, but parties are also constrained by collective cabinet responsibility from breaking ranks with their partners to communicate to their supporters. This means that once a policy has been proposed, all members of the coalition must vote for it and publicly support it. Members who violate collective responsibility risk loss of portfolio or even the dissolution of the government.

What, then, are parties to do? With few exceptions, political economic research has been relatively silent on this point.[3] Here, we will learn how parties are able to communicate with their supporters during the legislative review phase of the policy-making process – the period of time following the initial submission of a cabinet proposal to the legislature, but before it receives its final vote. In this part of the process, draft bills are openly debated, proposing ministers are questioned, and amendments may be considered. Rigorous and even contentious debate and scrutiny are tolerated without violation of collective responsibility, meaning that cabinet participants are at last free to needle and antagonize their partners in coalition, showing their supporters that they are steadfast in their commitment to represent their interests and fight for their core policy positions.

---

[3] Exceptions include Martin and Vanberg (2008) and Sagarzazu and Klüver (2017).

Of course, most voters do not observe this process directly without prompting from the news media pointing them toward a particularly interesting or scandalous outburst – only the most die-hard political junkies subject themselves to watching parliamentary debates or committee proceedings. Rather, antagonistic debates and rigorous legislative scrutiny help to reshape the broader media narrative on cabinet partners' interactions. The more contentious their interactions in legislative review, the more media will relay this contentiousness to voters. Voters, in turn, assimilate this information into their perceptions of cabinet parties as compromisers or dissenters and update their impressions of the parties' ability or propensity to stand firm for their supporters.[4] The more accommodating the parties are of one another, the more voters will update their perceptions of the parties as compromisers, and perhaps even conclude that they are selling out their supporters for a "ministerial Jaguar." The more confrontational the parties, the more voters will update their perceptions of the parties as dogged advocates of their supporters' will. Parties act. Voters react. Parties adapt. Voters update. And so on and so forth until election when the cycle begins anew.

Before delving into the specifics of the theoretical argument or the observable implications of that argument for the behavior of voters and parties, it is worth discussing how it is that our understanding of coalition governance has grown and evolved to this point and what the promise of studying the dynamics of party–voter interactions throughout the life of coalition governments may be. That is, while I believe we can agree that it is important to learn how voters understand and react to multi-party policy making and how these reactions feed back into cabinet party choices and behaviors, if for no other reason than the fact that the majority of the world's democracies are routinely governed by coalition cabinets, it is also worth considering what this pursuit may contribute to other areas of political economic research and how the arguments made here are informed by, and potentially recontextualize, previous contributions.

---

[4] This general framework is supported by recent research by Adams, Weschle, and Wlezien (2020) who show that media accounts of conflict and cooperation between political parties are highly correlated to changes in voters' perceptions of those parties' policy stances. In Chapter 8 we will assess the connection between media narrative and party actions in the legislative review phase more directly. To preview, the evidence suggests that media messaging is, indeed, conditioned by these actions.

2

Motivation and Promise

> Had gravity been a trifle stronger, the universe itself might have collapsed like a badly erected tent... Had it been weaker, however, nothing would have coalesced.
>
> Bill Bryson (2003, 15)

Gravity is an apt metaphor for the central argument of this book. Each coalition cabinet must regulate its own gravity or its own cohesiveness. The centripetal force of a multiparty government must be strong enough that its members are able to see eye-to-eye on a broad array of issues such that they may govern effectively, efficiently, and push the country toward their shared vision of its future. And yet, its centrifugal force must be strong enough that its members are able to convince their supporters that they have not been abandoned – that each member party continues to scratch and claw for its supporters; continues to fight the good fight. Without enough gravity, a coalition government may dissolve. With too much gravity, a coalition government may collapse under its own weight – degrading the perceived competence of member parties or obscuring their policy brands such that their short- and long-term electoral prospects are endangered.

This tightrope that coalition members have to walk is not sui generis in representative democracy, rather, merely another example of the collective action problem. How can we maintain discipline, or coordinated behaviors, in the face of actors with dissimilar interests and incentives? This is the question that drives Kam's (2009) study of party discipline in Westminster parliaments, Cox and McCubbins's (2005) study of agenda control in the US House, and is at the root of a great many applied problems of social choice. Further more, we know that, in maintaining legislative organization, discipline can be costly for the disciplined (Canes-Wrone, Brady, and Cogan 2002; Carson et al. 2010) and that this creates powerful incentives for differentiation (Slapin et al. 2018; Fortunato 2019b), which are likely to be rewarded by the electorate (Wagner, Vivyan, and Glinitzer 2019). Coordination, whether it is compromise across parties, or compromise within parties, is often critical to achieving policy goals, but also often at odds with the electoral incentives of individual actors.

These are the competing incentives that make multiparty governance fascinating. The simple, unavoidable need for parties to compromise and cooperate faced off against their supporters' ceaseless demand for dissent and disagreement. This is what animates the study of coalition. Indeed, the canonical model of cabinet formation is motivated by this simple question: how can coalition parties possibly come to trust one another when the demands of their individual bases of support are so great? How can parties with differing supporters, demanding distinct policies, ever commit to co-governance? Ironically, the case can be made that the answer Laver and Shepsle (1990, 1996) provided to this question molded a path of inquiry that would lead us away from the dynamic struggles of gravitational maintenance and into a world in which these cross-pressures are satisfied (or nearly satisfied) at the formation of the cabinet.

Subsequently dubbed the "ministerial dominance" or "ministerial autonomy" model of coalition formation and policymaking, Laver and Shepsle (1990, 1996) argue that the only way parties can consent to co-governance[1] in the face of their incentives to demand their most preferred policy at all times is effectively to recognize that demand openly and accede to it. That is, the fundamental problem Laver and Shepsle are intent upon solving is the inherent lack of credibility of commitments to policy compromise.[2] Policy- and office-seeking parties' incentives to demand their most preferred outcome are so strong that the authors believe any commitment to deviate from that demand is incredible and

---

[1] And also the only way that the parliament consenting (or not) to the formation of a government can trust its stated policy objectives.

[2] Though voters are never explicitly mentioned in the original 1990 article, Laver and Shepsle do later clarify in their 1996 book that policy-seeking and vote-seeking are intrinsically linked and that vote-seeking parties have substantial long-term interest in maintaining a stable policy brand. Of course, their focus is not on the interaction between voters and parties, as ours is here, so their engagement with the issue is reasonably limited.

should therefore be rejected. The solution, then, is to embrace this incentive and, rather than forge commitment to a grand compromise over all policy areas, forge a *division* of all policy areas wherein each minister with portfolio can act as a dictator. Or, in their words:

> ... a proposal that promises to enact the preferred policy position of the person (party) nominated for each relevant portfolio is credible in the sense that it depends only on giving ministers the power to do what they expressly want to do. Any proposal promising that a minister with wide-ranging power over the relevant policy jurisdiction will act against expressed preferences is less credible (1990, 874).

This rather brilliant innovation set the agenda for coalition research for decades and gave us an elegantly modeled and argued permission structure to effectively assume away the business of multiparty governance from the study of coalition governments. That is, the field was so convinced by Laver and Shepsle's arguments over how coalitions are *formed*, that we overwhelmingly applied that same rationale to how coalitions *govern*. In other words, if we concede that ministers are dictators within their jurisdiction, then we can predict with substantial accuracy the policy output of any coalition cabinet. All we need is an accounting of the parties (or perhaps individuals) running each department. Therefore, the most pressing questions to answer should be: which governments (or allocations of ministerial portfolios) are negotiated and how long will they survive? Answering the first question will allow us to understand and forecast the *direction* of policy change and answering the second will allow us to understand and forecast the *depth* of policy change. And so the field set upon answering these questions.

Over the following years a wellspring of research on the making and breaking of governments was opened, attracting some of the sharpest minds in political economy and producing some of the most rigorous theoretical arguments and innovative empirical tests. Austen-Smith and Banks (1990) showed us that the stability of any government is defined by how preferred its portfolio allocation is to available alternatives. Complimentary research by Strøm (1990b) taught us the logic of minority governance by uncovering the structures (and strategic incentives) that lead opposition parties to tolerate a cabinet they have the power to topple, while Baron (1991) modeled the impact of formation dynamics on relative policy influence, and Strøm, Budge, and Laver (1994) set the groundwork for understanding the critical impact of diverse institutional contexts.[3] Importantly, all of this work was "standing on the shoulders of giants," so to speak, building on previous contributions by De Swaan (1973), Schofield and Laver (1985), Luebbert (1986), and many others, but owing in particular to pathbreaking work by Riker (1962) and Shepsle (1979).

These theoretical innovations went hand in glove with attempts to test their predictions empirically, notably led by Franklin and Mackie (1984) and Warwick (1996). These steady advances would ultimately result in the introduction of McFadden's (1973) conditional choice model to political science by Martin and Stevenson (2001), which would become the workhorse of the field. Relatedly, theoretical and empirical advancements on the question of portfolio allocation broadened our understanding of differential policy salience (Warwick and Druckman 2001), formateur advantages (Ansolabehere et al. 2005), and pre-electoral pacts (Carroll and Cox 2007).

Concurrent with this growth in our collective understanding of government formation, political economists were hard at work on the theoretical and empirical determinants of government longevity. Through the 1990s, this literature was resolving a decades long disagreement between rival camps advocating competing approaches to the question – the so-called attributes and events debate. The attributes camp saw coalition durability as primarily a function of a government's characteristics at the time of formation (e.g., Warwick 1979). The events camp, on the other hand, saw coalition durability as primarily a function of shocks to the political economic environment in which coalitions govern (e.g., Browne, Frendreis, and Gleiber 1984). The resolution to this debate was the synthesis of the two approaches into a unified model wherein the characteristics of the coalition make it more or less able to survive stochastic shocks to its environment, *and* said shocks may also reshape the characteristics of the cabinet and its alternatives and therefore the cabinet's appeal vis-à-vis replacement alternatives. Seminal theoretical modeling by Baron (1998), Laver and Shepsle (1998), and Lupia and Strøm (1995) is notable in settling this debate.

Just as in research on coalition formation, theoretical advances in durability research were accompanied by empirical advances. Some have even argued that, on the question of coalition durability, the empiricists ran out ahead of theorists (e.g., Fortunato and Loftis 2018). Indeed,

---

[3] It should be noted that many of the easily testable implications of the theoretical constraints discussed by Strøm, Budge, and Laver (1994) have yet to be tested.

King et al. (1990) presented an empirical model unifying the events and attributes perspectives a few years before Lupia and Strøm (1995) began the work or harmonizing them theoretically. King et al.'s innovation was followed by Diermeier and Stevenson (1999, 2000), who introduced a competing risks approach to the empirical study, noting that cabinets may dissolve into new elections or simply be replaced and that these two types of risk must be properly modeled, both theoretically *and* empirically, in order to be understood.

The final mountain to climb, empirically, would be rectifying the selection problem of durability analysis. In short, governments are formed based on expectations for their longevity, and failure to account for these expectations may induce bias into our estimates and understanding of the correlates of stability. Like the other empirical challenges, these selection effects had also been noted in the theoretical research (e.g., De Swaan 1973; Laver and Shepsle 1996). Building on notable work by Merlo (1997) and Diermeier, Eraslan and Merlo (2003), Chiba, Martin, and Stevenson (2015) proposed a joint modeling approach to the selection problem, in which distributions describing formation and duration are joined by a copula function so that they may be estimated simultaneously with overlapping, distinct, or mixed vectors of predictors.

There are, of course, scores of articles and books on the birth and death of governments that are not mentioned here. The purpose of this chapter, however, is not recounting what we know about coalition, but discussing what we do *not* know and that is how multiparty governments function and interact with voters *between* formation and dissolution – how they monitor, maintain, or augment their internal gravity. This pursuit is primarily a twenty-first century phenomenon. Indeed, even when scholars did consider the actual business of making policy, they tended to do so under the presumption of ministerial autonomy, which tended to obscure focus away from intracoalitional dynamics. For example, scholars like Huber (1996) and Heller (2001) continued to run down the implications of the ministerial dominance model through the process of proposing and ultimately voting on legislation to discover how institutional parameters, aside from positive and negative agenda control and informational asymmetries stemming from the cabinet's control of the bureaucracy, contribute to the government's dominance of the policy-making process. These studies, and their counterparts, tended to couch the central struggle as one between the government and the parliament, and found that government may impose its will upon the chamber via procedural force or last-mover advantages, and so on.

Thies (2001), however, proposes an alternative angle to multi-party governance, exploring how governments can *overcome* ministerial autonomy, rather than how ministerial autonomy may be enforced. He argues that junior ministers (alternatively called cabinet secretaries in some parliamentary contexts) may be organized to counterbalance poten-tially "hostile" ministers – ministers who are ideologically extreme or have preferences that are quite dissimilar from their partners in coalition – or, to spy and report back to the cabinet on the activities of poten-tially hostile ministers such that they may be constrained by the cabinet as a whole. Subsequent research suggests that junior ministers are widely deployed in several European countries for these purposes (Lipsmeyer and Pierce 2011).

Thies's contribution, along with contemporaneous research by Müller and Strøm (2000) on the use of contracting and intra-cabinet commit-tees for constraining hostile ministers on salient issues, is something of a turning point for the literature, one that would pave the way for the comprehensive work on coalition governance – that is, the actual busi-ness of governing – by Martin and Vanberg (2004, 2005, 2011). Martin and Vanberg, like Thies before them, see ministerial autonomy as the primary challenge to multiparty governance rather than its guiding prin-cipal. As we are here, Martin and Vanberg are motivated by the central tension of coalition that demands that, "while they make policy jointly, parties that participate in coalition are held to account separately. Each coalition party must compete for votes under its own label" (2011, 3). This research is integral to our understanding of multiparty governance on several fronts, but there are two contributions that are particularly salient for our purposes here.

First, Martin and Vanberg bring voters back into the discussion. They acknowledge the powerful electoral incentives that parties have to subvert coalition compromise and how these incentives should shape ministerial behavior. In sum, the importance of protecting party brands and appearing competent in policy bargaining provides ministers with strong incentive to propose their most preferred policy rather than the compromise hammered out in coalition negotiations. Because of this, proposing ministers cannot be trusted and institutional mechanisms must be organized to constrain them. In other words, electoral incentives drive policy-making choices and, therefore, partisan interactions within the governing coalition.

The second contribution lies in the solution to this problem. Mar-tin and Vanberg propose that the *legislature* is capable of solving this problem. This is a relatively new development to the subfield, which had a tendency to write off parliaments as "rubber stamps" to executive decision-making, *particularly* in the case of majority (relative to minority) governments. Of course, there is previous research on the salience of legislative institutions, particularly on the role of strong committees in empowering opposition parties to influence government policy (e.g., Strøm 1990b; Powell and Whitten 1993; Powell 2000), and Martin and Vanberg build on this scholarship to show that these same institutions may be leveraged to mitigate ministerial drift, to drag a policy proposal back to the coalition compromise through amendment procedures.

Let us briefly discuss how these innovations are integral to the development of this book. First, bringing voters back into the day-to-day grind of coalition policymaking. Voters provide the counterweight to political expedience. If not for the sanctioning presence of voters, parties would only be too willing to collaborate on the extraction of office benefits and may even compromise away their core principals to facilitate efficient cooperation. Of course, many readers will recall that voters often motivated coalition theory. Indeed, Laver and Schofield (1990, 5) choose to open their seminal book on coalition politics with a case study on the electoral penalty suffered by the Irish Labour Party in 1987 due to compromises made in coalition, concluding that, "Labour's plight shows quite clearly what happens when a gap opens up between the policies with which a party is associated when it is in government and those its voters want at election time." But Martin and Vanberg are among the first to give voters their due in motivating partisan behaviors in the *policy-making* (rather than government-making or -breaking) process.

Second, Martin and Vanberg remind us of the power of parliamentary institutions to shape the policy-making process and show us how the parliament provides the venue to balance incentives. That is, there is much to multiparty policymaking that is inherently unobservable. Coalition negotiations – both the initial formation of the government and subsequent policy negotiations over the life of the government – routinely take place behind closed doors. It is unclear how coalitions barter over what to do, how to do it, and when. We cannot observe the bargaining that takes place leading up to and throughout the drafting of a legislative proposal.[4]

---

[4] There some exceptions to this general rule, however. One of the reasons Becher and Christiansen's (2015) work on dissolution threats is so interesting and informative is because they study these threats in the case of Danish minority governments, where the

But we can observe the debate and scrutiny of that proposal in its parliamentary review and this observability is crucial because it allows parties to communicate with their supporters.

Martin and Vanberg set to exploring this rediscovered terrain in a 2008 article. Here, the authors discuss how parties can use parliamentary debate to " ... [reconcile] the tension between the need to compromise on policy with the need to maintain the party's public profile with respect to certain policy commitments" (502–503). They examine the length of parliamentary speeches and find that the more ideologically dissimilar a pair of coalition partners, the more they will speak on the floor of parliament to send differentiating signals to their supporters; to control their gravity. This is the heart of coalition politics, balancing the competing incentives of policy, office, and votes (Müller and Strøm 1999).

However, what we will learn over the remainder of this book is that these choices are not inherently constant-sum, that there are outcomes outside of the ternary unit simplex for parties that play their cards right. Parties can, in fact, participate in coalition without hollowing out their base of support if they are able to manage the internal gravity of their political union. In order to understand how this can happen, however, we must first correct the most enduring oversight in the literature: we do not understand how voters perceive and think about coalition policy-making. For all of our research on coalition formation and termination and all of the advancements we have made in recent years understanding how parties balance their private policy interests (or the interests of their supporters) with the demands of multiparty governance, we have paid only cursory attention to how voters view these processes.[5] But without a model of the coalitional voter, we cannot hope to properly model the behavior of coalition participants.

---

kind of bargaining that typically takes place behind closed doors becomes public as the prime minister negotiates with opposition parties to form majorities one bill at a time.

[5] Of course, there are many reasons for this. One reason is a lack of data stemming from administrative inertia in national election studies. Until the late 1990s, election study respondents in parliamentary systems defined by multiparty governance were not asked for their coalition preferences or expectations and, until the early 2010s, these respondents were never asked for their perceptions of the processes of multiparty governance. Another reason is that many scholars were content to abide by the prevailing wisdom, in both prospective and retrospective voting models, that voters were simply incapable of understanding coalition governance (e.g., Downs 1957; Powell and Whitten 1993). Subsequent research has shown that this is not the case and that voters are capable of understanding coalition formation and allocating responsibility for policy outcomes to coalition participants (Fortunato and Stevenson 2018; Fortunato et al. 2020).

Herein lies one of the key contributions of this book, the merging of institutionalist explanations of party strategy with the behavioral study of voters' perceptions and choices. We must first take the time to consider, both theoretically and empirically, how voters perceive and react to coalition policymaking, or, more specifically, coalition compromise. Once we learn how voters perceive and react to coalition compromise, we can improve our theoretical understanding of how parties will craft their vote-maximizing strategies for their policy-making behavior – how cabinet participants will (or should) comport themselves through the legislative period in order to improve their expected electoral performance.

Rather than assuming that voters are extravagantly informed and able to perfectly perceive all party behaviors and incentives – precisely the kind of voter that Downs (1957) dismissed as incredible – or assuming that voters are completely uninformed know-nothings, we will build a model of a reasonable and *realistic* voter that, while capable of observing policy-making behaviors, does so intermittently, imperfectly, and typically indirectly. In other words, we begin with the assumption that voters possess some information about the goings-on of the policy-making process, but that this information is likely derived from mediated reporting rather than direct observation – that voters get political information from news reports or possibly second hand from their more interested and better informed friends and family. This assumption will force us to consider what kinds of information the typical voter is exposed to and, therefore, the typical information that we may expect voters to possess.

The promise of this approach is three-fold. First, such a detailed consideration of the coalitional voter is, in and of itself, a step forward in understanding voter behavior and democratic accountability in the majority of the world's democracies. To this point, the study of voters in coalition systems has tended to forego discussion of coalition governance. There are very notable exceptions, to be certain – take Kedar (2005), Duch and Stevenson (2008), Duch, May, and Armstrong (2010), Hobolt, Tilley and Banducci (2013), and Spoon and Klüver (2017), for just a few examples – but, more often than not, research has been reticent to engage in how multiparty government formation and policy-making processes should reshape voters' typical information set (relative to single party governance contexts) and, more to the point at hand, how voters should respond to the compromise and collective policy-making that multiparty governance requires. We have only just begun to study the manner in which voters perceive coalition compromise

(Fortunato 2019a), or, how voters may attribute responsibility for policy outcomes made collectively by several parties (Fortunato et al. 2020). In the first pair of empirical chapters, we will take a much closer look at the reactions that voters have to coalition compromise in both a lab setting and "out in the wild."

Second, as mentioned, a better understanding of the coalitional voter is critical to a better understanding of cabinet party incentives and behaviors. This book argues that the electorate is the gravitational force pulling cabinet partners away from one another – that parties act with an eye toward shaping the manner in which voters *perceive* them in order to shape the degree to which voters *support* them. As such, we need to think through the type of political information voters are likely to receive and possess (as well as the source of this information), before we can think about how parties are likely to signal voters. That is, if voters are imperfectly informed, and the source of their imperfect information is likely to be media reports of government or party activity, how does this shape the strategies that parties adopt to control (or at least influence) the manner in which voters perceive them?

The answer that this book provides is that government parties make systematic, *sustained* efforts in open fora to shape the media narrative about their working relationship with their coalition partners. Simply standing up in front of a microphone and stating once, for the record, that a particular policy proposal is disagreeable, is unlikely to make a dent in the overarching media narrative. On the other hand, a protracted effort to mark up and amend that particular policy in conjunction with extended, antagonistic debate over its merits on the floor of parliament, may, over the long term, be successful in bending the media narrative arc in the desired direction. Taken together, these two points are the core contribution of this book.

Third, once we have moved forward our understanding of coalitional voters and cabinet parties' responses to them, we can attempt to retrofit previous scholarship to this new understanding. That is, if we gain a better understanding of voters and specifically how they perceive and respond to coalition compromise, then our substantive interpretation of previous (specifically empirical) findings regarding both voters and parties may be updated and recontextualized.

How may this work? A core theoretical argument in this book, which is empirically supported in a variety of tests, is that voters' distaste for coalition compromise erodes both their perceptions of the competence (or *valence*) of the compromising parties, as well as the trustworthiness or perceived credibility of their policy promises. If we find that perceptions of compromise are the norm, then the attendant degradation of parties' perceived competence may help explain the so-called cost of ruling – the empirical regularity that incumbent governments lose votes more often than the economy falters in coalition systems (Paldam and Skott 1995; Stevenson 2002). As we will discuss in detail later on in this book, the prevailing explanation for this regularity relies on the fairly heroic assumption that the median voter is a consistent policy loser – that governing coalitions never span the median and that government policy outputs are systematically unacceptable to the median voter. The theoretical argument and empirical evidence presented here imply a much more reasonable explanation for this regularity: coalition governance demands compromise and, try as they may, parties are often unable to mitigate the entirety of the damage inflicted upon their valence image and policy brand as a result of this compromise.

Similarly, if we accept that coalition compromise can degrade the extent to which voters are willing to accept or trust the policy promises made by governing parties (as is also argued rather convincingly, albeit somewhat differently, by Bawn and Somer-Topcu 2012), then we can revisit past research on the credibility or impact of party platforms in parliamentary democracies with fresh eyes. Given the potential constraints on the credibility of governing parties, we should expect that they have less incentive to alter their policy positions. This may be another reason why we observe more change in the advertised policy positions of electoral "losers," who tend to be in opposition, than electoral "winners," who tend to be in government (e.g., Somer-Topcu 2009; Schumacher et al. 2015; Van Der Velden, Schumacher, and Vis 2018) – it is possible that it is not merely that poor performance motivates opposition parties to change their platforms, but also that the constraints of office-holding reduces cabinet members' incentives for the risk-accepting behavior of changing their platforms.

Further more, once we take seriously the fact that voters cannot be perfectly attuned to each and every political statement or interaction, previous inconsistencies in the extent to which voters are estimated to respond to changes campaign platforms begin to make more sense. For example, Adams and Somer-Topcu's (2009) finding that voters' responses to platform changes are substantially lagged suggests that repetition and reiteration of the platform is necessary for it to break through. Subsequent research suggests that these signals may dissipate quickly (Somer-Topcu 2009), never permeate at all (Adams, Ezrow, and

Somer-Topcu 2011), or simply be overwhelmed by other, more visible behaviors (Adams, Ezrow, and Somer-Topcu 2014; Fortunato and Adams 2015; Fernandez-Vazquez and Somer-Topcu 2019). In other words, these seemingly disparate empirical findings may simply be an artifact of the information environment in which voters operate – they have limited time and energy to devote to politics, but do, in fact, receive and incorporate moderated signals, particularly when those signals regard salient events.

This type of retrofitting of previous empirical findings is an important part of the scientific endeavor because it helps to better understand what it is, precisely, that we are learning. Does the new finding suggest that previous conclusions were potentially misinterpreted or underinterpreted? Does the new finding offer additional support for previous conclusions or perhaps add nuance to them? Of course, it is equally important to ask what the new finding suggests about potential future research. In the concluding chapter, we will spend a fair amount of energy running down the implications of the book's theoretical arguments and empirical evidence for recontextualizing past research as well as suggesting new research. While the former is to some degree necessary for telling a complete story, the latter is a concerted effort to move the literature forward and hopefully provide a starting point for scholars in search of an agenda.

3

Parties and Voters under Coalition Governance

The overarching argument of this book is simple. Voters do not care for compromise and cooperation between coalition partners in the policy-making process and they are willing to punish parties for these behaviors. This threat of punishment drives cabinet partners toward conflict with one another in an attempt to manage their internal gravity and mitigate potential electoral losses. The specific reasons why voters do not care for compromise and how perceptions of compromise can trigger both short- and long-term electoral costs for cabinet parties will be made clear as the book progresses. We will also discuss in more detail how parties can act to influence the manner in which they are perceived by the electorate. For now, let us be clear about the core assumptions of the argument.

First, it is assumed that voters are attentive to policy-making processes and outcomes and that the information they glean about these processes and outcomes shape the manner in which they perceive parties. We are not assuming that voters are *perfectly* informed, however. Far from it. We are simply assuming that some information regarding what policies the governing coalition has produced and how it has made those policy choices filters through to voters.

Second, we assume that voters use this information to update their perceptions of the policy positions and general competence of the parties involved and that these perceptions are factored into voters' choices at the ballot box. That is, voters' views of cabinet parties on at least these two dimensions are malleable and subject to change, given the behaviors of these parties while in government. As such, the choices that parties make in the policy-making process have electoral consequences, for better or worse.

Third, we assume that parties may factor voters' perceptions (or their expectations for voters' perceptions) into their choices – to act with an eye toward the electorate, attempting to control the manner in which voters perceive them and the policy-making process. As these perceptions influence evaluations of policy stands, competence, and credibility, parties that are able to influence these perceptions may also be able to influence their electoral fortunes. While the specifics of these assumptions may be new to some readers, their general shape is old hat and uncontroversial – they could just as easily be so stated: (1) voters are attentive to party choices; (2) voters factor party actions into their vote choices; (3) parties act to please voters. Together, these assumptions imply attentiveness, accountability, and responsiveness.

What will set the argument apart from extant research is not the assumptions undergirding it, but the focus on multiparty policymaking throughout the legislative period. That is, we will focus, specifically, on the manner in which voters perceive the process of two or more parties coming to policy agreements, and how the parties, then, respond to these voters' perceptions in "real time," rather than the typical approach which only allows for voter–party interactions at electoral intervals. In other words, while the overwhelming majority of previous research has focused on how voters respond to collective coalition policy outputs – i.e., estimating how changes in economic productivity or unemployment affect the choice to support the incumbent cabinet or chief executive – this book will focus on how voters respond to individual coalition partner contributions to policy processes and outputs – i.e., how ably a particular partner has asserted itself in policy negotiation, or, how well a partner has protected the integrity of its policy brand. And, while extant research has nearly always focused on party reactions *between* legislative periods – typically asking whether parties adjust their electoral strategies to changes in voters' preferences – we will study party reactions *throughout* legislative periods.

Further more, the nature of these interactions will be defined by the institutional constraints that coalition governance places on party behaviors. There are two particularly salient constraints. First, no one party may act as a dictator, making compromise inevitable, whether it is issue-by-issue compromise, as theorized by Martin and Vanberg (2011) or whether it is a compromise resulting from the aggregation of individual policies in which alternating parties act (more or less) autonomously, as theorized by Laver and Shepsle (1996). That is, while it is certainly possible that one party may get exactly what it wants at some time, the nature of multiparty governance precludes any one party from getting exactly what it wants *all* of the time.

Second, coalition parties are bound by collective responsibility, a series of rules prohibiting cabinet partners from openly discussing closed-door policy negotiations or speaking ill of the government's policy choices after proposals have been passed into law. These rules constrain the types of differentiating behaviors in which government parties may engage in order to protect their brand to particular windows of the policy-making process – specifically, the time following a draft bill's proposal, but before its final passage vote, when it may be debated, scrutinized, and amended.

This overarching theoretical argument, in its most general form, is summarized in Figure 3.1. Parties form coalition cabinets, negotiate policy proposals,[1] and then shepherd those policies through the review and markup period before voting on the legislation and finally implementing it. The manner in which parties comport themselves through these processes and the content of the policy outcomes that the processes ultimately yield shape the manner in which voters perceive the policy preferences and the competence of the parties involved. This is process **A** in Figure 3.1.

Voters' perceptions of the policy brands or competence of cabinet parties then feed back into the policy-making process, conditioning the manner in which parties behave. If voters are perceiving the parties as

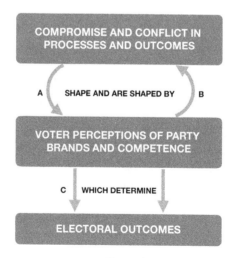

FIGURE 3.1 General argument

[1] Or, negotiate the distribution of agenda rights within and across policy jurisdictions.

too compromising, inferring that they are not fighting the good fight for their supporters, then the parties may have incentives to quarrel with one another in order to fight that perception. If compromised policy outcomes are leading voters to update their perceptions of the policy brands of the parties, inferring that the partners in cabinet are much more similar in their preferences than the parties would like, then the parties may have incentives to take positions against one another's policy proposals in order to protect the distinctiveness of their policy brand. This is process **B** in Figure 3.1.

Of course, cabinet parties are so strongly motivated to take these actions because the manner in which they are perceived by the electorate will ultimately determine their electoral fates, as given by process **C**.

With the general framework in place, we can begin to discuss in more detail why it is that voters dislike compromise, what it is that parties can do to inoculate themselves from being punished for compromise, and what happens when parties fail or succeed. We will also discuss characteristics of voters that may reshape their tendency to encounter information on compromise and conflict in the policy-making process or their tendency to punish or reward parties for these behaviors. Likewise, we will also consider how differing institutional constructs that condition the formation of coalition cabinets, alter the capacity of coalition partners to monitor and police one another, or shape the degree to which voters are able to observe various aspects of the policy-making process which may affect the specific shape of interactions between coalition partners and between parties and voters. Importantly, this discussion is aimed at clarifying, contextualizing, and extending the core theoretical argument, not setting the stage for the empirical tests to come later in the book. Indeed, testing many of the observable implications of this discussion is beyond the scope of this project, where case selection is geared toward holding constant many of the parameters we will discuss to ease data requirements and simplify analysis.

WHY VOTERS DISLIKE COMPROMISE

There are two central risks to coalition compromise for governing parties. The first is that voters may observe the process of compromise or the outcome of that process and perceive that their preferred party has been taken advantage of or failed to put up enough of a fight. Here, each policy negotiation has potential to create winners and losers, but in general these negotiations are more likely to result in voters being disappointed, rather than satisfied, with the outcome. Why is this? There are three reasons: optimism bias, informational asymmetry, and, of course, accurately perceived incompetence.

Humans have a natural tendency toward optimism that leads us to systematically underestimate the probability of unwanted or unpleasant events and overestimate the probability of wanted or pleasant events. In the social psychological and public health literature, this concept is typically credited to Weinstein (1980), who documented this tendency in people's overly positive expectations for future professional success, home value appreciation, and the academic aptitude of as-yet unborn children, as well as their overly negative expectations for developing a drinking problem, being the victim of a crime, and getting a divorce.[2]

Even in high-information markets, such as sports betting, where accurate forecasts are freely available, people are simply unable to overcome their natural optimism and systematically make overly optimistic bets on their preferred team (Babad and Katz 1991; Zuber et al. 2005). This optimism bias should, all else being equal, make the supporters of a cabinet party ill-equipped to process the inevitable: their preferred party will be unable to simply impose its will upon its partners in government, and, as a result, these voters will be denied their most preferred policy outcomes – the same outcomes that they were no doubt promised over the course of the campaign. Importantly, this natural inclination toward optimism bias means that parties need not actually be incompetent representatives or weak negotiators in order for their supporters to come away with the impression that they are. Because voters are inclined to anticipate outright success, disappointment may be unavoidable.[3]

What of the aforementioned informational asymmetry? In short, voters are likely to have more information about the policy preferences of the party they have most recently supported than that party's partner in coalition. To the degree that voters are attune to specifics and nuance in campaign platforms, they should come to know the specifics and nuance

---

[2] See Helweg-Larsen and Shepperd (2001) for a detailed review of the early literature on optimism bias. I also note that some may credit Kahneman and Tversky (1977) with "discovering" optimism bias when they first identified the planning fallacy.

[3] This is a fundamentally different kind of relationship between parties, voters, and expectation management than we would expect from an American politics perspective. The typical Americanist would likely expect voters to simply choose to interpret that their preferred party has dominated the policy negotiation process and "reward" them accordingly – a type of motivated reasoning (e.g., Redlawsk 2002; Taber and Lodge 2006). However, the nature of American partisanship is sui generis and those behaviors simply do not travel outside of the American case with sufficient regularity to consider them here. This becomes more clear in the empirical analysis later in this book.

and their most preferred party's platform more readily than other, less preferred parties. This informational asymmetry may make it difficult for voters to appreciate bargaining victories. For example, let us assume that some party A wants to set policy at 5 and their equally sized partner in government, party B, wants to set policy at 10. The two parties bargain and negotiate and the ultimate policy outcome is a 6. To the perfectly informed, this outcome is a stirring success for party A. However, to the supporter of party A, who understood fully that A's most preferred outcome was 5, but did not know what party B's most preferred outcome was, it may seem that party A was unsuccessful in negotiation. Such a voter may infer that party B's ideal policy was 6 and that it won the negotiation outright, meaning that party A was the unequivocal loser. Furthermore, a supporter of party A that did not know party B's most preferred outcome and inferred any position less than 10, would give party A less credit than it deserves for its bargaining tenacity. In the aggregate, these types of errors may cancel each other out, but still make it quite difficult for parties that are competent to successfully credit claim on their bargaining victories.

Finally, it may be the case that some party A is simply able to consistently get the better of some party B in policy negotiations, and, in this case, supporters of party B will be rightly disappointed. This type of disappointment is the one that seems to be most discussed in popular political discourse. Nonetheless, it will not be a central focus of the book. This is because accurate perceptions of bargaining prowess, unlike perceptions driven from informational asymmetries or optimism bias, are both normatively "good" (in general, we want voters to punish poor representation) and complementary, meaning that for every party B that gets punished due to real negotiation losses, there should be some party A that gets rewarded due to real negotiation victories. What is more interesting, both in terms of the cognitive dynamics of voters and the motivations for parties, are the *unearned* perceptions of incompetence that are a difficult reality of multiparty governance given both the information or attention constraints of the electorate and its natural biases toward optimism.

The second risk to coalition compromise for governing parties is that their policy brand will be tarnished. This may occur when voters begin to update their perceptions of what parties in coalition actually stand for. Fortunato and Stevenson (2013) discuss this process at some length (as we will in the chapters to come), but, in short, the formation of a governing coalition is likely to be seen as the announcement of two or more parties' intention to find common ground between them on which they can work toward policy compromise. Moreover, the nature of the policy-making process is such that nearly every policy outcome will not reflect the preferences of any one cabinet party, but, rather, the *aggregated* preferences of all members of the governing coalition. If voters update their perceptions of the policy brands of governing parties based on the policy outcomes of governments, then coalition participation should, over the long run, result in significant changes to how parties are perceived.

If we assume that parties construct their policy brands strategically, in order to maximize electoral support, then the erosion of these brands is likely to impose electoral costs on parties. Relatedly, if some party ascends to office on the basis of campaign promises to pursue specific policy outcomes, but the institutional constraints of multiparty policy-making conspire to produce outcomes other than what was promised, voters may not only update their perceptions of where that party stands, but they may also update their perceptions of how trustworthy that party is when it announces its intentions in the future.

HOW PARTIES FIGHT PERCEPTIONS OF COMPROMISE

In light of the long- and short-run penalties that cabinet parties risk as a function of coalition compromise, or, more specifically, *perceptions* of coalition compromise, they have substantial incentive to appear uncompromising or even in conflict with one another. But creating this conflict is difficult under coalition because parties are bound by collective cabinet responsibility, a series of rules that constrain the behaviors of coalition participants. In particular, these rules forbid the revelation of closed-door discussion, especially the type of intracabinet policy negotiations that precede the proposal of draft bills to the parliament. The rules also prevent parties from expressing distaste over the cabinet's policies once they have become law.

Given that (a) parties may not keep their supporters abreast of ongoing policy negotiations *before* draft bills are proposed to the parliament, (b) parties may not share their disappointment with draft bills *after* they have become law, and (c) parties are certainly forbidden from simply casting aspersions on their partners in government outside the context of policy discussion, how may they communicate their true preferences or preference dissimilarities from their partners in government? How may they show their supporters that they are fighting the good fight? The answer proposed in this book is that they use the period between a bill's submission and its final passage vote, the period of legislative review during which bills are debated, scrutinized, and amended. These processes of legislative review provide a temporary, and targeted, respite from collective responsibility in which cabinet partners are free to openly air their policy disagreements. Indeed, they may even feel compelled to instigate discord on areas of relative agreement in order to differentiate from one another and to signal their supporters that they have not forgotten their campaign promises and that they are steadfast in the pursuit of promised outcomes.

What does this differentiation look like in practice? It is simply conflict. It is heated debate in the plenary, pointed questions of ministers in subpoenaed testimony in committee hearings, and bold amendments in legislative review. Wherever the process allows for confrontation and conflict, we should observe it, provided that three conditions are met. The procedures must be sufficiently (a) open, (b) salient, and (c) individualized to meaningfully shape media narrative in order to observe differentiating conflict and, the degree to which these criteria are met can and should vary cross-nationally according to institutional structures. I explain each of these three parameters in turn.

By "open," I mean both *observable* and *unconstrained*. That is, procedures that may be viewed directly, either by voters or media (and reported on directly and transparently), and that do not inhibit the ability of legislators to express themselves, or, for lack of a better term, to mix it up. The first portion of this is more or less self-explanatory. Legislative procedures that happen privately, behind closed doors, cannot be used as fora to signal supporters or shape media messaging. There is a great deal of variation in the openness of committee meetings across European parliaments, as documented by Strøm (1998). While Finland's Suomen Eduskunta and Switzerland's Bundesversammlung have committee meetings that are closed to even other members of parliament, Ireland's Oireachtas and the Dutch Tweede Kamer have committee meetings that are completely open to the public.[4] We may therefore expect Irish committee meetings to be more heated and antagonistic than Finnish committee meetings, all else being equal, because of the differing audiences.

When it comes to behavioral constraints, differences in parliamentary debate are informative. For example, plenary debate is *observable*

---

[4] This even includes noncitizen tourists.

in all Western European parliaments, but the rules guiding debate (or ministerial questions) may make it more or less conducive to molding media narrative or directly signaling one's supporters. Russo and Wiberg (2010) provide an excellent accounting of these parameters. Of note here are rules that constrain "spontaneous questions" – questions that are not submitted in writing before the plenary session – and rules that place governors on debate for both spontaneous questions and pre-submitted questions. These institutional structures make some parliaments, like Austria's Nationalrat or Portugal's Assembleia da República, ideal for allowing for confrontation, while Germany's Bundestag and Spain's Congreso de los Diputados have institutional structures that make open confrontation quite unlikely. This is particularly interesting given that the Nationalrat and Bundestag are fairly similar in their institutional structure apart from their debate rules, as are the Assembleia da República and Congreso de los Diputados.

By "salient," I simply mean procedures that have policy implications, provide information on the policy-making process or parties' preferences, or are otherwise interesting to voters. Open committee meetings, legislative amendments, and issued committee reports both provide information and bear policy implications and should therefore be considered salient. Although it is almost certainly the case that the overwhelming majority of voters will never observe these meetings, amendments, or reports *directly*, they are a critical part of the policy-making process, should be observed and discussed by elites, and should therefore inform the overarching media narrative. Prime ministers' questions in the House of Commons, on the other hand, are not always salient to the policy-making process, but, nonetheless, can be very entertaining and therefore of interest to voters.

Finally, by sufficiently "individualized," I mean procedures that leave a record of individual action, where the "individuals" may be either MPs or party contingents. This is an important, if not immediately familiar criterion. The area most prone to contextual variability here is the commission of committee reports, which are often the instrument of record for the proposal of legislative amendments. Reports (in their entirety) may be attributed to the "committee" as a whole in countries with consensual rules, requiring majority support for the final report while not allowing formalized dissent from the minority (e.g, France's Assemblée Nationale); they may be attributed to the "majority" or "minority" in countries that do allow for minority dissent (e.g,

Norway's Storting); or, they may be attributed, in piecemeal to individual legislators or party contingents where proposed amendments within the reports are listed with their respective sponsors (e.g., Denmark's Folketing). See Döring (1995) and Strøm (1998) for more detail on these differences.

When these three criteria are met, we should observe parties engage in differentiating conflict in order to protect their image of competence or policy brand. In this book, we will examine the proposal of legislative amendments and the dynamics of parliamentary speech. We will also consider the extent to which these behaviors are manifest in the media narrative of partisan interactions and whether variation in the media narrative corresponds to variation in electoral performance. In other words, we will not only analyze whether parties engage in differentiating behavior in predictable ways, but also whether these behaviors are successful in mitigating electoral losses.

POTENTIAL MODERATORS

The general argument – that voters do not like coalition compromise and cabinet parties are therefore incentivized to squabble with one another to fight off perceptions of compromise – presumes that parties and voters are attentive to one another, but we need not presume that attentiveness and responsiveness are universal. We need not believe that all voters' receive the same information and respond to it equally, or that all parties send the same signals and face the same repercussions, particularly given that there are institutional structures and observable characteristics of both parties and voters that should moderate these relationships.

Which characteristics of parties or voters are potentially salient moderators? In sum, they are contextual features that potentially change the distribution of information on the policy-making process and its transfer from source to receiver; and features of voters that make them more or less likely to receive information and more or less prone to punish compromise. In this section, we will walk through both the individual-level and contextual-level characteristics that should condition the behaviors of voters and parties alike. The discussion will yield several simple, empirically testable expectations for observable behavior. A few of these expectations will be tested or prodded at in this book; however, most will be left untested. Nonetheless, the discussion should help clarify the general argument and also begin to lay the groundwork for future research.

Voter Characteristics

The most salient features of voters are their political interest and their relationship to members of the governing coalition. Interest will condition the extent to which voters are observing the incumbent coalition, or how much information regarding the policy-making process are they prone to receive.

This particular door may swing both ways. On the one hand, voters that are more attentive to political discourse should be more likely to receive information regarding the various policy compromises made by the cabinet participants. This includes the declaration of the coalition's intent to compromise, as given in the public coalition agreement, as well as case-by-case compromises made throughout the cabinet's term of office. These compromise processes, of course, produce compromise outcomes, which are also more likely to be observed by the politically interested. Quite simply, where compromise is made, it is more apt to be observed by those that are more attentive to politics.

The same can also be said of differentiating signals. When parties use procedure, the legislative review process, or parliamentary speeches to try to signal their competence, resolve, or "true" policy positions, these signals are also more likely to be received by more politically interested voters.

What does this mean for perceptions of compromise – are the politically interested more likely to observe compromise or observe differentiation? In expectation, where all signals are equally observable, the most politically interested would observe stasis. That is, because differentiation is not costless, parties should engage in it in proportion to their expectations for the electorate's perceptions of compromise. The more real policy negotiation and outcomes portray compromise, the more parties must differentiate in order to protect their brand. Where all of these actions are equally observable, the politically interested should receive compromise and differentiation signals in roughly equivalent doses.

However, this is unlikely to hold in the real world, for one very important reason: the interested are more likely to understand that real outcomes are both more credible and salient than theater. Though the evidence suggests that the most politically interested are less reliant on cheap, summary heuristic devices when updating their perceptions of parties (Fortunato and Stevenson 2013), they most certainly are more likely to understand that with the formation of a coalition cabinet, compromise is a foregone conclusion. Further, while each antagonistic speech portends a fairly credible signal of dissimilarity in preferences and each legislative amendment portends a concrete indication of preference dissimilarity, each realized policy outcome is affirmative evidence of a successful compromise, with real political economic consequences that the interested are more likely to observe and understand. The only signal of disagreement as credible as policy outcomes is stalemate – an inability to overcome differences. Of course stalemate is rare and often a leading indicator of government dissolution.

What this means is that the most politically interested should *perceive* more compromise, on average, than their less interested counterparts – an expectation that we can informally assess here, but truly requires a subsequent, dedicated study. However, given some level of perceived compromise, we should expect the politically interested to be less likely to punish the incumbent for it, relative to their less interested counterparts. Why? Because, just as the politically interested are more likely to possess a better understanding of politics that leads them to discount signals of disagreement relative to actual policy outcomes when updating their perceptions of the cabinet parties, they are also more likely to appreciate that compromise is simply an unavoidable reality of coalition governance. As such, they are less likely to be surprised or disappointed by compromise and more likely to have a higher tolerance for it. We can see evidence to this effect in Chapter 5; however, a dedicated study spanning a larger number of countries would be a welcome contribution.

Voters' relationship to the incumbent government is also likely to condition both perceptions of compromise and reactions to compromise. We expect previous supporters of cabinet member parties to be less tolerant of compromise than those that did not vote for the coalition parties. This is because previous supporters have entered into an agreement with these parties. They have been presented with a campaign platform and been promised some set of outcomes, and have, in a manner of speaking, paid in advance for those outcomes in the voting booth. When the outcomes inevitably fall short of expectations (campaign promises), previous supporters are more likely to be disappointed and punish the cabinet relative to those who did not previously support members of the incumbent government and have no such relationship (or agreement) with the incumbent government. Chapter 5 will also present evidence that this is indeed the case and go into some detail in discussion of both the reasons for this relationship and its broader implications which include a net vote loss for all coalition cabinets in expectation.

It is less clear whether previous cabinet supporters are more or less likely than their non-supporter counterparts to perceive compromise in the first place. On the one hand, it is possible that supporters have more fine-grained expectations for policy-making behavior and outcomes, particularly regarding the policy promises made by the specific party that they voted for, making them more apt to perceive realized outcomes as subpar. On the other hand, the type of differentiating signals that parties are incentivized to send should be targeted specifically to these voters – parties should go out of their way to demonstrate to their previous supporters that they are fighting the good fight and staying true to core principals. This would lead us to believe that, if cabinet parties are reasonably successful in sending differentiating signals through legislative review, debate, and so on, then previous supporters, the targets of such signals, should perceive less compromise than non-supporters, all else being equal. Later in the book, we will see that there is suggestive evidence for this tendency in the data; however, this evidence is inconclusive. Given that, we should, for the time being, view this question as an open one.

Institutional Characteristics

There are a series of institutional or contextual factors that should constrain parties' abilities or tendencies to send differentiating signals to their supporters. As noted earlier there is interesting institutional variability on the openness of both parliamentary debate and committee scrutiny that should direct the allocation of parties' differentiating actions within countries and their overall ability to signal differentiation across countries. More specifically, when legislative scrutiny in committee is not open or individualized, but parliamentary debate is, parties should expend more effort on differentiation via debate and vice versa. Where openness and individualization are constrained across all venues, the overall degree to which differentiation is possible is also constrained. In this book, we will focus on countries that are quite similar in their institutional structures (with the exception of a targeted study of the United Kingdom) in an attempt to avoid these kinds of contextual differences while laying out and testing the core argument. However, subsequent work on coalition dynamics will hopefully be able to begin to engage this kind of institutional variability.

Interestingly, the rules that constrain the openness of the scrutiny process overlap with the rules that enable "coalition policing" – the use of legislative powers and procedures to limit the ability of one's partner in government to force their ideal policy proposals through the legislative process unmolested. This means that the cross-sectional opportunity for differentiation is closely linked to the cross-sectional opportunity for coalition policing. This creates what may, at first blush, look like an interesting competition for party bandwidth – should they focus on policing or differentiation? – but may also be a serendipitous complementarity: policing and differentiation may often be one and the same. Again, analysis here is focused on systems that are quite similar on these parameters, but this regularity presents a very interesting puzzle for future research on the strategic allocation of partisan resources to untangle.

Further complicating this is the potential that legislative institutions are also likely to condition the extent to which opposition parties may influence policymaking. In this book, we touch upon this by briefly considering the role of pivotal opposition parties. As we will see later in the book, in the chapter on legislative review, the theoretical arguments draw sharp predictions for how the behavior of minority cabinets – both in crafting the initial policy proposal and in guiding behavior while the bill is scrutinized in committee – is constrained by having to extend negotiations to some opposition party in order to secure a legislative majority for the proposal. The same sharp predictions, however, do not extend to other parliamentary behaviors, such as speechmaking. Further more, it is not immediately clear how pivotal opposition parties, or opposition parties of varied levels of institutional strength opposing a majority government, will change our theoretical expectations for how voters perceive coalition governance and how these perceptions change the incentives and choices of governing parties.

Does the opposition's ability to exert policy influence contribute centripetal or centrifugal force to the "natural" gravity of a coalition cabinet? Both alternatives are possible. On the one hand, influential opposition parties may reorient the salient axis of disagreement to government versus opposition rather than cabinet partner versus cabinet partner, making it more difficult for coalition partners to differentiate from one another and contributing to the force of their internal gravity. On the other hand, such opposition may also reorient the nature of "score keeping" away from internal cabinet negotiations and toward cabinet–opposition interactions such that the signal of compromise by individual cabinet parties is overtaken by signals of collective wins and losses in dealing with the opposition. Using measures of conflict and cooperation derived from media reports of political interactions, as we will in Chapter 8, would be an efficient approach to this question, provided that the range of countries could be expanded to accommodate a sufficient level of cross-sectional variability in opposition strength.

A final pair of salient and interesting contextual covariates is the country's experience with coalition and the typical nature of coalition bargaining. It seems clear that voters in countries with long, uninterrupted histories of multiparty governance (e.g., Denmark or the Netherlands) would engage governing parties differently from their counterparts in countries with very short (e.g., Spain or New Zealand) or quite varied (e.g., Greece or Portugal) histories of multiparty governance. It is tempting to believe that this familiarity is likely to make voters more forgiving of coalition compromise as they are more likely to have learned that compromise is a fundamental requirement of successful coalition governance – compromise has been a vital part of their political socialization. On the other hand, it may also be the case that parties in such countries have more experience managing the internal gravity of coalition and are therefore better equipped to prevent disappointment on the part of their voters. In other words, it may be that voters are more forgiving of compromise, or that parties are better able to conceal their compromise in these more experienced contexts. Likewise, it may also be that the disappointment with compromise, due to the psychological factors we discussed above, can never be managed or socialized away.

Whether coalitions tend to be the product of pre- or post-electoral bargaining may also have powerful consequences for the manner in which voters' expectations are set and therefore the manner in which they interpret the subsequent policy-making behaviors and outcomes over the government's time in office. Instead of campaigning individually, making distinct promises to disparate groups, parties that enter into pre-electoral coalition agreements can coordinate on a common message and prepare their supporters for compromise by committing to a specific set of mutually agreed upon policies in advance. This fundamentally changes the relationship between voters and parties – voters are no longer paying in advance for policies to be pursued by a single party, but are paying in advance for joint policy ventures. Importantly, these joint ventures are more likely to be delivered with less drift than individual party promises, meaning that, on average, the difference between what voters are promised and what they receive will be less under pre-electoral relative to post-electoral coalition.

Even within the set of cases where parties agree to pre-electoral coalition, however, there is substantial variability in the nature of the pacts that we observe. It has been common, for example, in France and Italy, for parties to unite under a common (though perhaps temporary) banner, commit to a common electoral manifesto, and even merge party lists (as in Italy), or strategically withdraw candidates from districts (as in France) to concentrate on a single candidate from the party pair (or group) to maximize the union's total seat share. Most agreements, however, are not this strong. More typical are agreements of the type we tend to see in Sweden, where ideologically compatible parties on the left or right, make it known in advance that they intend to form a government if they win a sufficient number of seats, but do not formally collaborate on platform or electoral strategy. There are also instances in which a party will not announce intent to coalesce with a particular partner, but merely note that they are open to the idea, as in Norway, leading up to the 2009 election, when the Conservatives announced that they were willing to consider coalescing with the Progress Party, a primarily anti-immigrant party that had become more popular over the last decade.

From these announcements of openness to the quite strong, active pre-electoral coordination, we should have varying predictions for the degree to which voters' expectations for, and reactions to, policy-making behavior and outcomes will change. Under the most strict pre-electoral coalition agreements, the type that actually changes the commitments parties are making to the electorate, we would expect much less punishment for compromising behaviors and outcomes, because the compromise was baked into the campaign and selection process. But any tempering effects of pre-electoral pacts on voter reaction to compromise should be decreasing with the strength of the agreement. The less ex ante policy commitments (and campaign tactics) are altered by the agreement, the less we should expect the agreement to soften voters' inclination to punish compromise. We can get some traction on a more general form of this expectation in Chapter 5 by comparing the degree to which pre- and post-electoral coalitions are punished for compromise. However, again, the cross-sectional variability is small and a dedicated study would be a valuable step forward.

Of course, in all coalition governments, parties may take on one of several nominal roles: Parties with cabinet seats that provide the prime minister (prime ministerial), parties with cabinet seats that do not provide the prime minister (junior partner), and parties without cabinet seats that consistently vote for the government's legislation to help it achieve a majority (support). Untangling how these roles affect voters' expectations of behavior or outcomes, parties' actual ability to deliver those outcomes, or parties' capacity to respond to their supporters' demands for more conflict or differential is a difficult task.

For example, the research on multiparty policymaking suggests that prime ministers have more policy influence than junior partners (e.g., Thomson et al. 2017; Naurin, Royed, and Thomson 2019). As such, one may think that the compromise penalty may be less for prime ministerial parties, because they are actually more likely to "win" competitions over policy than their junior partner counterparts. However, we have also learned that voters will *expect* prime ministerial parties to have more policy influence (Fortunato et al. 2020), and they may therefore be held to a higher standard. On the other hand, perhaps true wins and losses are less important than the appearance of wins and losses, and, here, controlling political narratives or media messages may be more important. Given the advantages that come with being head of government, perhaps the prime ministerial party is much better at controlling the media narrative. There is some evidence to this effect. For example, Fortunato and Adams (2015) find that voters perceive junior partner parties getting pulled into the ideological halo of prime ministerial parties and there is also suggestive evidence to that effect in the analysis in Chapter 5. Moving forward, more research is needed to understand how voters may differentially hold prime ministerial and junior partner parties accountable for compromise and how well equipped each party type is to fight off perceptions of compromise, given the tools at their disposal and voters' expectations for those negotiation outcomes. Of course, subsequent study would also be needed to differentiate the incentives and behaviors of external support parties from junior cabinet partners.

Closely related to differences in role is the size of the cabinet more generally, in terms of number of parties. The modal coalition size is two parties. However, coalitions of three or more are not uncommon. It is possible that, as the number of parties grows, the complexity of policy negotiations may grow in kind, making it increasingly difficult not only for voters to follow the process of policy bargaining or attribute responsibility for outcomes, but also for the parties to create differentiating signals that cut through the clatter. The interesting question here is whether the increased complexity obscures signals that portray compromise (e.g., the process of forming a cabinet and then bargaining over, passing, and executing new policy) and signals that portray differentiation equivalently. One possibility is that larger coalitions increase the complexity of policymaking to the point where elites find it less efficient to attribute actions to individual actors (e.g., the Christian Democrats or the Social Democrats) and more efficient to attribute actions to groups (e.g., the government or the opposition). This simplifying choice could make differentiation substantially more difficult for cabinet members, but also, as discussed earlier, reorient the salient dimension of conflict from *within* the coalition to *between* the government and opposition.

All of this discussion is meant to serve two purposes. The first is to prompt readers to speculate through the many implications of the central argument of the book and how these implications may be conditioned by variability in the observable characteristics of voters and governments. We may find this a useful exercise not only because it contextualizes the argument, but also because it lays the foundation for future research. There are a lot of substantively significant and interesting possibilities to chase down and the hope is that drawing attention to a handful of them will prompt our colleagues to begin the process.

The second purpose of this discussion is that it makes clear the necessity for simplification in the remainder of the book. This project is ambitious. Studying voters experimentally and observationally, studying parties' behaviors in parliament at the micro-level and macro-level, and then trying to marry the two approaches is a fairly large endeavor. Walking through how, to take just one example, different institutional structures guiding the issuance of committee reports can increase the complexity of theoretical and empirical modeling really drives home the need for careful case selection in the observational analysis.

THE PLAN OF THE BOOK

How does multiparty policymaking influence the internal gravity of coalition governments and how do cabinet members attempt to take control of their internal gravity? Over the next two chapters, we will investigate voters' reactions to coalition policymaking, and compromise in particular. This analysis will facilitate a more complete (though, of course, still incomplete) understanding of the centrifugal forces in multiparty policymaking. How strongly does compromise seem to pull coalition participants toward one another in the eyes of voters, forcing cabinet partners to thumb one another in the eye in order to protect their electoral prospects? Do voters prefer compromise and the damage it inflicts to ideological brands to gridlock and ideological purity? Answering these questions will allow us to pivot back to the parliament to understand how these centrifugal forces can be satisfied without tearing the government apart.

The book proceeds by making this basic argument in parts. We begin the investigation by examining how voters react to compromise in the policy-making process in two ways. First, in Chapter 4, we assess how compromise influences voters' perceptions of parties' representational competence and their policy brands with an experiment administered in the Netherlands and in the United Kingdom in the midst of the Cameron and Clegg government's tenure. We will learn that voters do, in fact, equate compromise with representational incompetence. Further more, the results of the experiment also suggest that compromise erodes parties' carefully selected policy brands, causing voters to believe that they are more ideologically similar to their partners in government.

Following up on these findings, Chapter 5 proposes an empirical test for evaluating the effects of perceived compromise on incumbent support. Using panel data from Denmark, Germany, the Netherlands, New Zealand, Norway, and Sweden that allows us to track how voters' perceptions of parties change over their time in cabinet together, we will see that voters are only too willing to punish parties for compromise in the policy-making process. Perhaps just as important is the variation in punishment tendencies within the electorate. The data reveal that previous supporters of the cabinet – the citizens who have paid in advance for policies promised by cabinet participants by lending their votes in good faith – are substantially more likely to dole out punishment when they have perceived compromise.

The book then, in Chapter 6, pivots from the electorate to the legislature to assess whether, and how, parties may try to mitigate these losses for perceived compromise by differentiating from one another in the legislative review phase of the policy-making process. This also proceeds in two parts. First, we look to political systems with long histories of coalition governance, countries with parties who have, presumably, come to understand that balance between compromise and conflict is critical and do their best to behave in accordance with their supporters' demands. Analyzing the data on the legislative scrutiny of over 2,200 cabinet proposals in Belgium, Denmark, and the Netherlands over a period of several decades, we will see that, as cabinet participants are perceived as getting "too close" to their partners in coalition, they become more antagonistic in legislative review. The more similarly cabinet partners are perceived, the greater the threat to their brand (and therefore electoral fortunes). The greater the threat to their brand, the more incentive they have to differentiate from one another. The more incentive they have to differentiate from one another, the more they will amend one another's legislation.

In the second part of this analysis, in Chapter 7, these theoretically effective behaviors are contrasted to how the Conservatives and Liberal Democrats (especially the Liberal Democrats) handled themselves during the first Cameron cabinet from 2010 to 2015. Qualitative accounts of party strategies and quantitative analysis of behavior in the legislative review period – including an analysis of legislative speeches and a first-of-its-kind analysis of the depth and duration of the parliamentary scrutiny of cabinet proposals – reveal that, even though the Liberal Democrats understood quite early that they were eroding their brand, they were simply too slow to adapt their behavior to fight off voters' souring perceptions of their competence and trustworthiness. The result of this failure to adapt was the Liberal Democrats' disastrous performance in the 2015 parliamentary elections where they saw over 65 percent of their vote share and over 85 percent of their seat share evaporate.

The culmination of the general argument of the book and the two split-phase analyses of voters' reaction to coalition compromise and parties' behavioral responses to these reactions in parliament, is a macro-level test of the simple hypothesis that coalition members that are able to craft a reputation for resisting compromise in the policy-making process fare better at the ballot box. Chapter 8 tests this hypothesis by comparing quantitative estimates of coalition parties' behavior on a "conflict-cooperation" dimension that is derived from an analysis of media reporting on political interactions to these parties' electoral performance. The analysis suggests that more antagonistic parties are, in fact, more successful at the polls, even after accounting for the cabinet's economic performance. These findings, taken together with the theoretical and empirical analyses in the preceding chapters, paint a convincing picture that supports the overarching argument of the book: voters dislike and punish compromise and this incentivizes parties to fight off perceptions of compromise by differentiating from their partners in government. However, the arguments and evidence also suggest a distressing level of inefficiency in coalition policymaking, one that previous models of coalition governance do not imply. This implied inefficiency is discussed at some length and used as a bridge to mapping out potential avenues for future research, the bulk of which dominates Chapter 9.

4

Perceptions of Coalition Compromise

> ... it is the winning that seems more important to them.
>
> Henri Tajfel and coauthors (1971, 174)

Compromise, in the abstract, is an attractive practice. The willingness and ability of parties with dissimilar policy preferences to compromise is a necessary condition for policy change in divided and multiparty government and critical to addressing new hurdles. Indeed, in many cases, compromise may be necessary to simply *maintain* the function of the state. [1] More to the point, voters overwhelmingly report that they favor compromise in the policy-making process to divisive, contentious partisan conflict (e.g., Ramirez 2009; Harbridge, Malhotra, and Harrison 2014). However, there is a discordance between voters' views of compromise in the abstract and their reactions to compromises made by the parties or representatives that they have supported (Harbridge and Malhotra 2011). More specifically, voters seem to view compromise at the institutional level as favorable; however, when it comes to concessions made by a particular party, they tend to view it as weakness or worse. Hibbing and Theiss-Morse write at some length about voters' perceptions of compromise and present evidence that a majority of American voters believe "compromise [is] the equivalent of selling out on principals" (2002, 136).

Although nearly all of the extant research on voter reaction to compromise is focused on the American case, the basic intuition remains

---

This chapter and Chapter 5 adapt and extend a previously published article (Fortunato 2019a). Portions of these chapters therefore paraphrase or borrow directly from that article.

[1] Take, for example, the US government shutdowns of 1995 and 2013.

the same. Policymaking in the United States under divided government is similar to coalition governance in that multiple parties must reach a common ground. Thus, it is plain that compromises must be made – they are simply a political reality. As such, it is, on the one hand, unreasonable for all voters to *expect* that the party they supported will be able to avoid making any compromises at all. On the other hand, however, it is not unreasonable for voters to *hope* that their party will be able to avoid making concessions or to be disappointed if they perceive the party as making too many concessions. It is only natural to want as many "wins" as possible in any competition, and multiparty policymaking is a competition over a finite pool of influence.

In this sense, winning concessions from, or granting concessions to, one's partners in governance is a demonstration of competence. The more concessions won, the more competent is the party as a representative of its supporters or steward of its platform. This notion underlies the dilemma of coalition governance. How can parties coexist in cabinet when their motivations for smooth governance and extracting benefits of office pull them toward cooperation, but their electoral motivations push them toward intransigence (Strøm 1990a)? The ministerial dominance model of coalition policymaking (Laver and Shepsle 1996) argues that a division of jurisdictions with complete discretion can resolve these conflicts and allow parties to credibly commit to a type of policy compromise in advance of the cabinet's formation.

Here, the compromise is a division of ministerial portfolios where any one party acts as dictator in its own jurisdictions. In a sense, the parties may only consent to co-governance by embracing their selfishness and committing to a division of policy making authority that assumes ministers will never cooperate and will never compromise – that they are completely autonomous actors, unwilling to make proposals that deviate from their ideal point. In this way, the "coalition compromise" is simply a commitment to partitioned self-indulgence.

More recent work views this solution as potentially suboptimal as the gains from delegation in one policy area may be too small to counterbalance the losses in another. Alternatively, it may be that coalition parties are simply averse to ceding complete influence in any jurisdiction. Such work theorizes that a comprehensive compromise may be reached (i.e., where the coalition parties reach a common policy goal in each jurisdiction) and that institutions such as detailed coalition agreements with procedural enforcements (Strøm and Müller 1999; Eichorst 2014), junior ministers (Thies 2001; Lipsmeyer and Pierce 2011), or legislative committees (Martin and Vanberg 2011; Carroll and Cox 2012) may be utilized to mitigate ministerial drift – the propensity of ministers to flout compromise and propose, instead, a policy closer to their own ideal point in order to demonstrate competence and reap policy benefits from slack in the review process.

This work has found empirical evidence that such monitoring of institutions can be used successfully to mitigate ministerial drift. This means that even when parties consciously seek conflict or the abandonment of compromise, policy outcomes, as well as processes, are unlikely to reflect this – compromise by force is compromise nonetheless. Further more, because much of the business of enforcing compromise occurs in the parliament, in the legislative review phase of the policy making process, these actions are easily observable. Finally, subsequent research has provided empirical evidence that this "coalition compromise" model of multiparty policymaking better explains the actual behaviors and outcomes we observe than the two competing models (Martin and Vanberg 2014): the "legislative median" model (e.g., Baron 1991; Morelli 1999) and the ministerial dominance model (e.g., Austen-Smith and Banks 1990; Laver and Shepsle 1996).

These findings are significant here because they imply that voters are very likely to observe or infer compromise and there is research to support this implication. Fortunato and Stevenson (2013) argue that the compromise necessary to make coalition governance work will lead voters to view the coalition partners as moderating ideologically (toward each other) and find empirical evidence supporting this argument. This argument has been reconfirmed in subsequent replications by Falco-Gimeno and Fernandez-Vazquez (2020) and Adams, Ezrow, and Wlezien (2016). There is also evidence that expectations of compromise shape voters' expectations for policy outcomes. Duch, May, and Armstrong (2010) as well as Fortunato et al. (2020) provide evidence that voters expect coalition policy outcomes to be a weighted average of partner preferences. In sum, we know that compromise is essential to coalition governance and we know that many voters perceive this compromise, yet we do not know how voters respond to it.

For simplicity, assume that all coalition policy-making behavior falls somewhere on the spectrum between compromise and conflict. A party that is perfectly compromising concedes all contested policy points to its partner in coalition. A party that is perfectly conflictual will refuse to cede any policy points to its partners, even if that results in stalemate. It is possible that voters would value compromising behavior for its utility in moving policy forward. Similarly, it is possible that voters could punish conflict for its obstructionism and the stagnation of government. As discussed earlier, there is evidence from the American case that, in the abstract at least, voters value compromise in the interest of progress and have a distaste for gridlock.

These reactions, however, are unlikely. As noted, compromise is simply a political reality in coalition governance as it is in the American case when the executive and legislature are controlled by different parties or when the Congress is divided against itself. But voters do not have to like compromise. Indeed, if voters view policy bargaining (as political economists tend to) as a series of competitions for limited policy influence, an easy compromise or an accommodative bargaining process may be viewed as a weak-kneed concession rather than a pragmatic decision made in the interest of progress. As the policy-making process and political outcomes are inseparable, "[compromising] processes may produce outputs that are more akin to losses than wins for a particular party, especially if the alternative is standing firm" (Harbridge, Malhotra, and Harrison 2014, 328–329). In other words, voters may always imagine some counterfactual where the result of policy negotiation is getting everything they want and blame their representatives for failing to deliver.

This possibility makes it particularly important to bear in mind that the relevant audience to coalition bargaining is the cabinet's supporters – the voters who have paid in advance for policy advocacy by giving their votes in good faith to one of the cabinet parties. Once in government, those parties have an obligation to their supporters to honor their promises and to rigorously fight for the policies laid out in their platform. As Powell (2000) argues, voters understand entry into coalition government assures parties the opportunity to bargain for the policies they campaigned on. Thus, the separation between winners and losers, *within* coalition, is a function of the parties' abilities to win those bargaining rounds – to *avoid compromise*. By standing firm in the negotiation process, parties may be able to extract additional policy concessions from their partners and therefore deliver on the policy promises they made to their supporters during the campaign.

In this way, the quality of representation a cabinet party delivers to its supporters – its ability to honor its end of the implicit (sometimes explicit) agreement it has with its supporters that, in exchange for votes, certain policies will be pursued – is defined, at least in part, by its bargaining ability. Parties that compromise or yield policy concessions to their partners in coalition can very easily be painted as ineffective governors.

Getting into cabinet does not assure a party's supporters their preferred outcomes, it only allows that party the opportunity to bargain for them. Given this, voters should, on average, associate compromise with poor representation.[2]

Anecdotal examples of parties suffering popularity losses due to voters' perceptions of the process and outcomes of policy bargaining abound. For example, Germany's Free Democratic Party (FDP) suffered robust damage to their base of support in 2010 following what was widely interpreted as a sound defeat in bargaining over tax reductions with Angela Merkel and the Christian Democratic Union (CDU/CSU) during Merkel's second cabinet (Poguntke 2011). That year, the FDP's popularity would consistently fall to 5 percent (the threshold for representation in the Bundestag) or less, for the first time in well over a decade. The FDP would then go on to lose another round of high-profile negotiations, this time over the phasing out of nuclear energy in the aftermath of the nuclear disaster at Fukushima. Their popularity would never recover and they were trounced in the elections of 2013, failing to clear the 5 percent threshold for the first time in their history and losing all of their seats in parliament.

Denmark's Socialist People's Party (SPP) suffered similarly due to bargaining failures. In the lead up to the 2011 elections, the SPP had campaigned hard for a new toll road surrounding Copenhagen. The toll system was meant to:

reduce auto-mobile traffic in downtown Copenhagen, mitigate the environmental problems that auto-mobile exhaust was causing, and generate more money to expand and improve the collective traffic network (Bille 2013, 56).

Bille (2013) writes that, even though the SPP was able to get the plan adopted into the coalition agreement between themselves, Prime Minister Helle Thorning-Schmidt's Social Democrats, and the Social Liberals, the Social Democratic Finance Minister was able to block the final policy from being passed. This very public defeat humiliated the SPP and began the erosion of their popularity that would, over the course of the government, be cut in half, causing them to lose 56 percent of their seats in the following elections in 2015.

---

[2] It is important to note that this type of scrutiny does not apply to parties outside of cabinet. Because opposition parties are excluded from the policy-making process, they are never presented with the opportunity to honor their commitments and, therefore, never penalized for failing to honor them.

But of course, these anecdotes are not conclusive evidence. Furthermore, the most readily available examples are the parties suffering at the polls due to their participation in coalition with (as discussed earlier) stories of outright losses in the bargaining process, rather than stories of mutually beneficial (or detrimental) compromise. As such in the analysis to come, we will examine responses to compromise where there are no explicit "winners" and "losers" experimentally stripping out the baggage of party reputations, partisan affinities, and histories of co-governance. Subjects will be presented with a policy impasse and one of the three outcomes: a specific compromise that moves policy forward, an ambiguous compromise that moves policy forward, or gridlock. Their reactions to the randomized resolutions will allow us to test the argument that voters equate compromise with representational failure.

Hypothesis 1 (Representational Efficacy) *Voters who perceive a compromising cabinet are less likely to believe that coalition parties are properly representing their supporters.*

To the extent that Hypothesis 1 holds, parties should suffer a competence or credibility penalty. Voters may perceive them as incapable of securing the policies that they promised to their supporters. Relatedly, voters may also infer that the parties never meant to keep their promises in the first place and are simply untrustworthy. Both of these penalties are likely to result in electoral losses. But these are not the only losses they may suffer. Recall that Martin and Vanberg's (2008) primary concern regarding compromise was its ability to erode the party's brand:

> compromise obscures the relationship between the policies a party supports as a member of the government and its 'pure' policy commitments. As a result, participation in coalition has the potential to undermine a party's carefully established profile (Martin and Vanberg 2008, 503).

This point is critical. Not only do parties risk electoral losses by consenting to compromise due to the propensity of their supporters to perceive compromising as indicative of weakness or incompetence, but they also risk damaging their brand. That is, when the processes of coalition policymaking – the protracted compromise at the formation of the cabinet, intense internal negotiation over the structure of the legislative agenda, and the process of legislative review – conspire to deny any one participant from getting exactly what they want (given that preferences between coalition partners over the issue in question are dissimilar), voters will only observe policy outcomes that are out of alignment with the campaign platforms of individual member parties.

As outcomes continue to be discordant with voters' priors over the policy preferences of cabinet parties, it is only natural that voters would begin to update their perceptions of where the parties stand ideologically and it is only natural that they would update with the assistance of simplifying heuristics. Why is this? Monitoring the day-to-day business of governance, including debates of policy proposals and their legislative scrutiny, is difficult and time-consuming. Voters have limited resources (and, presumably, limited desire) to keep up with the daily grind of the policy-making process. Substituting a simplifying heuristic that parties striking policy compromises must have moderated toward one another in one way or another is substantially easier than collecting and parsing detailed information on the policy-making process in order to extract relevant data with which they may draw inferences about the evolving policy positions of parties. Indeed, Fortunato and Stevenson (2013) present compelling argument and evidence that voters not only do precisely this, but are, in general, also correct to do so.

On the other hand, even if voters are sufficiently attentive to the political process that they are, in fact, *able* to observe all of the cabinet's policy outcomes, it is still easier to simply infer that all coalition members support each outcome. That is, rather than attempting to monitor each phase of the policy-making process to assess which parties are more or less supportive of each cabinet proposal to make more fine-grained inferences about potential change in their policy positions, voters simply check in every now and then on the policies that the cabinet has produced and use this information to update their perceptions of where the parties stand ideologically in a relatively uniform manner – assuming, for example, that all coalition members are equally enthusiastic about all proposals.

Again, what we know about coalition policymaking suggests that, at least at a superficial level, this would yield relatively accurate inferences. In nearly every cabinet, all member parties hold a de facto veto over each policy proposal.[3] Each member party may have the power to prevent the proposal from being submitted to the parliament and each party most

---

[3] Oversized coalitions are the exception.

assuredly has the power to prevent its success at the final passage vote.[4] Therefore, the existence of a new policy is evidence of consent of each member party – or, at the least, we could infer that each party prefers that policy outcome to the cabinet's dissolution. As such, a voter that uses the information in those policy outcomes to update their perceptions of the policy preferences of the member parties would be justified in doing so. After all, actions speak louder than words. When faced with the choice of how to interpret what parties *say* against what parties *do*, sensible voters will likely choose to give more weight to the latter. As Key famously wrote:

Voters may reject what they have known; or they may approve what they have known. They are not likely to be attracted in great numbers by promises of the novel or unknown (1966, 61).

Given the rationale for why voters would (should) update their perceptions of parties' ideological positions in response to their participation in coalition, the question of *how* they will do so is simple. Voters should perceive coalition partners as moderating toward one another. That is, if the manner in which voters update their perceptions is derived from signals regarding the parties' compatibility from the formation of the government or information about evolving preferences gleaned from the cabinet's policy outputs, then perceived moderation toward the government's ideological core is the only sensible result. It is unreasonable for voters to observe a center-left party coalesce with a center-right party and, as a result, infer that the center-left party is actually *more left* than they had initially believed. Similarly, because the cabinet enjoys perfect agenda control, there can (in expectation) be no policy change outside of the ideological range of the government. Therefore, the only updating information available to voters in the formation and policy output of a coalition government should cause them to perceive partners in government as moderating toward one another ideologically. As such, the empirical expectation that we will test is:

Hypothesis 2 (Ideological Change) *Voters who perceive a compromising cabinet are more likely to believe that coalition parties are moderating their ideological positions toward one another.*

---

4 Barring the replacement of a cabinet parties' vote with opposition support, that is.

AN EXPERIMENT ON COALITION COMPROMISE

To isolate voters' reaction to coalition compromise, we want an experimental design that will effectively strip out voters' partisan dispositions, their perceptions of the trustworthiness of those parties, and the parties' history of co-governance. In other words, we want to begin with a clean slate, removing all expectations and affect from the party system to isolate voters' perceptions of compromise in a vacuum.

The experiment was administered to voting-age citizens of the United Kingdom in June 2012 and of the Netherlands in September 2012.[5] The experimental setup posits the formation of a new country, which is never identified by name. The "new country" has its own party system that is populated by a group of generically named parties: the Christian Democratic Party, the Green Party, the Conservative Party, the Liberal Party, the Social Democratic Party, the Independence Party, and the Labour Party.

The first task that the subjects are asked to perform is to give their perception of where those parties lie in the left-right space (the order of the parties in the response matrix was randomized) with no additional information. Of course, the names themselves are fairly informative, which we will see in a moment. The full text of the prompt is as follows:

A new country has been formed. In this country there are several political parties: the Christian Democratic Party, the Green Party, the Conservative Party, the Liberal Party, the Social Democratic Party, the Independence Party, and the Labour Party.

Using only the information given above, please answer the following question about the parties in this country: On a scale of 0-10, where 0 is the most left and 10 is the most right, where would you place each of the parties? If you do not know, please guess.

After the respondents have recorded their guesses as to where parties stand in the policy space, they are introduced to a coalition cabinet that is governing the country. They are given the names of the parties and told about a few of the policy commitments the parties had made during the recent election campaign. These commitments imply that the parties generally see eye-to-eye regarding spending, but also imply a disagreement in the budget-making process. More specifically, the text reveals that the

---

5 Note that the United Kingdom had been governed by a coalition of the Conservatives and Liberal Democrats for a little over two years at this point. Thus, while the United Kingdom is nowhere near as comfortable with the idea of coalition governance as the Netherlands, UK citizens are at this point familiar with multiparty governance.

cabinet parties – the Christian Democrats and the Independence Party – have both promised their supporters that they would reduce government spending. However, the text also tells the subjects that the parties have promised to pursue this overarching goal in different ways – one party prefers increased privatization of health care and increased university tuitions, while the other prefers alternative, unspecified routes to reducing government spending and specifically rejects health-care privatization and tuition increases. It reads as follows:

This country is currently being governed by a coalition of the Christian Democratic Party and the Independence Party. Before the election, the Christian Democratic Party campaigned on a platform of reducing government spending by increasing the role of the private sector in providing health care and allowing universities to raise their tuitions. The Independence Party also campaigned on a platform of reducing government spending, but promised its supporters that it would not allow the private sector to have a greater role in health care, would keep university tuitions at their current levels, and would find other ways to reduce spending.

All subjects have received the same information to this point. After being presented with the identity of the coalition, and their common and differing policy promises, the respondents are randomly assigned to one of three experimental treatments, each of which is a policy-making outcome.

The first treatment informs the subjects that the parties were able to reach a compromise and pass a new budget, but gives no specifics on the precise terms of that compromise. Thus, the subjects learn that both parties were able to deliver on their broader promise of reducing government spending; however, the subjects are given no information about who gave what in the budgeting negotiations. This is called the "compromise" treatment in the discussion below:

[compromise] When it came time to set a budget, the Christian Democrats and the Independence Party were flexible on their promises regarding health care and education and were able to reach a compromise.

The second treatment also informs the subjects that the parties were able to strike a deal; however, this treatment notes the terms of the negotiation. More specifically, in this outcome, the parties agreed to increase tuitions, however they chose not to increase the level of privatization in health-care provision. Thus, the subjects learn that both parties were able to deliver on their promise of reducing government spending and that each party gave and received one policy concession in working toward the larger goal. This is called the "logroll" treatment in the discussion below:

[logroll] When it came time to set a budget, the Christian Democrats and the Independence Party negotiated a trade. The Christian Democrats and the Independence Party agreed on a budget that raises tuitions but does not increase the role of the private sector in health-care provision.

The third and final treatment informs the subjects that the parties were unable to reach a compromise and were therefore unable to pass a new budget. Here, the subjects learn that both parties were unable to deliver on their promise of reducing government spending, but they also learn that neither party was forced to make a concession in the bargaining process. This is called the "stalemate" treatment in the discussion below:

[stalemate] When it came time to set a budget, the Christian Democrats and the Independence Party both held fast to their promises regarding health care and education and were therefore unable to agree on a new budget.

Note that in no treatment is there a clear "winner" or "loser" in the budgeting negotiations, yet the signals of compromise and conflict are clearly differentiated with the compromise and logroll treatments on one side and the stalemate treatment on the other. After the respondents were treated with bargaining resolutions, they were asked to evaluate how well each party represented its supporters in the negotiations on a scale of 1–5, where the response matrix labels 1 as "not well at all" and labels 5 as "very well" and the order of the parties in the response matrix was randomized:

On a scale of 1–5, how well do you think the Christian Democrats and the Independence Party represented the preferences of their supporters?

Finally, the subjects were asked to place each of the seven parties in this system on the 0–10 left-right scale once again (and once again, the order of the parties was randomized in the response matrix).

Table 4.1 demonstrates the balance of treatment assignment across the gender, age, and ideological self placements (on a 0–10 scale) of the respondents. What we are wanting to see here is that, if the treatments were properly randomized across respondents, then there should be very

Table 4.1 *Balance statistics by treatment*

Treatment	Female	Age	Self placement
Stalemate	0.489	45.550	5.037
Logroll	0.471	44.493	5.043
Compromise	0.498	45.861	5.192

Table 4.2 *Effect of policy-making outcomes
on perceived quality of representation*

Response summaries	Mean (SD)
Stalemate	3.050 (1.238)
Logroll	2.943 (1.019)
Compromise	2.904 (1.033)
$N = 2,909$	

little difference in the observable characteristics of the respondents across the treatment groups. As the table shows, the randomization device was successful and achieved balance on these demographic characteristics of the subjects. The mean values on each of the characteristics are quite similar across treatments and not one of the differences across treatments are statistically significant.

First, let us examine the subjects' responses to the representational quality question. Recall from our previous discussion that the theoretical expectation is that voters will equate compromise with poor representation – that concessions yielded in the policy-making process, even if they advance the greater goals of the party, are likely to be interpreted as bargaining failure. The empirical expectation, therefore, is that subjects receiving the compromise and logroll treatments will have lower evaluations of representational quality than subjects receiving the stalemate treatment, even though the stalemate treatment results in both parties *failing* to achieve their broader goal of reducing government spending.

Table 4.2 summarizes the subjects' raw responses by treatment. The recovered rank-ordering suggests that stalemate is preferred to logroll

Table 4.3 *Comparing across treatment groups*

Comparison	Difference (certainty)
Stalemate – Logroll	0.107 ($p = 0.039$)
Stalemate – Compromise	0.146 ($p = 0.005$)
Logroll – Compromise	0.039 ($p = 0.402$)
$N = 2,909$	

and that logroll is preferred to compromise.[6] Moreover, only the subjects receiving the stalemate treatment issue an average evaluation that is positive, or above the response scale median, subjects receiving both the logroll and compromise treatments return evaluations that are negative on average, or below the response scale median.

The rank-ordering of stalemate > logroll > compromise is supported by the difference of means testing as well (although the difference between the logroll and compromise treatments is not statistically significant). Table 4.3 gives the results of pairwise comparison of the responses by the treatment categories. Both comparisons of logroll and compromise to the stalemate treatment show that voters have a statistically significant aversion to compromise in the policymaking. This is robust support for theoretical arguments made earlier that voters equate political compromise with poor representation and this holds even in the context of this experiment where failing to compromise over smaller points of difference explicitly meant the parties would fail to accomplish their larger policy goals. Further more, it should be noted that the audience before whom the parties are bargaining have *no investment* in the outcome of the negotiations. These negotiations are taking place in an imaginary country, between fictitious parties, on behalf of non-existent supporters. Still, the audience punishes the parties for compromising on their commitments, even when this compromise is in pursuit of a larger goal. This implies, as complementary research on the American case by Tomz and Van Houweling (2012) also suggests, that campaign commitments

---

[6] Though the differences across treatments may appear small, one must bear in mind that the setup is intentionally abstract. The subjects have no history with the parties and will not be exposed to the effects of any policy. These responses are therefore purged of any "baggage" of socialization into the political system, political preferences, perceived risk posed by the outcome, and so on.

are meaningful to voters and that there are real costs associated with breaking them.

The data also reveal that the subjects do not have statistically differentiable preferences between general, unspecified compromise and compromise that is more specific, allowing subjects to observe the horse-trade.[7] This too is salient as it implies that there is no benefit to showing supporters how the sausage is made – no benefit for explaining the particulars of a compromise. This may come as a surprise to some readers whose expectation may have been that voters are more willing to accept a compromise if a party can make the case that it is in pursuit of a larger goal. But, still, it is most likely too difficult for parties to make the case that the larger goal they achieved would have been impossible in the absence of compromise. Thus, whether voters are informed that there has been some unspecified compromise or some specific compromise, they are equally likely to believe that the party issuing the policy concession has in some sense failed its supporters. This suggests that, in terms of popular support, there may in fact be no upside to engaging in policy compromise – at least in terms of voters' perceptions of representational competence.

Let us now consider how the subjects updated their perceptions of the cabinet members' policy positions in response to the policymaking prompt. The arguments made above imply that voters should use compromise cues to infer that the parties have moderated ideologically toward one another – that they *are* more similar than previously supposed or that they *have become* more similar than previously supposed.

First, let us have a look at how the voters perceived the parties in the ideological space. Figure 4.1 shows the mean placements of the parties both before and after the revelation of the governing coalition and its policy-making disagreement. The panels are rank-ordered from left to right and the *t*-statistic for the difference in the pre- and post-treatment placements (light and dark bars, respectively) for each party is given at the top of each panel.

As the figure shows, the voters perceive an ideological rank-ordering of Labor Party < Green Party < Social Democratic Party < Liberal Party < Independence Party < Christian Democratic Party < Conservative

---

7 It is fair to note that it is possible that we may observe statistically significant differences in a larger sample of subjects, or, when more or less publicly popular policies are the focus of the log roll. That is, if a party with a popular position concedes that point to a party with an unpopular position in pursuit of a larger goal, we may expect that the party conceding the popular position is punished more significantly.

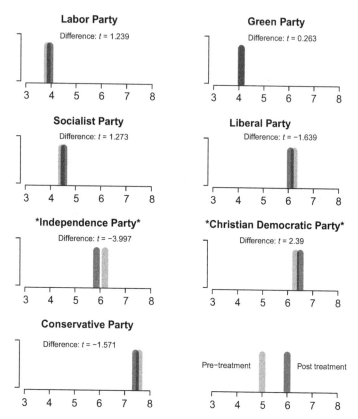

FIGURE 4.1 Subjects' placements of the parties: light bars are pre-treatment; dark bars are post treatment

Party, which is a fairly reasonable rank-ordering to recover given that political ideologies typically associated with parties bearing variants of those names.[8] The figure also shows that the only differences in pre- and post-treatment placements that reach traditional levels of statistical significance ($|t| \gtrsim 2$) are the Christian Democratic and Independence Parties, our governing coalition and the only two parties for which any policy preference information was revealed.[9] However, respondents

---

[8] The only real disagreement on the placements between UK and Dutch samples was over the Liberal party, where UK subjects placed it far to the left of Dutch respondents. This makes sense given the relative differences between Dutch (Volkspartij voor Vrijheid en Democratie) and UK (Liberal Democrats) Liberal parties.

[9] It is also worth noting that the only other parties that come close to having statistically significant changes in their perceived ideology bracket are the coalition partners on either side. It is possible that the revelation of the coalition reverberated through its neighbors to some degree.

Table 4.4 *Effect of policy-making outcomes on change perceived distance between coalition partners*

Response summaries	Mean (SD)
Stalemate	0.458 (2.227)
Logroll	0.045 (2.165)
Compromise	-0.157 (2.087)
Total $N = 1,542$	

update the two as more *dissimilar* rather than as more *similar* on average. Why? The reason is that, even though respondents learn that these two parties have coalesced, they receive this information in the context of a policy *disagreement*. It is probable that perceptions of ideology elicited *after* revealing the coalition partnership, but *before* revealing the budgeting impasse, would show that subjects update the two as more similar. We parse these changes in perceived similarity across treatment groups and this clarifies the impact of the disagreement on respondent perceptions.

This parsing is given in Table 4.4, which shows the changes in the subjects' perceptions of the coalition partners ideological distances across the three treatments. These values are simply the differences in the absolute distances perceived between cabinet parties across pre- and post-treatment responses: $|CD_{post} - Ind_{post}| - |CD_{pre} - Ind_{pre}|$. Thus, positive values indicate that the subject believes the parties are *more* ideologically *distant* after the treatment than before, and negative values indicate that the subject believes the parties are *less* ideologically *distant* after the treatment than before. We know from the total summaries in Figure 4.1 that subjects across all treatments, on average, perceived a widening of the ideological distance between cabinet partners. However, the results given in Table 4.4 suggest that this is almost entirely due to the powerful effects of the stalemate treatment – effects roughly three times the magnitude of the next most powerful treatment, the compromise treatment.

Indeed, Table 4.4 reveals a rank-ordering in treatment effects that conforms more readily to what many readers' natural expectations may be: Stalemate > Logroll > Compromise. That is, on average, the subjects

Table 4.5 *Treatment effect comparison on perceived dissimilarity*

Comparison	Difference (certainty)
Stalemate–Logroll	0.414 ($p = 0.003$)
Stalemate–Compromise	0.615 ($p < 0.001$)
Logroll–Compromise	0.202 ($p = 0.127$)
Total $N = 1,542$	

perceive an increase of about one half of one unit of left-right distance (in a 0–10 space) between the coalition partners when treated with the stalemate outcome. Subjects receiving the compromise treatment, on the other hand, perceive a significant contraction of the distance between the coalition partners, while those that receive the logroll treatment manifest effectively no change. Table 4.5 shows pairwise comparison across treatment groups with certainty estimates.

The estimates reveal that there are – as above in the representational quality analysis – significant differences between the stalemate treated and the logroll and compromise treated; however, there is no statistically identifiable difference between the logroll and compromise treated. While stalemate treated perceived the parties as significantly more dissimilar than both logroll and compromise treated; the differences between logroll and compromise treated are statistically negligible. However, even though the difference between the logroll and compromise treatments fails to reach the traditional level of statistical significance, the recovered rank-ordering across all treatments is quite robust (i.e., a non-parametric bootstrap exercise reveals that the rank-ordering in treatment effects is manifest with strikingly high certainty) and the difference in the average treatment effect between logroll and compromise is *substantively* significant. That is, while those receiving the logroll treatment do not seem to update their perceptions of ideological difference at all, those receiving the general compromise treatment do update and they update in a significantly negative fashion, shrinking the distance between the two parties.

What can we learn from this? Most importantly, the data suggest (although they are certainly not conclusive) that even though parties may not be able to mitigate representational competence penalties exacted in response to compromise by relaying the specifics of the negotiation, they *may* be able to mitigate the damaging effects to their policy brand by relaying the specifics of the negotiation. This is important for several reasons. First and foremost, it suggests that voters may be attentive to nuance in bargaining interactions in the policy-making process. This is important because it implies that, second, parties may be able to preserve the integrity of their policy brand throughout the process of coalition governance by making appeals to their supporters and the broader electorate. This may take the shape of publicly discussing the costs and benefits of specific policy decisions, or, more likely, by simply sending differentiating signals to the electorate, making clear which portions of the policy they like and dislike. Of course, that is one of the most central points of this book – that parties must adapt their behavior in the policy-making process to account for the potential damage that coalition compromise may inflict upon their brand. The impact of coalition governance on the electorate is about more than the outcomes alone, it is also about process.

DISCUSSION

The goal of this chapter was three-fold. First it aimed to advance a rationale for how voters in coalitional democracies are likely to react to compromise and why. The discussion above suggested that voters are likely to view compromise as manifestation of poor representation. This may happen one or both of two ways. It may be that voters equate compromise with incompetence, believing that parties who yield policy concessions to their partners in coalition do so because they are unable to best their counterparts at the bargaining table and must therefore accept a suboptimal resolution. It may also be that voters view compromise as a sign of untrustworthiness – that parties are either willing to sellout their campaign promises in the policy-making process in pursuit of some other goals, or, that they have misrepresented their policy preferences in the first place.

The second and third goals of this chapter were to test how compromise would affect voters' evaluations of the representational competence of coalition parties and how compromise may alter the electorate's perceptions of the ideological positions of coalition participants. To this end, an experiment was conducted where subjects are introduced to a simulated country, party system, and coalition government. They are then told about the policy promises made by the two members of the governing coalition and presented a budgeting disagreement between the two parties which is rooted in their campaign promises. After being presented with the disagreement, the subjects are treated with one of three randomly assigned resolutions to this dispute: a stalemate treatment in which the parties cannot overcome their differences and no new policy is passed; a logroll treatment in which each party gives and receives one policy concession in order to come to an agreement and pass a new budget; and a general compromise treatment, in which the subjects are told that the cabinet partners were able to forge an agreement over the new budget, but no specifics are given over the shape of that compromise.

Subjects receiving the logroll and compromise treatments gave significantly lower evaluations of the parties' success in representing their supporters than subjects receiving the stalemate treatment, *even though the stalemate resulted in an overall policy-making failure*. Further more, subjects receiving the logroll and compromise treatments also perceived the cabinet partners as having grown significantly closer in the left-right space than subjects receiving the stalemate treatment, although, there is suggestive evidence that parties may be able to protect their brand by communicating the mechanics of the compromise to their supporters. In sum, the results of the experiment suggest that voters do not care for compromise in the policy-making process, that voters will have lower evaluations of the representational competence of parties that compromise (even if compromise advances a larger goal), and that voters will update their perceptions of the policy profiles of cabinet participants in response to compromise. Moreover, all of these effects manifest even in the sterile environment we have created for the experiment in which the parties and stakes are imaginary.

These results are similar to previous studies on the American case that provide experimental evidence that voters are averse to compromise (e.g., Harbridge and Malhotra 2011; Harbridge, Malhotra, and Harrison 2014), but this is the first time such evidence has been offered in the context of coalition governance where compromise is an unavoidable reality. In forming a multiparty cabinet, the participants are publicly announcing their intention to embark upon a series of broad and wide-ranging policy compromises with their partners in government, often enumerating the policies they intend to pursue in a public coalition agreement.

And voters must, on some level, understand that each parties' votes are required to pass policy and, as a result, that no party is likely to get everything it wants on each and every item on the agenda. It is simply unreasonable to expect that a party engaged in coalition governance will be able to avoid compromise on each dimension and it is similarly unreasonable to be surprised when compromise inevitably occurs. Even if one subscribes to the ministerial dominance model of coalition governance where compromise on specific policies is avoided, the allocation of ministerial portfolios at the outset is still a product of compromise. Further, even if voters are willing to forgive this original sin, perceiving a coalition government in which no party must compromise means that voters would have to attribute each and every policy to the party controlling the relevant ministerial portfolio and for nearly all citizens this is simply asking too much.

And yet, here we are, with evidence in hand that compromise is equated with representational failure. It may not be fair-minded for voters to expect that coalition compromise can be avoided altogether. It may not be sensible for voters to be surprised at the revelation of coalition compromise. On these matters, reasonable people can disagree. However, the widespread expectation that compromise is completely avoidable within the parameters of a system of governance built upon rules and incentives seemingly designed for the sole purpose of making compromise inevitable is not what social scientists would call ecologically rational and this expectation therefore provides a poor explanation of the results uncovered here.

That having been said, we can absolutely forgive voters a level of *disappointment*. As any New York Knicks fan can tell you,[10] we would be foolish to head into the start of each and every season expecting our broken yet beloved Knicks to win the championship, or even to win their division. However, each and every year, despite reasonable *expectations*, we find a way to muster high *hopes*. Deep down, we know that our treasured Knicks will not be competitive for the title, but we *hope* that we are wrong; we *hope* for the best. And these high hopes have a way of making the realities of the present day National Basketball Association all the more painful to bear. Every season we conjure high hopes and these high hopes ultimately lead to disappointment which, in turn, fosters dissatisfaction with the players, the coaches, and with team management. Maybe

---

[10] At least any Knicks fan about the time of this writing in 2020 My hope is that the discussion here will seem alien to future generations of Knicks fans.

the players are not as good as we thought they were. Maybe the coaches drew up those terrible plays purposefully, not realizing how unsuccessful they would be. Maybe the executives cannot fairly and accurately evaluate the talent and capabilities of their players and coaches. Players get traded, coaches get fired, executives are forced to resign, and, in the process, any incremental improvement in the team's long-term prospects can be dashed.

In sports, just as in politics, short-term disappointments leveled by overly optimistic expectations have a way of sabotaging progress toward long-term improvement. It is difficult for teams to devote resources to the development of young players when their fans – their core constituency – demand wins right now, just as it is difficult for parties to strike compromises to move their broader agenda forward when their supporters may count these incremental advancements as losses.

Of course, these fan and supporter reactions are in no way, shape, or form unique to professional basketball or politics. Humans are pathologically optimistic and therefore regularly disappointed. Optimism bias is one of the most robust social scientific findings we have discovered and it holds across an array of disciplines, wherever expectations are salient to decision-making. We underestimate the probability of car accidents (DeJoy 1989). We overestimate the probability of long, healthy lives lived with lasting relationships (Weinstein 1980). Of course, we are overly optimistic about our financial prospects as well (Puri and Robinson 2007). The evidence presented here suggests that voters in coalitional democracy are, essentially, human and are therefore prone to optimism, which induces disappointment with the unavoidable realities of multiparty policymaking. Of course, voters understand that compromise is unavoidable. Of course, voters will not be surprised by compromise. But voters may still get their hopes up only to be disappointed. They may still confuse execution with intent; conflate outputs with inputs. And so each new compromise erodes supporters' confidence in their chosen representatives. Each new compromise causes supporters to question what it is, truly, that their party is wanting to accomplish.

5

Costs of Coalition Compromise

Their parties compete in mass elections, as firms compete in mass markets, by developing brand names.
    – Gary W. Cox and Mathew D. McCubbins (2005, 32)

Does it matter that voters are averse to coalition compromise? In the previous chapter we learned that voters tend to (1) equate compromise with representational failure and (2) infer from compromise cabinet members' ideological moderation toward one another. While these results from the laboratory provide evidence for our theoretical arguments regarding how citizens should react to compromise, those reactions matter little if they do not manifest in alterations to real world voting behavior. Attitudes that do not shape actions are, for all intents and purposes, irrelevant. Therefore, the goal in this chapter is to assess whether perceptions of coalition compromise manifest changes in voting behavior and, if they do, determine the nature and magnitude of those changes, and their distribution across the electorate.

The core argument is that compromise and cooperation lead to the erosion of a cabinet member's individual brand by degrading both the distinctiveness (and trustworthiness) of their ideological position as well as their ability to credibly claim responsibility for policy successes – by eroding voters' perceptions of their representational and bargaining competence. By examining data from panel surveys administered in Denmark, Germany, the Netherlands, New Zealand, Norway, and Sweden,

This chapter and Chapter 4 adapt and extend a previously published article (Fortunato 2019a). Portions of these chapters therefore paraphrase or borrow directly from that article.

our analysis will reveal that perceptions of compromise in the electorate exact harsh penalties on cabinet participants, in excess of 2 percentage points of their joint vote share. Further analysis reveals that these penalties are concentrated among the cabinet's previous supporters and the politically disinterested, results that bear important implications for the cabinet's ability to mitigate these losses.

COMPETENCE AND CREDIBILITY

Perceptions of compromise should lead to penalties for cabinet parties on two levels: by eroding voters' perceptions of their competence and also by damaging the credibility of their policy promises. As such, one of a party's primary motivations to eschew compromise is to signal competence. By resisting the coalition compromise and needling one's partner in government, parties can send the message to their supporters that they are tireless agents, unrelenting in their pursuit of their campaign promises. This intuition that voters associate antagonistic policy-making behaviors with representational competence, or at least have a preference for resisting compromise, is supported by the experimental results presented in the preceding chapter and also has support from the extant literature on the American case (e.g., Harbridge, Malhotra, and Harrison 2014).

Going a step further, the idea that there is (typically psychological) value to "winning," or causing the other side to lose, beyond the actual outcome of a negotiation is fairly commonplace in the social science literature writ large. People like to win and they like to win even more when it means that someone else has lost. For example, in a series of dispute resolution games, Loewenstein, Thompson, and Bazerman (1989) find that a player's evaluations of their outcomes are conditioned, not only by the cardinal value of their own yields, but also by the *relative difference* between her own yields and their partner's yields. Meaning that, holding constant one's own payoffs, the greater the (positive) difference between their own payoffs and their partner's payoffs, the higher their utility. Or, given that you have won, you will be increasingly happier the greater your opponent has lost. Building on this contribution, Thompson, Valley, and Kramer (1995) find that player utility *increases* with their opponent's disappointment and *decreases* with their opponent's happiness. Further, these effects are exacerbated when the opponent is a member of an out-group – a finding that speaks directly to political negotiations between parties. These studies imply that policy outcomes may be viewed more favorably when they are won through hard bargaining or represent a "loss" to other side.

While these results have come from somewhat abstract laboratory experiments, they tend to just "feel true" to many of us. And again, sports provide an apt reference point. We tend to enjoy the game more when our team wins and there is no sweeter victory than victory over a hated rival. And we need not let intuition do all of the heavy lifting here, sport psychologists have studied this for decades (e.g., Zillmann, Bryant, and Sapolsky 1989; Zillmann and Paulus 1993). Going even further, there is political economic research finding evidence that salient or unexpected wins or losses by one's preferred team can have deep and far-reaching behavioral consequences, and condition, for example, the sentences handed out by judges in juvenile courts (Eren and Mocan 2018), the fervor of stock market investment (Edmans, Garcia, and Norli 2007), incidences of domestic violence (Card and Dahl 2011), and, yes, even voting (Healy, Malhotra, and Mo 2010). Team affiliations, or social identities more generally, can be powerful drugs.

Though there is not a direct corollary in political research between voter attitudes and wins in policy negotiations, there are studies that provide indirect support for this notion; most saliently in the literature on satisfaction with democracy and trust in government by Anderson and his colleagues. For instance, Anderson and Guillory (1997) show "losers" – those that in the most recent election supported a party that found itself in parliamentary opposition – are less satisfied with democracy than "winners." In addition, the authors show that policy-making institutions that constrain the majority by giving influence to the minority mitigates this difference in satisfaction between winners and losers. In other words, satisfaction with democracy is proportional to one's preferred party's ability to assert its will upon the parliament. Related research finds similar effects for trust in government, patterns of perceived democratic legitimacy, and preferences for institutional change (Anderson and LoTempio 2002; Anderson et al. 2005).

The central point to this discussion is that wins and losses matter to voters. And, as such, the connection between perceptions of compromise and perceptions of competence is fairly clear. A compromise is not a victory.[1] Winners win and losers lose and what separates the two is

---

[1] To reiterate a central point: given our natural penchant for optimism and competitiveness, compromised outcomes are substantially more likely to be perceived as a loss than a win.

ability – competence. But loss of perceived competence is just one half of the risk parties run by compromising. A party that is quick to compromise may find itself punished because voters have come to believe it lacks principles. There is precedent for this intuition in the extant literature as well. The desertion of compromisers has been noted by researchers analyzing the performance of parties whose primary focus is on principled stands, that is, "niche" parties. Theoretical and empirical research on these parties has found that they are most successful when they present themselves in sharp contrast to the parties that typically dominate government (e.g., Meguid 2005; Ezrow 2008). For example, in their analysis of the electoral fortunes of niche parties, Adams et al. write that,

> niche parties' activists are strongly policy oriented and are therefore highly resistant to ideological 'compromises' in their party's policies...[that] may tarnish the party's standing along such 'valence' dimensions of voter evaluation as competence and reliability (2006, 515).

The authors find that, as a result, niche parties are punished for ideological moderation. Note that this is moderation of their *platform* only and does not take into account actual legislative behaviors. That is, niche party voters are not punishing for poor representation, they are punishing for ideological compromise of the party's brand.

In this way, compromise may influence voters' perceptions of party credibility. During campaigns, parties make promises to their potential supporters and these promises may be viewed as more or less credible given the previous behaviors of parties in coalition. Parties that are viewed as dominating the policy-making process in the last legislative period may be perceived as more credible than parties that are seen as too compromising or overly accommodative of their partners. This notion of credibility or discounting the promises or policy statements of parties is not new to the comparative literature. Building on Grofman's (1985) discounting model, Bawn and Somer-Topcu argue that voters are likely to discount the policy statements of members of the incumbent cabinet, because, "[p]articipating in government routinely requires parties to make compromises, to accept ideologically uncomfortable necessities, to deliver less than they promised, less than voters hoped for" (2012, 437). This intuition is no secret, nor is it limited to academic research. Indeed, Nick Clegg discussed this openly at the Liberal Democrats' annual conference about halfway into their period of co-governance with the Conservatives:

...the fact is governing together in the public interest carries a cost. Making compromises; doing things you find uncomfortable; challenging some of your traditional support – these are the dilemmas the Conservatives are coming to terms with, just as my party has had to (2013).

Not too dissimilar from the central arguments of Bawn and Somer-Topcu (2012), Lupu (2013) also presents a discounting model, albeit one focused on partisan attachments in the Americas. Here, voter perceptions of party brand or ideological position, where voters hold preexisting beliefs over the location of parties, are updated with new information as the parties are observed. Lupu's concern is brand dilution; how much will new information, discordant with voters' prior beliefs, erode the party's brand? He finds that information that reinforces party position, reinforces voter identification with that party, but that information discordant with expectations or prior beliefs of position, erodes identification that there is a loss of core support associated with off-brand or brand-blurring behaviors. Even more saliently, the information in this case regards the formation of party alliances that degrade brand distinctiveness.

Though partisanship is substantially weaker in Europe than in the Americas (Shively 1972; Mair and Van Biezen 2001), Lupu's underlying logic is particularly relevant here. Why would brand loyalty persist when party behaviors erode brand distinctiveness and create an increasingly crowded marketplace? Further more, if a party promises some policy x to its supporters, but its inability to successfully bargain for x, or merely the political realities of multiparty governance conspire to produce some policy $y \neq x$, it is eminently reasonable that the party's policy statements be discounted in the future, just as Bawn and Somer-Topcu (2012) argued.

This research reiterates and gives empirical support to the concerns Martin and Vanberg (2008) raised over the potential of compromise to obscure a party's policy image. Each time a cabinet member agrees to a compromise with its partner in government, it is sending signals to the electorate that are discordant with its strategically selected policy brand. Voters, in turn, may begin to question their understanding of the party's brand and intentions. Did the party misrepresent itself during the campaign? Did its policy priorities change after entering government? Or, is the party simply incapable of delivering upon its promises? In any event, voters would be justified in discounting future policy commitments from this party as its behavior has demonstrated that its commitments are incredible.

In sum, compromise could prove costly for a cabinet party on two distinct levels: First, voters may associate compromise with an *inability* to win policy concessions from its partners in cabinet; a competence penalty. Second, voters may conclude that a compromising party has changed its policy preferences or perhaps misrepresented its preferences during the previous campaign; a credibility penalty. How do these penalties manifest in the vote choice?

Let us assume that voters have preferences for parties defined by competence and ideological proximity. As in typical selection models of performance voting (in particular Alesina and Rosenthal 1995; Duch and Stevenson 2008) voters may learn about the competence of the incumbent party by observing its performance over the previous legislative term and utility over opposition parties is the complement to incumbent utility – it is decreasing with incumbent competence and increasing with incumbent incompetence. The wrinkle here is that competence refers not only to policy outcomes and managerial prowess (summarized as economic growth in the empirical models to follow), but also to the policy-making *process*, meaning that voters take into account the outcome *and* how it was produced. As such, voters may punish incumbent coalition members for being too compromising in the policy-making process – for appearing incompetent in policy negotiation or for failing to vigorously pursue their platform and thus failing to adequately represent their supporters – and these punishments may manifest even when overall cabinet performance (e.g., economic growth) is positive. Indeed, when parties are perceived as being too compromising, they can be easily scuttled into a "no-win" situation in regards to policy outcomes. When performance is good, they are unable to claim credit for having been bullied in policy negotiations by their partners in government and the good performance is attributed entirely to their partners. When performance is poor, however, they may *still be blamed* for not halting the passage of bad policies over which they held veto power.

Compromise tendencies also factor into proximity considerations by influencing parties' perceived credibility. As discussed compromise can obscure a party's ideological position or discredit their pronouncements. A party that is quick to compromise clouds its policy image and voters may become less certain about what type of policies the party actually wants or become suspect of its desire to deliver them. Thus, voters may discount the policy pronouncements of members of the incumbent coalition if they are perceived to have been too compromising in the previous legislative period.[2] This is of particular concern to voters who are risk averse in their choices and may be frightened away from alternatives who have obscured their policy image with compromise. As in the competence component, voters only have information about incumbent coalition members' propensity for compromise.

We can derive three hypotheses from this discussion: a generalized compromise hypothesis that ignores distinctions between competence and credibility, and a pair parsing the two.

Hypothesis 1 (General Compromise) *Voters are less likely to support incumbent parties they view as compromising.*

Hypothesis 2 (Competence) *Voters will discount the performance of incumbent parties they view as compromising.*

Hypothesis 3 (Credibility) *Voters will discount the policy positions of incumbent parties they view as compromising.*

DATA AND MEASUREMENT

Testing these hypotheses requires a measure of how compromising voters believe the members of the incumbent cabinet have been over the last legislative term. Unfortunately, no national electoral study to date has asked about voter perceptions of compromise in the policy-making process.[3] As such, a proxy must be developed. Fortunately, we are not without guidance in building such a proxy. Fortunato and Stevenson (2013) argue that voters, in response to the compromise of coalition governance, update their perceptions of coalition partners as being more ideologically similar than pairs of parties that are not coalesced. The reasons why perceptions of compromise would manifest spatially can be quickly resummarized. First, compromise signals an ideological flexibility that obscures a party's "pure" position on the issues (Martin and Vanberg 2008). Second, com-

---

[2] Note that this refers to credibility, or trustworthiness, not expectations for future policy moderation that require the voter to forecast likely future coalitions as in Kedar (2005). As such, one would not expect voters to prefer compromising parties that are distant to them more than uncompromising parties that are distant to them.

[3] Indeed, parliamentary election studies ask surprisingly few, if any, questions about the actual business of governing, particularly coalition policymaking.

promise presents new information that voters may use to update their perceptions of where parties stand and this new information can often be at odds with previous perceptions (Lupu 2013). Third, the compromise and cooperation necessary for coalition governance may, in some cases, motivate coalition partners to converge on their policy preferences (Adams et al. 2013). Finally, the available research on coalition policymaking suggests outcomes will most often reflect coalition compromise, rather than the preferences of any individual party (Martin and Vanberg 2014). This means that, to the extent that voters monitor outcomes to infer the preferences of coalition parties, the typical voter is likely to perceive coalition partners as moderating toward one another.

Empirically, Fortunato and Stevenson (2013) find robust evidence that perceptions of cabinet parties are influenced by coalition policy making and that voters are likely to perceive compromising parties as becoming more similar spatially. This is a finding that has recently been reconfirmed by Adams, Ezrow, and Wlezien (2016), who show that voters also update their perceptions of parties' preferences on European Integration in response to coalition formation, as well as by Falco-Gimeno and Fernandez-Vazquez (2020), who find that coalitions are most informative, or have the largest impact, when they are off-brand or unexpected. The latter result is of course reminiscent of Lupu's (2013) research. Thus, both the literatures on coalition policy making and voter behavior suggest that voters' spatial placement of parties may be leveraged to construct a measure of *perceived compromise* – that parties who are perceived as ceding concessions to their partners in the policy-making process will be "pushed" toward those partners in the policy space or that parties who are perceived as intransigent in the policy-making process will be "pulled" away from their partners. Of course, we need not rely on this previous research to justify such a measure, we need only refer back to the previous chapter where we found that *compromise* signals caused our subjects to update their perceptions of coalition partners as having moderated *toward* one another relative to the *conflict* signals that caused our subjects to update their perceptions of coalition partners as having moved *away* from one another.

All together, the extant research and our experimental findings from the previous chapter present a compelling case for the idea that if we are able to track how individual voters have changed their perceptions of the ideological position of a cabinet party in reference to its partner over their time in government together, we can proxy for how compromising that voter believes the party has been over the legislative period. This means that we must be able to measure how voters perceive partners in coalition at the formation of their government as well as at the termination of their government. We need panel data.

To test our empirical expectations, nine parliamentary election panel surveys have been gathered. These surveys were conducted in six countries with similar policy-making institutions and intracabinet norms (Müller and Strom 2003): Denmark (2001–2005), Germany (2002–2005; 2005–2009), the Netherlands (1982–1986; 1986–1989; 1989–1994), New Zealand (2005–2008), Norway (2001–2005), and Sweden (1991–1994).[4] The governments and their member parties are summarized in Table 5.1, where the first listed member controls the premiership.

Each survey administered its first component in the days immediately prior to or following a parliamentary election and its second component about the subsequent election. This allows us to measure voter perceptions of the cabinet's member parties at the time the government is formed and after it has served its term. These values (left-right placements of the cabinet parties) are used to construct our proxy for *perceived compromise*. This measure quantifies the degree to which a voter perceives that one coalition partner has ceded compromises to another by capturing how far the voter has "pushed" the policy position of the focal party toward the partner party over the course of their time in cabinet together.

Consider a two-party cabinet composed of *Party A* and *Party B*. For *Party A*, we compare how far a voter perceives the position of *Party A* to be from the position *Party B* at the time the cabinet forms ($|A_1 - B_1|$) to how far the voter perceives the position of *Party A* to be from *Party B*'s original position after the cabinet has served its term ($|A_2 - B_1|$). We compare the two perceptions of *Party A* (A_1 and A_2) to *Party B*'s original position (B_1) to account for the possibility that voter perceptions update jointly. That is, the voter may push *Party A* toward *Party B*'s original position and also vice versa if they perceive both parties conceding policy points to one another. Choosing the original position for each party to serve as a reference point accounts for this tendency.

---

4 These surveys were administered by the Danish Election Project, the study of Political Attitudes, Political Participation and Voting Behavior in Reunified Germany, the Dutch Parliamentary Election Study, the New Zealand Election Study, the Norwegian Election Study, and the Swedish National Election Study, respectively. Of course, a cabinet replacement between the first and second wave of the survey would make measuring perceived compromise impossible. None of the surveys used here has this problem; however, surveys from the Netherlands and Norway were discarded due to this issue.

Table 5.1 *Cabinets included in analysis*

Country	Cabinet	Members	Tenure
Denmark	A.F. Rasmussen I	Venstre; Det Konservative Folkeparti	2001–2005
Germany	Shröder II	Sozialdemokratische Partei; Grüne	2002–2005
Germany	Merkel I	Christlich Demokratische Union/Christlich-Soziale Union; Sozialdemokratische Partei	2005–2009
Netherlands	Lubbers I	Christen-Democratisch Appèl; Volkspartij voor Vrijheid en Democratie	1982–1986
Netherlands	Lubbers II	Christen-Democratisch Appèl; Volkspartij voor Vrijheid en Democratie	1986–1989
Netherlands	Lubbers III	Christen-Democratisch Appèl; Partij van de Arbeid	1989–1994
New Zealand	Clark III	Labour; Progressive Party	2005–2008
Norway	Bondevik II	Kristelig Folkeparti; Høyre; Venstre	2001–2005
Sweden	Bildt	Moderata samlingspartiet; Kristdemokraterna; Liberalerna; Centerpartiet	1991–1994

The measure, then, takes the following form for *Party A*: $|A_1 - B_1| - |A_2 - B_1|$, or, the absolute difference between *Party A* at election *one* and *Party B* at election *one* less the absolute difference between *Party A* at election *two* and *Party B* at election *one*. Thus, positive values indicate perceived compromise, and negative values would indicate the opposite (differentiation via intransigence), as positive values denote that the voter has pushed *Party A* toward *Party B* over the cabinet's tenure.

When there are more than two parties in coalition, perceptions of *Party B* are replaced by the mean perception of all of *Party A*'s coalition partners. Since this measure is so important to coming analysis, it is

Table 5.2 *Exploring* perceived compromise. *Model is a hierarchical linear regression. Higher values of the DV denote greater perceived compromise*

Covariate	Parameter	SE
Intercept	−7.568	(2.486)
CMP compromise	−0.031	(0.044)
Preelectoral coalition	0.024	(0.107)
ln(cabinet duration)	0.999	(0.348)
Junior partner	0.126	(0.101)
Prior cabinet supporter	−0.067	(0.038)
Economy	−0.015	(0.018)
Distance	−0.176	(0.018)
Political interest	0.065	(0.018)
Ideological extremity	−0.007	(0.013)
Between cabinet parties	0.736	(0.044)
Random intercept: *var*(respondent)	0.783	
Random intercept: *var*(party)	0.219	
N	12,772	
ln(likelihood)	−24,447	
AIC	48,923	

worth taking a moment to examine its correlates. Table 5.2 assesses the correlates of perceived compromise by regressing the measure on several characteristics of the cabinet and member parties. These are, in order, the degree to which cabinet partners have moderated their positions – as expressed in their manifesto-derived preference estimates – toward one another (*CMP compromise*), whether or not the parties signaled their intent to cooperate before the first election by announcing a *pre-electoral coalition*, how long the cabinet's term in office was (*cabinet duration*), and whether or not the party in question was a *junior partner* or held the premiership. The model also includes a series of characteristics of the voter whose perceptions we are assessing: whether or not they are a *prior cabinet supporter* (voted for the incumbent at the first election), their perceptions of the *economy*, their ideological *distance* from the focal party, their level of *political interest*, their own *ideological extremity*, and whether or not they situate themselves within the cabinet's ideological range (*between cabinet parties*).

The results in Table 5.2 suggest that changes to parties' electoral manifestos between elections (at least in the short term) do not affect voters' perceptions of compromise, nor does the formation of pre-electoral coalitions. The cabinet's duration, however, does affect perceptions of compromise and the effect is strongly positive. This is intuitive and speaks to previous theoretical results that we will discuss later in the book (i.e., Stevenson 2002). The longer a party spends in coalition, the more policy it makes with its partners, the more concessions it's forced to endure, the more voters perceive it as compromising.

Being a junior partner, rather a prime minister is positively correlated to perceived compromise, but only weakly so. Economic outcomes seem to have no impact on perceptions of compromise, but previous cabinet supporters and those that are ideologically distant from the government tend to perceive less compromise in the policy-making process, while those with higher levels of political interest and those that fall within the ideological range of the cabinet tend to perceive more compromise. It should be noted that there are only a handful of cabinets in the sample and, as such, estimates on cabinet or party-level covariates should be taken with a grain of salt as there is little cross-unit variation on those variables. That said, we should bear in mind that the *perceived* characteristics of parties do vary within and across units and so we can be fairly confident in those relationships.

Getting back to the task at hand, assembling the data needed to analyze the effects of perceived compromise on vote choice, let us consider the variables we need to test our hypotheses. In addition to perceived compromise, the data assembled allow us to measure voters' perceptions of economic performance (*economy*, where higher values indicate better performance), which will act as a summary measure of the perceived quality of incumbent performance. Of course, they also allow us to measure how close the voters perceive themselves to each of the parties spatially (*distance*).[5] Thus, we are able to test the *competence* hypothesis by interacting perceived compromise with economic perceptions and test the *credibility* hypothesis by interacting perceived compromise with distance.

As our voters have several alternatives to choose from, a conditional choice model is most appropriate and a mixed logit model (Train

---

[5] The scales used to measure perceptions of economic performance and party position vary a bit across surveys (three or four and ten or eleven point scales, respectively). To account for this, these values are rescaled before the surveys are aggregated and moved to have a minimum value of zero to make for easier interpretation of the interactions. Omitting this rescaling or changing economic evaluations to a dummy variable indicating positive/negative perceptions, has no effect on the substantive results.

2003; Glasgow, Golder, and Golder 2011) is estimated. The model regresses each respondent's vote choice (where the choice set is all parties included in the survey) on a vector of covariates, which vary over individuals and parties and allow for the estimation of random coefficients on each covariate at the level of the choice. The random coefficients allow us to assess how individuals may place differing weights on certain variables when making their choice. In other words, we can allow some voters to place more weight on compromise than others, or, some voters to place more weight on economic performance than others. These different weights can then be compared, which will come in handy when we consider some individual behavioral differences later.

The model includes perceived compromise, economic perceptions, distance, an indicator for incumbent coalition status, and interactions of incumbent status and distance to account for the possibility that incumbents are simply less credible as a function of their time in cabinet, regardless of their tendency to compromise, as Bawn and Somer-Topcu (2012) suggest. The model also contains interactions of perceived compromise with economic perceptions and distance to parse the effects of competence and credibility and test our second and third hypotheses. Recall that the expectation is that perceived compromise will be negative and that perceived compromise and its interactions with economic perceptions and distance will be negative. More specifically, the *competence* hypothesis is supported if the interaction of perceived compromise and economic perceptions reveals that the level of support gained by incumbent parties due to the performance of the economy is eroded by perceived compromise – that their ability to credit claim on these gains has been damaged. The *credibility* hypothesis is supported if the interaction of perceived compromise and distance reveals that the support lost by incumbent parties due to ideological distance is exacerbated by perceived compromise – that their ability to credibly commit to a set of policy promises has been damaged.

Because interpreting these kinds of models can be tricky when simply looking at the parameter estimates, the results are presented in Table 5.6 in the appendix and we will simply discuss the key findings and substantive effects here. In sum, estimates reveal that there is no *direct* punishment for compromise, rather, compromise exacts its costs by moving voters to discount the policy accomplishments or policy promises of incumbent cabinet members. That is, while the model does not support the *general compromise* hypothesis, it does support the *competence* and *credibility* hypotheses.

We can see evidence for this by examining Figure 5.1 which plots the change in the predicted probability of voting for the incumbent given an increase in perceived compromise over the range of both economic performance and ideological distance. In other words, these figures show (a) how the benefit of high-quality economic performance is eroded by perceived compromise and (b) how ideological dissimilarity is exacerbated by perceived compromise. There is no point at which the shift in perceived compromise significantly increases the probability of choosing the incumbent party and the change has a robust negative effect for nearly half of the range of economic perception and approximately two-thirds of the range of ideological distance. This corresponds to nearly half of the sample in both cases. That is, nearly half of the sample report values of economic perceptions and ideological distance great enough to cause a robust reduction in the probability of supporting the incumbent given the shift in perceived compromise (holding constant the corresponding values of economic performance and ideological distance). In sum, the data bear strong support for both the *competence* and *credibility* hypotheses, but no support for the *general compromise* hypothesis. This means that, while voters may not have a direct distaste for compromise strong enough to penalize an incumbent, compromise does change the way voters view the performance and policy promises of incumbent parties.

More substantively, parties that are viewed as compromising, unable to plausibly claim credit for the policies that encouraged growth, are rewarded significantly less for positive economic outcomes, while they are still punished for poor outcomes. Similarly, compromising parties are also punished more robustly for ideological dissimilarity – voters become increasingly uncertain of what it is, precisely, that parties stand for when they have appeared too willing to compromise on their positions over the legislative term and are thus increasingly averse to ideologically distant alternatives. Given the distance at which the penalty truly takes shape, a plausible substantive explanation may be that voters are willing to tolerate compromise to a degree from an incumbent party that is clearly most proximate to them, but when distances of alternatives begin to become negligible, the compromise penalty becomes manifest.

(a) Effect of perceived compromise on incumbent selection: economic performance

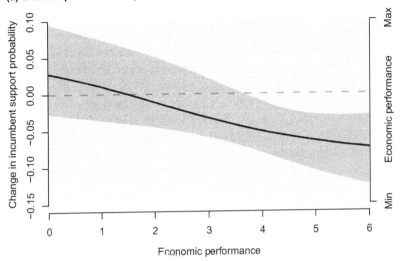

(b) Effect of perceived compromise on incumbent selection: ideological distance

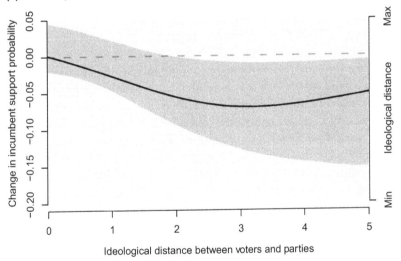

FIGURE 5.1 Testing the *competence* and *credibility* hypotheses. (a) Effect of perceived compromise on incumbent selection: economic performance. (b) Effect of perceived compromise on incumbent selection: ideological distance

In the face of these findings, the natural follow-up question is, just how large are the costs suffered by incumbent cabinets due to compromise? To answer this question, we will simulate several thousand "elections" to evaluate how many votes an increase in perceived compromise can cost the incumbent cabinet. For each simulated "election," we generate two sets of predicated probabilities. The first predicts the probability that each respondent supports a member of the incumbent cabinet given the true, observed values for each covariate, save perceived compromise, which is held at its true value less one standard deviation. The second predicts these probabilities after increasing each respondent's perceived compromise by one standard deviation from its true value. These probabilities are then used to calculate the number of votes the incumbent cabinet should receive under each of the two conditions (low compromise and high compromise) by comparing them to a randomly drawn cutoff. Then we simply subtract one from the other.

This process yields a total of 10,000 predicted incumbent cabinet vote changes resulting from the swing in perceived compromise. The distribution of changes is plotted in Figure 5.2. Note that, because the surveys are designed to be representative of the voting population at the time of administration, and the surveys are imputed for missingness, this exercise generates predicted changes that should be representative of the nine populations we are analyzing.[6]

Figure 5.2 shows that the predicted electoral loss for the incumbent cabinet given an increase in perceived compromise is high. Over 96 percent of the simulated elections result in a net loss for the incumbent with the mean prediction being a loss of about 2.5 percentage points of the incumbent's vote share – a total greater than the plurality winner's margin of victory in about half of the parliamentary elections in Europe in recent years. This means that the cost of compromise can be more than enough to cause incumbent losses sufficient to prevent the leading party from retaining plurality status and more than enough to prevent the reformation of the cabinet. To put this predicted loss in a more familiar context, it is roughly *twice* the loss one would expect from a 1 percent reduction in real GDP growth (Becher and Donnelly 2013).

Taken together with the experimental results from Chapter 4, the evidence is fairly conclusive that voters do not care for compromise. We have learned that compromise is equated with representational incompetence and that it can damage a party's ability to credit claim for policy accomplishments and credibly stake out strong policy stands. Additionally, these perceptions are not merely expressive feelings on the part of

---

[6] As recommended by Hanmer and Ozan Kalkan (2013).

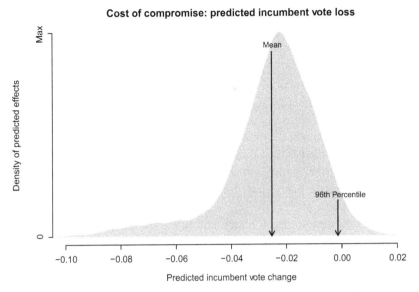

FIGURE 5.2 The predicted change in incumbent vote share resulting from a one standard deviation swing in *perceived compromise*

the electorate – the costs of compromise are real and they are large. What remains to be learned is how these costs are distributed across the electorate. Do all voters punish compromise similarly and, if not, where are the penalties most concentrated?

Who Punishes Compromise?

There is good reason to believe that some factors may make voters more or less likely to punish incumbent cabinet parties for appearing too compromising and this potential variation deserves exploration. In particular, it is likely that previous supporters of the incumbent cabinet, as they have paid in advance in a good faith exchange for the pursuit of certain policies, may be less tolerant of compromise than voters who did not previously support the cabinet. Indeed, a careful reading of the social-psychological literature discussed previously suggests that penalties should be larger among the "in-group," voters who previously supported a party that is failing to win policy negotiations or properly represent their interests; voters who allied themselves with the party in question. This is similar to arguments made in the behavioral literature by Harbridge and Malhotra (2011) and is echoed in the policy-making research by, for example, Martin and Vanberg (2011), who write that parties' legislative behavior is motivated by the demands of supporters in particular. Parties have made commitments to their core supporters; it is therefore this group that parties are ultimately trying to please in the parliament; and it is therefore also this group that will ultimately hold parties accountable for their (in)ability to impose their will upon the parliament. Our expectation, therefore, is that previous cabinet supporters will dole out greater punishment for perceived compromise than their counterparts that did not support the government in the previous election.

There may also be variation in punishment according to voters' level of political interest or sophistication. Compromise is, after all, an unavoidable reality of coalition. It is likely that this is a concept better understood by more politically interested voters. Further, it is the politically interested who are more likely to have been exposed, not only to coalition compromise, but to a more fine-grained narrative surrounding the compromise. Cabinet parties actively try to send signals to voters that they are fighting the good fight in parliament. They may debate their partners in government vigorously to signal their pure policy preferences and show that they are ideologically distinct from their partners. They may antagonize their partners' policy proposals in the legislative review process. These differentiating signals, meant to mitigate the potential costs of compromise, are substantially more likely to be received by voters who are highly attentive to the day-to-day business of governing. Our expectation, therefore, is that highly interested voters will dole out lesser punishment for perceived compromise than their less politically interested counterparts.

The data also allow us to consider the effects of priming the electorate for compromise by forming pre-electoral pacts. That is, parties may signal their intention to make particular compromises in advance of forming a government; indeed, in advance of the election itself. These signals may prepare voters for compromise and level out some of their less reasonable expectations or quell some of their more fanciful optimism, therefore mitigating their disappointment when the compromises are ultimately announced. These potential variations across cabinets that have and have not announced pre-electoral pacts are substantively interesting and can improve our understanding of the electoral repercussions of coalition policymaking as well as the logic of pre-electoral pacts and their ability to mold expectations for outcomes more generally.[7]

We can test our empirical expectations by leveraging the random coefficients estimated in the voting models above. As noted, each model allows for random coefficients on each parameter at the level of the choice, or voter, reflecting individual perturbations to the utility function. These random coefficients allow us to calculate differences in the effects of perceived compromise across each voter in the sample. These differences may then be regressed on a vector of individual and contextual characteristics, such as whether or not the voter previously supported the incumbent cabinet or whether the members of that cabinet announced a pre-electoral pact.

The process is as follows. First, we use the estimated random coefficients to calculate the change in the probability of choosing an incumbent party for each individual voter given the same one standard deviation swing in perceived compromise used previously and leaving all other covariate values constant at their observed levels. This probability change, punishment for compromise, is the dependent variable – the more negative its value, the greater the punishment for perceived compromise. The estimated probability change is regressed (via ordinary least squares) on a vector of individual and contextual covariates: the voter's ideological extremity, their level of political interest, whether they identify as a partisan, whether or not they previously supported the incumbent coalition, whether or not that coalition formed a pre-electoral pact, and fixed effects for each sample (with the 2001–2005 Danish panel serving as baseline). The results are displayed in Table 5.3 and they can be interpreted just as any regular linear regression model, bearing in mind that *negative* parameters indicate features that make voters *more* likely to punish for compromise, while positive parameters denote features that make voters more accepting of compromise.

The model results in Table 5.3 conform to the expectations discussed earlier and the estimates on the undiscussed variables are fairly intuitive. At the contextual level, the estimate on the pre-electoral coalition indicator is positive and robust, though its influence is smaller than several individual-level covariates. This means that cabinet parties may mitigate their expected punishment for compromise by priming voters to expect

---

7 In our data, pre-electoral coalitions are present in the following sample groups: Germany 2002–2005; Netherlands 1986–1989 and 1989–1994; Norway 2001–2005; and Sweden 1991–1994. These constitute about the half of our observations, all told.

Table 5.3 *Individual and contextual predictors of punishing compromise.
Negative estimates indicate* greater *punishment for compromise. Baseline
survey is Denmark 2001–2005*

Covariate	Model 1 Parameter	SE	Model 2 Parameter	SE
Prior Cabinet Supporter	−0.050	(0.020)	−0.050	(0.020)
Political Interest	0.004	(0.001)	0.004	(0.001)
Respondent Extremity	0.010	(0.002)	0.010	(0.002)
Partisanship	0.002	(0.001)	0.002	(0.001)
Pre-Electoral Coalition	0.012	(0.005)	—	(—)
Germany 2002–2005	−0.042	(0.011)	−0.029	(0.009)
Germany 2005–2009	−0.067	(0.016)	−0.067	(0.016)
Netherlands 1982–1986	−0.016	(0.006)	−0.016	(0.006)
Netherlands 1986–1989	−0.042	(0.011)	−0.029	(0.008)
Netherlands 1989–1994	−0.054	(0.014)	−0.041	(0.011)
Norway 2002–2005	−0.041	(0.010)	−0.029	(0.007)
New Zealand 2005–2008	−0.038	(0.007)	−0.038	(0.007)
Sweden 1991–1994	—	(—)	0.012	(0.005)
Intercept	−0.075	(0.019)	−0.075	(0.022)
N	5570		5570	
R^2	0.211		0.211	

it with the formation of pre-electoral pacts. Looking over the only other
contextual covariate, the fixed effects, it would appear that, on average,
Germans dole out the largest punishments for compromise and that the
partnership between the Christian Democrats and the Liberals (FDP) suffered more than the Grand Coalition between the Christian Democrats
and the Social Democrats that preceded it. That said, there are simply
too few cabinets in the sample to draw any meaningful inferences at the
contextual level and this small number of cabinets precludes analysis of
other interesting cabinet characteristics such as minority status, ideological compatibility, and so on. Although the sample is fairly evenly divided
between coalitions that did and did not agree to pre-electoral pacts, even
that result should be taken with a grain of salt.

There is, however, a much greater amount of individual-level variation on the included covariates so we can be a little more confident
about these effects. The largest individual-level difference is, by far, the
variation between those who supported the incumbent previously and
those who did not. Indeed, the average penalty among previous cabinet
supporters is about 150 percent the penalty levied by those who did not

support the incumbent in the last election. This result is encouraging, of course, given the nature of the arguments in this and the preceding chapter. If we found that non-supporters were the most likely to sanction compromise within the governing coalition, that would suggest that the theoretical arguments borrowed from the social-psychological literature on responses to bargaining across groups were a poor fit to the data.

Political interest also exerts the predicted effects, though they are by no means as strong. Respondents who report higher levels of political interest are significantly more accepting of compromise than the disinterested, suggesting that more politically interested voters have a more nuanced understanding of coalition policymaking that makes them more tolerant of compromise, or, that these voters are more likely to receive signals sent by parties in the policy-making process meant to soften the blow or mitigate the deleterious effects of compromise.

The remaining individual-level variables exert intuitive effects. A respondent's level of ideological extremity makes them less likely to punish the incumbent cabinet and those that have stronger, rather than weaker, partisan identifications (nebulous, though, that concept may be in multiparty parliamentary systems) are similarly less likely to punish the incumbent for compromise.[8] These results make sense for two reasons. First, there is a well-documented relationship between ideological extremity and partisanship and political sophistication (e.g., Luskin 1987; Prior 2005), and these factors may be tapping into knowledge effects not subsumed by the political interest measure. Second, very extreme voters are relatively unlikely to consider supporting incumbent cabinet parties, regardless of their propensity to compromise, simply as a function of their typical ideological distance or preference for less mainstream alternatives. Further, extreme voters and voters with stronger

---

[8] It is very important to note that partisanship in most proportional parliamentary democracies is an entirely different animal than partisanship in presidential or other single-member-district democracies. These partisan affinities are often fleeting and change with regularity. Indeed, in his seminal study on voting in the Weimar Republic, Shively concluded,

On the basis of the Butler-Stokes study of Britain and the Kaase-Schleth study of West Germany, as well as the present analysis of Weimar voting, I would suggest that such party identification must only rarely approach American levels and that what is often reported as 'party identification' in other countries is simply an expression of immediate voting choice (Shively 1972, 1223).

levels of partisanship are those most likely to have stable, reliable, choice propensities (e.g., Miller 1991; Scheve and Tomz 1999) – thus, their overall propensity to punish should be mitigated by the stability of their voting patterns.

Implications for the "Cost of Ruling"

One of the most pervasive empirical regularities in advanced democracies is that incumbent governments tend to lose votes, even after accounting for economic performance and institutional structure (Paldam and Skott 1995; Stevenson 2002). As Powell pointed out in his study of over 150 elections in twenty contemporary democracies:

> ... across a quarter of a century, the party or parties in office lost votes much more often than not... In only a quarter of the elections did the incumbents actually gain votes (2000, 47–48).

Nannestad and Paldam (2002) survey fifteen parliamentary democracies where coalition governance is the norm and estimate that this electoral "cost of ruling" averages over 2.5 percent. As discussed earlier in the chapter, these losses are not insignificant. In roughly 70 percent of recent elections, the plurality winner was determined by a margin similar to or less than the mean cost of ruling and in nearly 40 percent of recent contests, incumbents were unseated by such a margin.

However, despite widespread acceptance that the cost of ruling for coalition governments is real and important, we lack a theoretically coherent and empirically supported explanation for it. While there have certainly been attempts to explain this phenomenon, these efforts tend to suffer from one or more of three drawbacks that limit their explanatory power or applicability to the case of multiparty government. First, several theories are aimed at explaining behavior in the aggregate and so provide no explicit individual-level model of voting behavior that would support a convincing empirical test (e.g., Mueller 1970; Paldam 1986). Second, models that do provide a picture of the individual voter in their explanation tend to assume that voters are extravagantly informed and capable of making a diverse array of complex calculations (e.g., Paldam and Skott 1995), precisely the type of calculations famously dismissed as incredible by Downs (1957) and refuted by years of subsequent empirical work on voter knowledge (e.g., Bartels 1996). Third, many models are built upon foundational assumptions that, while perfectly acceptable for presidential or majoritarian contexts, are inappropriate for coalitional systems (e.g., Alesina and Rosenthal 1995).

The results above suggest an alternative explanation for the cost of ruling in coalitional democracies that avoids these three issues and is supported by the data. Voters dislike compromise and punish it at the polls. As a result, coalition government, which, by its very nature, demands compromise, will erode the support of its members. Before making this case more passionately, however, I first discuss the prevailing explanations and point out why they do not provide a good fit for parliamentary systems where coalition governance is the norm.

In the United States, the notion that executive incumbency is a disadvantage in midterm legislative elections has been wide spread for decades. Tufte's (1975) seminal work on midterm congressional elections is now over forty years old and was hardly the first to consider the issue; classic research by Key et al. (1955) and Campbell (1960), for example, discuss how the party of the president regularly loses congressional seats in midterm elections. Many works attributed the regularity of these losses to "surge and decline" effects, perhaps best captured by Converse's (1966) idea of a "normal vote." That is, if we consider each party's potential vote share as a distribution centered over some average vote share, then the greater the draw in *election$_t$*, the greater the probability of a lesser draw in *election$_{t+1}$*. Thus, the observed pattern of "surge and decline."

The surge and decline explanation was fairly quickly abandoned in favor of more systematic explanations for electoral outcomes that evolved out of the early literature on retrospective voting in the United States (e.g., Key et al. 1966; Fiorina 1981; Lewis-Beck 1988). For example, Tufte's (1975) theory, that midterm losses are driven by a mixture of presidential approval and real economic change, is one such example. This research has a clear parallel in the comparative literature, the cross-national economic voting literature, which attributes electoral change to voter evaluations of government performance, typically conditioned on institutional contexts (Powell and Whitten 1993; Duch and Stevenson 2008).

These performance voting models tend to generate good predictions for the electoral fortunes of incumbent cabinets conditioned on economic outcomes. The problem is that governments lose votes much more often than would be predicted simply by their economic performance. For example, Stevenson estimates that governments can expect to lose, on average, approximately 2 percent of their vote share, "even after controlling for various economic and political influences" (2002, 158).

A second prominent family of explanations for the cost of ruling is policy balancing. Here, voters have spatial preferences for policy and it is typically assumed that a large amount of voters find themselves near the middle of policy space, and, most often these models conceptualize competition between two parties that are anchored on either side of that continuum, more toward the extremes than the median. One example of this is Alesina and Rosenthal's (1995) American model that suggests voters will systematically vote against the party of the president in midterm elections in order to facilitate, on balance, more moderate policy outcomes via interbranch bargaining.

Paldam and Skott (1995) adopt the balancing approach to explain the cost of ruling more generally in their "median gap" model. The model assumes a simplified competition space in which voters have a choice between the two distinct alternatives. As such, elections may produce either "left" or "right" cabinets. Once a government is formed, it moves policy leftward or rightward over time and elections present an opportunity to reaffirm or reverse the direction of change. Therefore, far-left voters will always support the left alternative and far-right voters will always support the right alternative. But what of voters between the extremes? Paldam and Skott predict that moderate voters will *alternate* support between left and right alternatives in order that they may, on average and over time, obtain more moderate policies by denying left governments sufficient time to bring policy significantly leftward and vice versa.

In other words, we can think of policy outcomes as a pendulum. If we want to attempt to "anchor" that pendulum toward the center, but are deprived of the option of stopping its movement, what are we to do? The answer is that we can alter its direction as often as possible. The more quickly we change the direction of the pendulum, the smaller its average distance from the center. Paldam and Skott (1995) argue that, because so many voters place themselves about the median, a significant number of them will *always* vote against the incumbent in order to maintain moderate outcomes.

Though simple on their face, policy balancing models have substantive value as they predict the type of routine incumbent losses that we actually observe. Moreover, they help us understand voter behavior in a variety of contexts, not only under the condition of a simplified choice space where policy is altered over time as in Paldam and Skott (1995), but also in more complex institutional settings, such as a separated powers setting as in Alesina and Rosenthal (1995), or even under federalist structures as in Kedar (2006, 2009). There are, however, two hurdles in extending these models to coalitional systems. The first is informational; in the coalitional context, these models require an extravagantly informed voter capable of highly complex calculation. The second hurdle is that the foundational assumptions of these models simply do not fit the coalitional context. Let us think about this a little more deeply.

In the canonical policy balancing framework, the American case, moderate voters must (1) know who is in government, (2) have some perceptions of government policy output, (3) understand that the midterm election presents an opportunity to moderate policy – that is, have a model of the policy-making process with which they can understand the separation of powers, and (4) be able to select the party most likely to do so (meaning, have perceptions of the policy positions of the parties). Most would agree that these assumptions are fairly reasonable in the United States where there are only two relevant parties, thus a moderate voter need only to know the party of the president in order to know which party (not) to vote for (provided, of course, that they possessed a reasonably accurate understanding of the policy-making process). However, as the number of parties increases or the complexity of the policy-making process increases, so too does the difficulty of determining which party to support.

Consider policy balancing in coalitional systems, where there is no separation between the legislative and executive (and thus no midterm elections) and voters must account for cabinet formation. Just as before, the moderate voter must know (1) which parties are in government and (2) have some perceptions of government policy output. Given that they wish to moderate policy from where the current cabinet has brought it, the voters must now possess several more pieces of information. They must (3) have perceptions of the policy positions of all parties, (4) understand how votes are aggregated into policy – meaning that they must have some mental model of how multiparty cabinets are formed, (5) have expectations for which cabinets are likely to form and (6) what their likely policy outputs will be, and (7) use these factors to calculate which party to vote for in order to maximize the probability of policy moderation by indexing the probability of coalition inclusion by expected coalition output *for each party alternative*. Many doubt the ability of voters to make these calculations. Indeed, Downs famously concluded that, when faced with such tasks:

Eventually each voter either abstains, votes after cutting off his deliberation at some unpredictable point, or decides it is easier just to vote for his favorite party (1957, 163).

Clearly, such a complex decision puts tremendous strain on voters, but there is still more to it. Not only must moderate voters possess all of the relevant information and cognitive abilities listed above, but their information and calculations must be sufficiently accurate, and the number of such voters must be sufficiently high, as to bring about the levels of incumbent vote loss that we actually observe, even when controlling for economic performance and electoral institutions. Given the requirements of knowledge and cognitive ability that policy balancing models place on individual voters in coalitional systems, it is no wonder that they have received so little individual-level empirical testing outside of the American case.[9]

The second issue is perhaps even more troubling. Policy balancing models require that the median voter is categorically and enduringly denied their favored policy – that no cabinet may be formed to reflect their preferences – thus creating the need to alternate left and right cabinets to moderate policy over the long term. This assumption simply does not hold in coalitional systems. The structure of electoral institutions in these systems and the range of alternatives they provide are such that voters may elect a centrist cabinet and continue to reelect it over and over again if they wish. Indeed, there is ample evidence, from both the cabinet formation and democratic accountability literatures, that governing coalitions *regularly* span the party-system median and that policy outputs routinely reflect the preferences of the median voter (Martin and Stevenson 2001; Powell 2000, respectively). Without systematically denying moderates their preferred outcomes there is no need to alternate cabinets and therefore there is no routine incumbent vote loss.

The relationship between compromise and vote loss that we have discovered here, however, presents a much more reasonable (and systematic) explanation for the cost of ruling than policy balancing or surge and decline. And, though the specific application of the explanation is novel, it does harken back to earlier research – Mueller's "coalition of minorities" explanation for midterm election losses in the

---

[9] Kedar (2005) and Bargsted and Kedar (2009) present empirical tests of *prospective* voting models that take post-electoral bargaining into account, but these models do not explain systematic incumbent vote loss. Nor do policy balancing models that leverage federalist structures (Kedar 2006, 2009).

United States (1970; 1973). Mueller theorized that winning elections most often entails making promises to disparate groups of voters with disparate policy priorities. The process of governing, however, often means making tough decisions that are likely to alienate these groups in piecemeal. On balance, this should gradually build opposition in the electorate.

The process of voter alienation due to coalition compromise is similar, though it does not rely on parties assembling heterogeneous support coalitions. Parties make promises to their supporters during campaigns, but the political realities of multiparty governance make it difficult for cabinet parties to honor these promises or demonstrate that they are making their best effort to represent their supporters' policy preferences. Thus, coalition parties become more likely to lose support as perceptions of their tendency to compromise increase.

Because these perceptions can levy significant electoral losses, it seems possible that the nature of coalition policymaking itself may be to blame for the cost of ruling in coalitional systems. And there is more support for this explanation than the correlation between perceived compromise and vote loss. Recall that Stevenson observed that "the longer an incumbent government has been in power, the more votes it loses" (2002, 157–158). It should be of little surprise, then, that we found earlier that perceptions of compromise increase with the cabinet's tenure – the longer a government has been in power, the more compromising voters perceive its members to be, and therefore the more the incumbent can expect to be punished.

These complementary findings provide compelling evidence that the cost of ruling in coalitional democracies is rooted in voters' distaste for compromise and the unavoidable nature of compromise in multiparty governance. Unless parties are able to convince their supporters that they are not abandoning their policy promises, that they are not ceding concessions to their partners in coalition, and that they are fighting the good fight, electoral losses will come as a result. In the following chapters, we will discuss how parties may be able to send these signals without violating the norms of collective responsibility and therefore without risking the dissolution of the cabinet – a strategy that we will call "differentiation." We will also explore in detail, both qualitatively and quantitatively, a catastrophic failure of partisan differentiation and the resulting electoral aftermath, before moving on to a more comprehensive, macro-level analysis.

APPENDIX

Voting Model Descriptives

Descriptive statistics for the voting models are displayed in Table 5.4. The data are structured into respondent-choice rows, meaning that each survey respondent enters the data as many times as they have parties to choose from – this structure is necessary for the conditional choice models we will estimate. This means that the variables as characterized in Table 5.4 are measured at different levels. Incumbent party status is measured at the respondent-choice level, thus the table tells us that about 26 percent of the parties voters may choose from members of the incumbent cabinet. Ideological distance from alternatives is measured at the same level. Perceived compromise is only measured for incumbent parties, thus the descriptive statistics omit all of the 0 values that are observed for opposition parties.

Finally, economic perceptions are measured at the level of the respondent, or choice, but enters the model as an implied interaction with incumbent party status – meaning it can only take on a value of greater than zero for incumbent alternatives. Perceived compromise also enters the model as an implied interaction with incumbency. This is necessarily the case for conditional choice models in which attributes of alternatives are interacted with attributes of the choice, or chooser. Examples of this in the literature include the interaction of being the incumbent in the presence of a continuation rule in Martin and Stevenson's (2010) investigation of the role of incumbency in cabinet formation, or the interaction of a party holding the presidency in the presence of an investiture vote in Glasgow, Golder, and Golder's (2011) analysis of prime ministerial selection.

Table 5.4 *Descriptive statistics for voting model*

Covariate	Mean	SD	Min	Max
Incumbent coalition party	0.263	0.440	0.000	1.000
Perceived compromise	−0.188	1.719	-10.000	10.000
Distance	1.377	1.000	0.000	4.835
Economy	3.139	0.998	0.000	5.869

Note: Distance and economy are standardized and then moved to have minimum zero to aid maximization and interpretation of interactions.

Table 5.5 *Predictors of compromise punishment descriptive statistics*

Covariate	Mean	SD	Min	Max
Prior cabinet supporter	0.511	0.500	0.000	1.000
Political interest	3.905	1.002	0.000	8.766
Respondent extremity	0.000	0.999	−1.583	2.812
Partisanship	0.017	0.998	−2.639	2.808
Pre-electoral coalition	0.507	0.500	0.000	1.000
Germany 2002–2005	0.062	0.242	0.000	1.000
Germany 2005–2009	0.056	0.229	0.000	1.000
Netherlands 1982–1986	0.165	0.371	0.000	1.000
Netherlands 1986–1989	0.138	0.345	0.000	1.000
Netherlands 1989–1994	0.155	0.362	0.000	1.000
Norway 2002–2005	0.135	0.342	0.000	1.000
New Zealand 2005–2008	0.211	0.408	0.000	1.000
Sweden 1991–1994	0.078	0.268	0.000	1.000

Perceived Compromise Model Descriptives

The descriptive statistics for the analysis of perceptions of compromise are given in Table 5.5.

Full Mixed Logit Voting Model Results

In Table 5.6, the "Mean" columns are the mean parameter estimates (with standard errors below in parentheses) from the mixed logit models and may be interpreted as one would interpret typical conditional logit estimates. The "SD" columns summarize the variation in the random coefficients (reflecting individual-level perturbations in utility) estimated across choices (again, with error estimates below in parentheses). The raw results of the simple model support the *general compromise* hypothesis. The parameter estimate on perceived compromise is in the predicted direction, statistically robust, and substantively large. The log-odds change in the likelihood of supporting an incumbent party when perceived compromise swings from one standard deviation below the mean (−1.934), to one above (1.518).

To put these effects in more substantive terms, we can assess the impact of varying perceived compromise on incumbent support. We can calculate the effect of perceived compromise by holding all covariates constant at their true values and altering perceived compromise by one standard deviation below its true value for each observation to one standard deviation above its true value for each observation and computing

Table 5.6 *Effects of perceived compromise on incumbent support*

Covariate	Simple Model		Full Model	
	Mean	SD	Mean	SD
Incumbent coalition party	−0.120 (0.235)	0.701 (1.339)	−0.084 (0.234)	0.807 (1.285)
Distance	−1.708 (0.021)	0.880 (0.077)	−1.705 (0.057)	0.873 (0.069)
Incumbent × distance	−0.573 (0.157)	0.897 (1.146)	−0.585 (0.152)	0.860 (0.855)
Incumbent × economy	0.354 (0.047)	0.090 (0.173)	0.347 (0.047)	0.159 (0.097)
Incumbent × perceived compromise	−0.053 (0.021)	0.309 (0.080)	0.177 (0.097)	0.229 (0.463)
Incumbent × distance × compromise			−0.068 (0.032)	0.057 (0.097)
Incumbent × economy × compromise			−0.051 (0.023)	0.041 (0.084)
N(choices)	5,640		5,640	
N(total alternatives)	48,038		48,038	
log(*likelihood*)	−9051.863		−9041.211	

the probability of selecting an incumbent party for each of the two values. The change from one standard deviation below, to one standard deviation above the observed values results in a decrease in the probability of incumbent support by −0.026. That is, averaging across the sample, this change would reduce the incumbent government's share of the vote by 2.6 percentage points: A dramatic penalty.

Just looking at the simple model, however, does not tell the whole story because it does not allow us to determine the source of penalty. Are voters simply averse to compromise in general? Are they discounting the policy accomplishments of compromising parties? Or, are they viewing their policy pronouncements as incredible? The results of the interacted model allow us to parse these effects. These results suggest that there is no *direct* punishment for compromise, rather, compromise exacts its costs by moving voters to discount the policy accomplishments or policy promises of incumbent cabinet members.

6

Collective Responsibility and Differentiation

It is these distinctions that can then provide the compelling differentiation that allows brands to fulfill their potential.

Richard Woods (2004, 400)

We have devoted the previous chapters to discussion of the necessity for compromise in multiparty governance and learning about the harsh electoral costs that compromise can inflict. Still, it bears repeating that compromise *does* yield benefits. Cabinet parties that are cooperative with their partners in government are likely to find the policy-making process easier and more efficient. A harmonious coalition is able to maximize the benefits it derives from policy in a way that squabbling, inefficient coalitions cannot – each day a policy is delayed is a day its benefits cannot be enjoyed. Further, a cabinet party that is cooperative in crafting its legislative proposals by honoring the coalition compromise (rather than shirking the coalition agreement and initiating proposals at its own ideal point) may find that its partners reciprocate, just as parties that allow the proposals of their partners to pass through the legislative review process unmolested may be more likely to find their own policies receiving a similarly breezy treatment. And of course, coalition partners that are in sync and resist the temptation to quarrel over resources may also find it easier to dole out and enjoy the benefits of office – benefits that are primarily consumed by the party leadership; those that "call the shots."

There are benefits of compromise and cooperation that are less intuitive as well. Coalition is a repeated game. In some states, there are cabinets that seem to form over and over again. For example, since the

This chapter adapts and extends a previously published article (Fortunato 2019b). Portions of this chapter therefore paraphrase or borrow directly from that article.

formation of the Dutch Christen Democratisch Appèl (CDA) in 1977, it has formed ten governments with the Volkspartij voor Vrijheid en Democratie (VVD), despite the country's very large and diverse party system that often sees seats in parliament being won by ten or more parties. Austria has witnessed the formation of twenty governments composed of the Sozialdemokratische Partei Österreichs (SPÖ) and the Österreichische Volkspartei (ÖVP) in the post-war period. To the extent that a party hopes to once again govern with its current partners in the future, it is motivated to reaffirm its willingness and ability to compromise. To the extent that a party believes its current coalition will never reform, it may still wish to "play nice" in order to signal to potential future formateurs or junior members that it is a desirable partner in governance. After all, a partner that continually flouts the coalition bargain in its policy proposals or is regularly and overtly confrontational in the review process may be very likely to find itself in opposition after the next formation episode. Indeed, Tavits (2008) and Martin and Stevenson (2010) provide evidence that coalitions that terminate under friendly conditions are substantially more likely to reform, while those that end in squabbles are substantially less likely to reform, all else being equal.

But, of course, we know that appearing overly accommodative to one's partners, too willing to cooperate, or too quick to compromise can be ruinous come election day. So parties must differentiate – they must be able to signal to voters that they are fighting the good fight and doing their best to represent the preferences of their supporters by demonstrating that they are distinct from their partners in government. Indeed, this may become key to remaining in office after the next election or simply avoiding profound electoral losses. But cabinet parties face several obstacles in differentiating. First, parties cannot differentiate on issues that voters do not care about. For example, it makes little sense for a cabinet member to demonstrate that their views on international security are different from their partner's during peace time, just as discussions over how to best handle unemployment would be irrelevant in a state of full employment. Voters should only care about policy differences when these differences are relevant and so, given that time is a finite resource, parties should only attempt to make hay of disagreement on salient issues.

These saliency constraints exist in all contexts, of course. In the United States, for example, a Congressional minority can only credibly criticize the majority's stance on relevant issues that reach the floor for debate. The contexts of coalition governance, however, create even more problems for parties needing to differentiate. Even when the issues of debate are defined, the venues for debate *within* coalition are more scarce than debate *between* cabinet and opposition. This is because coalition members are bound by *collective cabinet responsibility*, a set of rules that determine the parameters of behavior for cabinet members (Laver and Shepsle 1994). These rules are so constraining, so important to the day-to-day function of coalition cabinets, that it is surprising how little discussed they are in the political economic literature and they most certainly warrant due consideration here. Let us begin with an anecdote.

COLLECTIVE CABINET RESPONSIBILITY

In March of 1999, Germany's Finance Minister and second in command of the Social Democratic Party (SPD), the leading party of government, Oskar Lafontaine resigned his post as Finance Minister and seat in the Bundestag, and renounced his offices in the SPD. Lafontaine had spent the previous three months privately warring with his Chancellor and party leader, Gerhard Schröder, over the shape of social economic policy in the only six-month-old government. Lafontaine was adamant that cabinet's priority should be alleviating unemployment and child poverty, while Schröder's focus was on the liberalization of the corporate tax and regulatory regime.[1] This discord had been raging behind closed doors for months, but Lafontaine's resignation was prompted by its public revelation. Mortified that the discord had been brought out into the open (and accepting that he could not win the fight with his Chancellor), Lafontaine chose to resign rather than continue the struggle in public and threaten the unified face of the government.

Though the disagreements between Lafontaine and Schröder were rooted in stark differences in their policy preferences, Lafontaine's resignation would almost certainly have been delayed, and may very well have been avoided altogether, if they were able to keep their disagreements private – if they were able to maintain collective cabinet responsibility.

Collective cabinet responsibility stipulates that the government present a united front on all policy matters, particularly after the policy has passed the parliament. In other words, all members of government are expected to support all government decisions and cloister any discord between member parties or individual ministers. Though these rules are

---

[1] This was, of course, the style of the time for Social Democratic and other left-center to left parties in modern, industrial democracies. See, for example, Tony Blair's Labour Party in the United Kingdom or Bill Clinton's Democratic Party in the United States.

typically informal – that is, unwritten – they are formally codified in several countries. The United Kingdom, for example, publishes its collective responsibility policies, including this example from the first Cameron cabinet, the coalition of the Conservatives and the Liberal Democrats formed in 2010, setting expectations for privacy in cabinet debate:

> The principle of collective responsibility, save where it is explicitly set aside, requires that Ministers should be able to express their views frankly in the expectation that they can argue freely in private while maintaining a united front when decisions have been reached. This in turn requires that the privacy of opinions expressed in Cabinet and Ministerial Committees, including in correspondence, should be maintained. (The Cabinet Office 2010, section 2.1).

And this example, also from the first Cameron cabinet, setting expectations on public support of cabinet decisions:

> The internal process through which a decision has been made, or the level of Committee by which it was taken should not be disclosed. Decisions reached by the Cabinet or Ministerial Committees are binding on all members of the Government. (The Cabinet Office 2010, section 2.1).

These are strong rules to abide by, even *within* parties, when preferences are dissimilar. But given what we have learned about how voters view compromise and the penalties they are willing to inflict upon cabinet members for appearing too compromising, collective cabinet responsibility in multiparty government can become an electoral straitjacket, effectively eliminating a cabinet member's potential to defend themselves.

This straitjacketing occurs because collective responsibility strips a member party of its ability to criticize its partners in government *or their policy proposals*, particularly once those proposals have become law. It inhibits parties from drawing public distinctions between their own preferences and those of their partners in public discourse. And, of course, once a policy comes to the floor for a vote, all coalition members must cast their ballot in the affirmative, and therefore may not differentiate with their roll calls as, for example, members of US Congress can, less they risk the dissolution of the government. Indeed, collective responsibility and party discipline are so strong that an individualized calling of the roll for all members is the exception rather than rule in many parliaments.

What are cabinet members to do, then, to try to mitigate electoral losses stemming from the compromise and cooperation necessitated by multiparty governance? The answer is that they may pursue differentiating behaviors in the only venue left to them by the constraints of collective cabinet responsibility, the legislative review period of the policy-making process.

THE LEGISLATIVE REVIEW PERIOD

The legislative review phase is the time between a proposal's submission to the parliament and its final vote. During this portion of the policy-making process – which itself follows a typically lengthy period of closed door, intra-cabinet negotiations over the proposal's content – draft bills may be openly debated on the floor of parliament, scrutinized in committee and the plenary (the process of which often includes ministerial questions or testimony of the anticipated effects of the legislation compelled from bureaucrats in the relevant department), marked up, and ultimately amended. In the process of this debate, scrutiny, and amending, parties may advocate for changes to the draft bill to defend the terms of the coalition compromise in the face of ministerial drift, or, more saliently here, advertise their criticisms of the draft bill to demonstrate competence, burnish their true policy preferences, and reinforce their ideological distinctiveness from their partners in government. In other words, cabinet parties may openly and aggressively push back against the policy proposals of their coalition partners in order to send signals to their supporters and protect their brand.

In practice, the legislative review period provides two fora in which cabinet parties may demonstrate how they differ from their coalition partners: legislative amendments and parliamentary debate.[2] Martin and Vanberg (2008) provide an exploration of parliamentary debate focusing on ideological dissimilarity and the electoral cycle. They argue and provide evidence that parties are motivated to signal to their supporters that they are different from their partners in government and that

---

[2] Sagarazu and Klüver (2017) propose that cabinet partners may use press releases, direct communications with their supporters, to differentiate from one another. They analyze which issues cabinet parties choose to emphasize over the course of the legislative period and find that partners generally discuss the same types of policies in the heart of the sessions, but diverge in the run up to election. Of course, their analysis is not concerned with demonstrating distinct *policy preferences* as is our focus here and neither do they argue that press releases are speaking directly to policy proposals or are substitutes for legislative scrutiny or debate. Indeed, they explicitly argue that these press releases are untethered from the legislative agenda. "Unlike speeches or questions in parliament, press releases are not bound by the parliamentary agenda and parties can choose independently what issues they want to talk about" (339).

these motivations should be increasing with the degree of dissimilarity in preferences between cabinet partners and proximity to the election.

This argument is intuitive and not too dissimilar from the arguments being made here. Nonetheless, the research design does not allow us to separate two competing motivations: the desire to signal competence and ideological positioning to the electorate and "true" policy disagreement. That is, the authors compare the length of parliamentary speeches (in words) given on a particular bill to a measure of the speaking party's ideological distance from the proposing minister and proximity to the election and find a positive effect, arguing that the need for differentiation is increasing with ideological distance and this effect is exacerbated by electoral proximity. However, it is almost certainly the case that parties that are more ideologically dissimilar from a proposing minister will find more aspects of the proposal distasteful and worth discussing on the plenary floor, which would cause us to recover that positive relationship between ideological distance and speech length regardless of the electoral imperative. Further, proximity to election may simply increase the relative value of signaling one's ideal point, apart from the dynamics of coalition compromise and cooperation.

What we would ideally want in our model is a measure of how *voters perceive* the ideological orientations of the coalition partners, *given* their true level of policy disagreement or the difference in the policy content of their ideological brands. In other words, we want to know the difference between the level of dissimilarity that voters perceive between two parties and the level of dissimilarity that those parties have strategically selected and advertised in the campaign platforms. Knowing this would allow us to infer the level to which coalition compromise has eroded the distinctiveness of the parties' ideological brands in the eyes of the electorate. This is the measure that should provide explanatory power for vote-seeking behavior in parliamentary speeches and legislative amendments.

Let us start here with an examination of legislative amendments in three parliamentary democracies with long histories of coalition governance: Belgium, Denmark, and the Netherlands. Legislative amendments are, by their very nature, expressions of dissent with a policy proposal – they mandate change. These demands for change may only be offered to an initiated proposal, which means that they are germane and salient to the political discourse of the day. Further more, amendments are costly – they require expertise, time, and labor to draft and propose. These costs mean that amendments cannot merely be considered "cheap talk." This is not to say that parliamentary speech is meaningless. Quite the contrary. Speaking time on the floor of parliament is a valuable resource used to voice dissent or support on various draft bills, attempt to stimulate public support for policy proposal, and communicate with voters or shape the media narrative on the government and its activities. Rather, this discussion is simply meant to drive home the point that we may consider amendments as credible differentiating signals sent by the reviewing party in reference to the proposal's authoring party.

More saliently, there is qualitative and quantitative evidence that proposing amendments sends differentiating signals that are likely to be absorbed by the electorate. For instance, most parliaments publish daily reports cataloging the events of each legislative-session day in the plenary as well as in committee meetings. These reports cover ministerial questions, plenary debate, the proposal and hearing of amending documents, and so on. These reports are vital resources for understanding politics in general and the policy-making process in particular in both scholarly research and popular press (e.g., Andersen 2016; Lund 2013). Increasing conflict in the review process is quite likely to make for a more antagonistic tone in media reporting of party interactions and new research analyzing the effects of this reporting on party interactions (such as the review process) suggests that these behaviors do, in fact, substantially shape media narrative on politics *and* that voters receive and assimilate these messages into their perceptions (Adams, Weschle, and Wlezien 2020). In the face of this evidence, we can proceed on the presumption that legislative review and scrutiny provide an avenue through which parties may communicate with their supporters and the broader electorate without risking violation of collective cabinet responsibility.

WHEN WILL PARTIES AMEND?

Let us first assume, as is standard in the literature on party competition, that the cabinet parties have arrayed themselves along the left-right spectrum such that they have maximized their expected electoral returns (e.g., Cox 1985, 1990). Now let us assume that voters perceive the parties' strategic self-placement, but will update their perceptions in response to signals from the policy-making process. Parties that appear to be cooperative or compromising will be updated as more similar, converging upon each other and shrinking the distance strategically placed between them. Parties that squabble and antagonize one another will be updated as more distinct, growing the perceived distance between them.

Recall that the arguments and analysis in the preceding chapters present compelling evidence that voters are more likely to perceive compromise, on average, than conflict. This is, of course, a function of coalition policymaking, which demands compromise. Indeed, Fortunato and Stevenson (2013) and Adams, Ezrow, and Wlezien (2016) provide evidence that voters update cabinet partners as more similar simply as a function of the coalition's formation. This means that the majority of cabinet parties face an immediate need to differentiate in order to maintain the distinctiveness of their brand – that most cabinet parties will need to differentiate in order to *preserve* the perceived distance between themselves and their partners and the legislative review process offers cabinet parties an opportunity to send such differentiating signals.

We can think of the utility a cabinet party derives from amending the legislative proposals of their partners in government as a function of three parameters: the electoral benefit, the policy benefit, and the cost of drafting and proposing the amendment. Here, electoral rewards are a function of the benefit of differentiation from the bill's authoring party – how much does the perception of concession, compromise, or ideological moderation toward the bill's proposer stand to cost the amending party at the polls? Or, how much has the strategically selected distance between the two parties eroded? As the perceived distance between the proposing party and the reviewing party closes (relative to their selected positions), the benefit of differentiation increases and therefore the probability of amending should increase in kind. We can write a simple utility function for a cabinet party in the legislative review process as:

$$U_a = (m - v) + p - c \tag{6.1}$$

where U_a is the utility a reviewing party derives from amending the legislative proposal before it. Here, p captures the policy benefit of amending. The simplest way to conceptualize this is as the distance between the reviewing party's ideal point and the policy proposal. As this distance grows, so too does the implied utility loss represented by the draft proposal, and therefore the greater is the benefit to amending. The costs of amending – analyzing the draft bill to predict its impact, the information investment required to write the amendments, and then the actual business of proposing and advocating for the changes – are captured by c. The distance between the reviewing party and the party of the proposing minister as perceived by voters is given as v, and m is the distance between the two as staked out in their electoral manifestos – their strategically selected policy positions. Holding p and c constant, the utility of differentiating through amendment is increasing when voters perceive the pair as more similar than their selected positions and it is decreasing when voters perceive the pair as more dissimilar than their selected positions. As such, for any constant value of m, the utility of amending increases as v falls. This yields a testable hypothesis:

Hypothesis 1 (Voter Perceptions) *All else equal, the more similarly a party pair is perceived, the more they will amend one another's legislative proposals.*

Before testing this hypothesis, however, we must first consider the other aspects of the above utility function. A richer discussion of the policy benefits of amending, as well as the potential costs will not only yield a better understanding of the scrutiny and markup process, but will also yield a listing of important covariates to consider in building the empirical model. This starts with the draft bill.

For parties endowed with ministerial portfolio, differentiation is accomplished through "ministerial drift," the act of purposefully defecting from the policy position of the coalition bargain (Huber and Shipan 2002; Indridason and Kam 2008). By offering a draft bill that disregards the coalition agreement, the minister signals to their party supporters that they are both sensitive to their policy demands and sufficiently competent to flout the constraints of their coalition partners. These signaling incentives should not be under-appreciated. Indeed, the credit-claiming benefits of ministerial drift are the engine of the Martin and Vanberg (2011) model of coalition policymaking. Ministers, they argue, endowed with substantial informational and procedural advantages, simply cannot resist the temptation to break with the coalition compact to attempt give their supporters the policies they crave.

These proposals, which break with the coalition compromise, can levy significant policy costs on the minister's coalition partner. The more distinct the minister's preferences from the preferences of their partner, the greater the costs. The greater the costs, the greater propensity of the minister's partner to amend the proposal in order to enforce the coalition bargain and mitigate their agency loss (Martin and Vanberg 2011). As such, one of the most important covariates in the model below is the ideological distance of the proposing minister's party from the coalition compromise (*compromise distance*). Relatedly, we must also include the ideological distance between the proposing party and the reviewing party as derived from their electoral manifestos (*CMP distance*). Recall that the electoral motivation of differentiation is determined by the distance voters perceive between the proposing and reviewing parties *relative* to their strategically selected distance.

An additional benefit of including this measure, the dyadic distance between the proposing and reviewing parties, is that it allows, for the first time, to empirically differentiate between amendments submitted to monitor the coalition compromise and amendments submitted by a party in an effort to drag the proposal toward its own ideal point. As Martin and Vanberg's (2011) amendment data are collected at the bill level – that is, they count the total number of article changes submitted to each bill by *all parties*, rather than the number of article changes submitted by each *individual party* to each bill – amendments motivated by the private policy concerns of individual parties are empirically indifferentiable from amendments motivated by coalition policing: both types of amendments should increase with the proposing minister's average distance from its coalition partners. The data analyzed here count amendments submitted by each *individual party* on a particular bill and are therefore able to parse these behaviors statistically. Because of this, we are able to execute a more explicit test of the coalition-policing model than has previously been possible.

Moving on to the costs of amending, extant literature on legislative institutions suggests that holding a committee chair empowers reviewing parties and substantially reduces the costs of legislative review. Döring (2001) discusses the substantial agenda-setting powers committee chairs possess and Strøm (1998) writes that committee chairs enjoy "expert staff assistance" that can substantially reduce informational and transaction costs in the review process. More recently, research by Carroll and Cox (2012) and Kim and Loewenberg (2005) argue that, as a function to these resources, holding a committee chair allows cabinet parties to efficiently mitigate the ministerial drift of their partners and, indeed, their empirical analysis shows that these so-called shadow chair are distributed just as we would expect given their ability to constrain ministerial drift.

This proposition was recently tested by Fortunato, Martin, and Vanberg (2019), who analyzed the degree to which ministerial proposals were amended conditioned upon the party controlling the committee chair. The authors find no difference in the number of amendments made to bills scrutinized by committees chaired by the party of the proposing minister and committees chaired by a partner of the proposing minister. This may be due to a minister's propensity to "auto-censor" their legislative proposals when faced with a shadow chair, or, more likely, that parties controlling committee chairmanships are loathe to use that power to prevent their partners in government from scrutinizing their own legislative proposals, less they risk retributive actions. The net effect of this would be to mute the amending "bonus"; one that cabinet parties enjoy when possessing the committee chairmanship (as the chair would not inhibit their partners from scrutinizing). These attenuative concerns are not manifest for opposition parties, however, and the authors do, in fact, find that bills scrutinized by committees chaired by opposition parties are amended significantly more than we would expect otherwise. The authors conclude that this demonstrates the power of the committee chairmanship.

Our empirical model must therefore include indicators for the identity of the committee chairperson; whether it is the party of the proposing minister, the reviewing party, another cabinet member, or an opposition party. As in the discussion between coalition policing and private policy motivations earlier, the more granular data employed here may allow us to learn something more about the role committee chairs play in legislative review. More specifically, because we can observe which parties are submitting each amendment, the data should allow more leverage in discovering whether committee chairs' primary influence is positive (increasing their party's ability to scrutinize), negative (inhibiting other parties with dissimilar policy preferences from scrutinizing), or both.

As monitoring devices, committee chairs have an executive complement in junior ministers. Thies (2001) and Lipsmeyer and Pierce (2011) present compelling evidence that "watchdog" junior ministers are placed in departments controlled by ministers who are ideologically distant from the coalition compromise and that this practice is more prevalent in countries that lack strong committee systems. Though each of the chambers we consider here do have strong committee systems, it is still important to account for the possibility that junior ministers are able to "spy and report" on ministers intent upon breaking with the coalition agreement and therefore reduce the need for policy-motivated scrutiny as Martin and Vanberg (2011) have found.

The costs of review extend far beyond institutional parameters. Committee chairmanships and advance information from junior ministers may be helpful, but the real work of amending comes at a substantial informational cost. Proposals must be understood and their effects forecasted. Ministers, of course, through their control of the relevant bureaucracy control the lion's share of these informational resources. For parties without ministerial portfolio, these informational costs are effectively labor constraints. Do parties have sufficient members on the relevant committee to interpret the initial proposal, identify the most salient points to take issue with, and then write and submit the amendments? Fortunately, committee seats (and legislative staff personnel) are distributed proportionately in the chambers we are analyzing. This means that we can account for these labor resources by including the reviewing party's parliamentary seat share in the empirical model.

A final consideration in modeling the costs and benefits of amending is whether or not the cabinet controls a majority of seats in parliament. This is critical as minority cabinets will not only be compelled to monitor ideologically dissimilar cabinet partners like their majority counterparts, but they must also appease some pivotal opposition party. This need to maintain opposition support for the legislative proposal should, on average, reduce the number of amendments we observe.

Consider a two-party coalition composed of m and r, the proposing ministerial party and reviewing party, respectively, where the coalition compromise position x, is located $m < x < r$, with some opposition party o. For an arrangement of the parties $m < r < o$ when the cabinet controls a majority and does not require the support of the opposition, the expectation would be that m proposes some policy p about its ideal point $m \leq p < x$ in order to capture credit-claiming (and potentially also policy) benefits and r would be compelled to amend the policy to drag it back to the coalition compromise x; this is the intuition of the Martin and Vanberg (2011) model.

In the case of a minority cabinet with the same arrangement $m < r < o$, o becomes pivotal. This means that m and r must maintain the support of o in order to pass their policy, making it much more likely that m makes an initial offer closer to x or perhaps even greater, $p \geq x$, in order to hold the support of o. This, in turn, shrinks the distance between the initial offer and the coalition compromise, $|p - x|$, therefore reducing the number of amendments that r must propose to monitor the coalition agreement.

We should observe a similar reduction in amendments given the arrangement $o < m < r$. Again, when the coalition controls a majority of the legislature, we would expect m to propose about its ideal point and r to rein the proposal back in to the compromise position by amending during the policy's review period. When the cabinet is a minority however, m may still propose about its ideal point, $p \simeq m$, but r is constrained in its ability to amend. This is because each amendment that r submits in order to drag the policy back to the coalition compromise increases policy's distance from o, therefore increasing the likelihood that o will reject the offer and vote against the proposal.

Finally, for an arrangement $m < o < r$, the placement of o between the two cabinet partners serves as de facto enforcement of the coalition compromise.[3] Taken all together, for any ideological rank-ordering of cabinet and opposition parties, we should observe fewer amendments submitted by a minority coalition relative to a majority counterfactual due to the cabinet's obligation to maintain pivotal opposition support.

In sum, we will need to assemble data that includes measurements of the following characteristics of amending parties, proposing parties, and coalitions: the distance that voters perceive between the amending party and the proposing party; the strategically selected distance that the amending party and the proposing party have staked out in their manifestos; the distance between the proposing party and the coalition compromise; the seat share of the amending party; the partisan identity of the chairperson of the relevant committee; whether or not the amending party has placed a junior minister in the department of the proposing minister; and whether or not the coalition possesses a legislative majority. Of course, we will also need to measure the degree to which the amending party proposes to change the draft bill.

DATA COLLECTION AND VALIDATION

The dependent variable for the analysis is the extent to which a cabinet party proposes to change a draft bill submitted by its partner in coalition. To collect this measure, information on over 2,200 legislative proposals introduced by cabinet ministers was gathered from three parliamentary democracies over a period of roughly twenty years: Belgium (1992–2010), Denmark (1991–2004), and the Netherlands (1995–2013). This is the largest such collection of data ever assembled and the sample includes all legislation on tax policy, spending, and the provision of social services – policy areas that should readily conform to a single, left-right dimension of political discourse. Other policy types, such as the ratification of

3 It should be noted that minority governments spanning a pivotal opposition party are rare.

international accords or transposition of European Union (EU) directives, for example, may tap dimensions orthogonal to national political discourse, and, as such, the positions of parties on those issues are much less likely to conform to a standard, unidimensional left-right. More importantly, the origin of this type of legislation is more likely to be exogenous to domestic political debate. Finally, the sample omits budgets and constitutional alterations as these are subject to special rules. Some readers may recognize these sampling choices as nearly identical to those made by Martin and Vanberg (2011).

Unlike, for example, Greece and Portugal, who have intermittent periods of multiparty governance, or Spain and the United Kingdom, who have almost no experience at all with multiparty governance, Belgium, Denmark, and the Netherlands are all quite well acquainted with coalition. Indeed, Denmark did not have a single-party government between 1981 and 2015, Belgium has been continually governed by coalitions for the last sixty years, and the Netherlands has not had a single-party government since the nineteenth century.

Importantly, Belgium, Denmark, and the Netherlands each have "strong" committee systems. Fortunato, Martin, and Vanberg (2019) describe five particularly relevant qualities of strong committee systems. First, the committees correspond to relevant ministries, that is, a one-to-one, or nearly one-to-one match between each ministerial department and each legislative committee. Meaning, for example, the Minister of Finance will report all of their bills to a Finance Committee. Second, the committees are of a reasonably small size, meaning that individual members of parliament do not become overburdened with committee assignments and may specialize and invest in expertise in one or few jurisdictions. Third, the committees are endowed with investigative powers, particularly the power to compel testimony by ministers, or other relevant bureaucrats, as well as subpoena relevant documents or commission research from outside experts. Fourth, the committees may freely amend or rewrite the draft bills before reporting them back to the plenary. And, fifth, the committees enjoy autonomy from ministerial and plenary meddling. That is, ministers may not veto proposed amendments or force the committee to prematurely report the bill to the floor before the committee has concluded its scrutiny. European countries with similarly strong committee systems include, for example, Austria, Finland, Germany, Luxembourg, Norway, Sweden, and others.[4]

---

[4] Interested readers should consult Mattson and Strøm (1995) and Martin and Vanberg (2011) for excellent discussion and data on the nature of committee system strength.

Belgium, Denmark, and the Netherlands provide particularly good test fora in part because they allow for the submission of amendments to cabinet proposals to be made by, and subsequently credited to, *individual parties*. In this respect, these countries are similar to a wealth of parliamentary countries at varying stages of development and, as such, the behaviors uncovered here generalize to a wide array of legislatures. Conversely, there is a small number of states with equally strong committee systems that do not produce a party-specific record of amendment submission. Instead, amendments are an output of the committee as a whole, as in Germany, or credited to the "majority" or "minority," as in Norway. In these states, parties must find alternate fora through which to differentiate, such as parliamentary debate, which we will discuss in Chapter 7.

For each bill in the collected sample, the proposing minister's party and department are recorded. There are a handful of bills with multiple proposing ministers – this is most common in Belgium – and for these bills the leading minister is recorded. Then, the number of articles in the original proposal is recorded. This is a very important exposure variable for the empirical model below as each article in the draft bill presents another potential point of disagreement for the author's partners in cabinet.

For the dependent variable, the number of article changes proposed to the draft bill by all coalition partners (except the party of the proposing minister) are counted and recorded. This means that amendments making simple typographical alterations, such as moving a comma or period in a currency sum, or fixing other small errors are not counted, as these changes are made exclusively by proposing ministers or rapporteurs in these countries. Also important is that amendments that are cosponsored by the party of the initiating minister are not counted. This practice is more common in Denmark, where the operating norms of governance call for consensual behaviors within the coalition for rectifying draft bill "errors" and reconciling discrepancies between the draft bill and coalition pact where the agreement makes very specific policy commitments.[5] Note also that each article change in each amendment document is counted independently and that parties may offer multiple amendment documents. That is, if the Dutch CDA proposes three amendment documents that respectively propose changes to articles 1 and 3; articles 2 and 3; and articles 2, 5, and 6 on a given draft bill, the CDA

---

5 This procedure is not commonly documented but was explained by a former Danish Minister of Finance during an interview conducted for this project.

will be credited with seven proposed article changes for that bill, even though there are redundancies in the articles being changed across the amendment documents. Multiple documents are most common in the Netherlands, somewhat common in Belgium, and nearly unheard of in Denmark where all amendments, offered by all parties, are nearly always aggregated into a single report.

The proposed article changes are counted in the same manner as in Martin and Vanberg (2011), with two exceptions. First, as noted, all changes here are attributed to a single party, whereas Martin and Vanberg sum all changes made by all parties and use the bill as the unit of observation. Recording the data in this manner is critical. Only by coding changes at the *party* level for each bill are we able to test our central hypothesis. The second difference is that these data count *proposed* article changes, whereas Martin and Vanberg record *implemented* article changes. Of course, their focus was policy outcomes, while our focus here is in signaling differentiation to the electorate and this coding difference reflects that divergence.

The independent variable of interest, the distance perceived by voters between the proposing party and the reviewing party, is calculated with survey data from the Eurobarometer, European Electoral Survey, and the Comparative Study of Electoral Systems surveys conducted between 1989 and 2013 in Belgium, Denmark, and the Netherlands. In each module, respondents were asked to place their country's political parties on an ideological scale. These placements are rescaled to a common 0–10 scale and a placement is estimated for each party in each survey via linear regression.[6] These individual party placements are then used to create a voter perceived (absolute) distance between each ministerial party and each reviewing party. For each bill, I use the distance estimate derived from the most recent survey. This variable is called *voter distance* in the tables to follow. The greater the distance, the more dissimilar voters believe the cabinet parties are. The smaller the distance, the more similar the parties are perceived and, holding the parties' strategically selected distance constant, the greater their incentive for differentiation in

---

[6] The models employed are intercept-only regressions where the constant estimate serves as the party placement and the standard errors are recorded to model the uncertainty of these placements. Of course, the intercept is equivalent to the sample mean. Alternative estimates, like modeling the perception for a "typical voter," such as a forty-five-year-old woman, with some college education, and so on, yields slightly different placements, but the effects in the final model remain. As such, I present the most simple estimates.

order to protect their brand. Thus, the expectation is that the parameter estimate on voter distance will be *negative*.

The data also contain variables capturing the policy incentives for amending discussed earlier. Recall that these are measures of ideological distance – the dyadic distance between the ministerial and reviewing parties and the ministerial party's distance from the coalition compromise. The first covariate represents both the strategically selected ideological distance between pairs of coalition partners and an individual reviewing party's incentive to amend in order to selfishly drag the draft bill toward its own ideal point. The second covariate represents the necessity to amend in order to enforce the coalition bargain.

Both of these measures are calculated with data from the Manifesto Project Database, which was formerly known as the Comparative Manifestos Project (CMP) (Volkens et al. 2017). First, the left-right policy positions (or "RILE" scores) and their standard errors are calculated for each party for each bill using the parties' most proximate manifesto according to Lowe et al. (2011). These positions are then used to calculate the absolute distance between the ministerial and reviewing parties. This variable is called *CMP distance*.

These party preference estimates are also used to construct the absolute distance between position of the proposing minister and the coalition compromise. This variable is called *compromise distance*. As is standard in the literature (e.g., Powell 2000; Martin and Vanberg 2011), the coalition compromise is calculated as a seat-weighted average of the policy positions of all parties in cabinet. The compromise distance, therefore, is given as:

$$\left| m - \frac{\sum_{i=1}^{n} x_i \times s_i}{\sum_{i=1}^{n} s_i} \right| \tag{6.2}$$

where m is the ideal point of the proposing minister, $i \in n$ indexes the parties in coalition, x_i represents the ideal point of coalition party i, and s_i represents the seat share of coalition party i. The coalition compromise model of policymaking predicts a positive relationship between the compromise distance and the number of observed amendments as a function of coalition policing.

The correlation of the distance between a pair of coalition partners as perceived by voters and as selected by the parties (given by their manifesto positioning) is shown in Figure 6.1, where the overall correlation is plotted with both linear fitted and LOWESS lines. Regressing

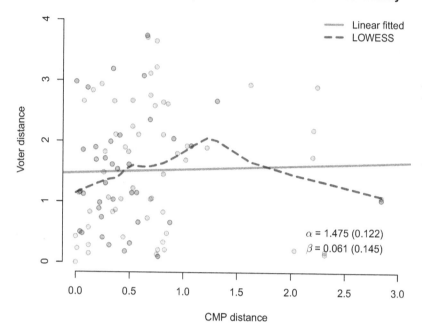

FIGURE 6.1 Comparing voter-perceived and manifesto distances. Each point represents one coalition partner dyad from the data. Dyads within a particular government are not recurring in the figure

voter-perceived distance on manifesto distance yields a positive, yet insignificant relationship which is given in the lower right-hand corner of the figure. Note that these two variables are measured on different scales.

As the figure shows, the correlation between the measures is positive, but only weakly so. Given the sample of parties displayed here, this is a sensible relationship. That is, the plot only includes cabinet partner dyads – parties that are sufficiently similar in their policy preferences to coalesce in the first place. If the plot also contained dyads including opposition parties then the recovered relationship between voter-perceived and manifesto distances would be strongly positive.[7] But the positivity

---

7 Indeed, if one examines the regression results given in table 3 of Fortunato and Stevenson (2013), it is plain that manifesto distances are a very strong positive predictor of voter-perceived distances when a wide array of parties are considered.

of the relationship (or lack thereof) is not the central focus of this figure. Instead, the point of the figure is to reveal the considerable variation between the similarity perceived by voters and the similarity manifest in the selected policy manifesto positions of cabinet partners. The process of coalition formation and policymaking is very disruptive to the positions that parties have staked out for themselves strategically in an attempt to maximize their vote share. Protecting against electoral losses requires that these disruptions be corrected by signaling the electorate. In a sense, the variation in this figure is the focus of the chapter.

The data used to construct the remaining variables were all collected from the respective countries' legislative databases, most often from the legislation itself, the Constitutional Change and Parliamentary Democracies (CCPD) project data (Strøm, Müller, and Bergman 2008) or the Parliament and Government Composition Database (Döring and Manow 2011). This includes the identity of the chairperson overseeing the reviewing committee – whether it is the party of the proposing minister, the reviewing party, some other cabinet party, or an opposition party. The data also include a binary variable indicating that the cabinet is a minority and a few exposure variables.[8] First, as mentioned, we must include the (logged) number of articles in the original proposal, as each article present another potential point of discord. The model also includes the (logged) number of days the bill spent under review, and a dummy variable indicating that the plenary session expired before the conclusion of the bill's scrutiny. Finally, the data include information on whether or not the reviewing party has placed a junior minister in the department of the bill's signatory to "spy and report" on the drafting process.

With these covariates in hand, we can use our data to replicate the main analysis from the Martin and Vanberg (2005) model of legislative review. This replication serves as a validation exercise for data collection process, and also gives us an idea of how externally valid our findings are. That is, if the patterns found in Martin and Vanberg (2005) hold in the data gathered here, then we can be more confident that the empirical regularities uncovered in the analysis to follow are not constrained to our three countries – that patterns of legislative review are fairly common across different samples, given that the institutional parameters are sufficiently similar.

---

[8] Bills submitted by caretaker cabinets are not analyzed as the electoral motivations facing caretaker cabinets are inherently different than typical governments.

The Martin and Vanberg model is replicated by collapsing our data from the party-bill level to bill level, simply summing all amendments offered by all cabinet parties for the dependent variable. The other covariates in the model are also transformed to the bill level as appropriate and follow the construction outlined in Martin and Vanberg (2005). The specifications are the same, less three exceptions. There is no opposition divisiveness variable in our model here as opposition amendments have been omitted. There is also no variable indicating the number of committee referrals as in the original model. This is because multiple committee referrals are vanishingly rare in the countries analyzed here. Indeed, going back to the original data used by Martin and Vanberg, it appears that multiple referrals are effectively limited to Germany. In their data, 99 percent of their German bills are referred to multiple committees, while only 3 percent of their Dutch bills are referred to more than one committee and, in the sample gathered here, there are no bills for which a second committee issues an independent report. Third, because there are several minority cabinets in our sample, a binary variable indicating such is included. Finally, a second model is estimated including the identity of the committee chair overseeing the bill's scrutiny – ministerial party, opposition party or the baseline category, a partner party to the submitting minister – following Fortunato, Martin, and Vanberg (2019), so that we may evaluate how the results here compare to those findings as well. Following both articles, a negative binomial regression is estimated, however, to account for the possibility that there are correlations across rows of data due to unmeasured factors at cabinet level, random intercepts are estimated for each of the cabinets in the data.

As Table 6.1 shows, Martin and Vanberg's (2005) primary finding – that amendment activity increases with the proposing minister's ideological distance from the coalition bargain – is manifest in this sample. The estimate is large and statistically significant. This is encouraging as it not only reaffirms support for their theoretical model in new data, but also suggests that the determinants of *policy-motivated* amendments in this sample are similar to the determinants in their original sample, even though the contexts from which the data are drawn are distinct. We can interpret the similarity in the empirical patterns discovered here to mean that the mechanics of legislative review are likely relatively common in parliamentary democracies with strong committee systems. Thus, the conclusions drawn from the main analysis can be reasonably inferred to travel outside of the sample countries.

Table 6.1 *Amendment data validation: replication of Martin and Vanberg (2005)*

	Main model		Chairs added	
	Parameter	SE	Parameter	SE
Compromise distance	0.954	(0.363)	0.980	(0.363)
Junior minister	0.943	(0.263)	0.923	(0.266)
Minister chair			−0.321	(0.292)
Opposition chair			−0.357	(0.276)
Minority	−3.661	(0.600)	−3.549	(0.615)
ln(days in review)	0.696	(0.126)	0.694	(0.126)
ln(articles)	0.670	(0.100)	0.695	(0.101)
Plenary expiration	−1.557	(0.944)	−1.546	(0.941)
Intercept	−4.021	(0.613)	−3.874	(0.622)
ln(θ)	2.247	(0.076)	2.240	(0.076)
Random intercept: var(cabinet)	0.795	(0.423)	0.841	(0.447)
N	2,209		2,209	
log(likelihood)	−1,578.337		−1,577.374	

This extends to the second set of estimates, modeled after Fortunato, Martin, and Vanberg (2019), which also confirms the original findings. That is, just as in the original article, there is no difference in the level of scrutiny observed between shadow chairs and chairs controlled by the proposing minister. Finally, note the strong negative effects of minority status, confirming the theoretical expectations regarding the constraints imposed by external support parties. For any ordering of ministerial party, reviewing party, and pivotal opposition party, we should observe a *reduction* in legislative amendments offered by cabinet parties.

MODEL ESTIMATION AND ANALYSIS

Let us transition back to original party-bill format of the data and testing of our central hypothesis. We will add two variables , in addition to our focal variables, to the models just estimated: seat share of the amending party and size of the cabinet in (logged) number of parties. The first covariate was discussed at length earlier – amending requires labor and, given the proportional allocation of resources in these chambers, a party's share of seats in the parliament provides a good estimate of these labor resources. The size of the cabinet is included because it may be the case that larger cabinets are simply more difficult for voters (or elites) to monitor. If this is true, then parties would derive less benefit from differentiation because the probability of those signals reaching the electorate would be reduced in kind. In other words, the clarity of responsibility shrinks as the number of parties in cabinet grows (Powell and Whitten 1993), and this may reduce incentives for differentiating behavior in the parliament.

The dependent variable is, of course, a count of the number of article changes offered by a given party on a proposal of one of its cabinet partners, so a count model is warranted, just as above. However, the structure of the data here presents a small hurdle. The data group bills across different countries and amendment propensities vary systematically across these countries with the Belgians amending more than the Danes and the Dutch amending more than the Belgians on average, commensurate with the differences in co-sponsorship and multiple document submission discussed earlier. To account for these broader contextual differences, fixed effects indicating country are included, where Belgium serves as the baseline. There are other interesting issues with the distribution of the data. However, discussion of these issues and how they are modeled are perhaps less interesting than the central results, so they are relegated to the appendix. Instead, we simply note that a Hierarchical Poisson model is estimated, allowing random intercepts at the level of the bill, because several parties often amend the same draft legislation, so there is potential for unobserved factors at that level. The model results are presented in Table 6.2.

The model bears strong support for the central hypothesis. Voter distance has a robust negative effect on amending – the more voters perceive the reviewing party as similar to the ministerial party, the more the reviewing party will amend, all else being equal. Holding all other covariates constant at their mean, the effect of a one standard deviation *decrease* in voter distance between a pair of cabinet partners, is a 9 percent (4%, 13% CI) *increase* in the predicted number of amendments. To put this in context, this is roughly 1/3 of the magnitude of the effect of a similar change in compromise distance (a 29 percent decrease in amendments). This is strong evidence for the hypothesis and supports the central argument that cabinet parties, limited by collective responsibility in their ability to highlight policy differences with their partners in government, use the legislative review process to communicate their ideological distinctiveness by voicing dissent with their partners' policy proposals.

The remaining variables in the model conform to expectations. The number of articles in the original draft bill and the length of the review

Table 6.2 *Amendment proposal model. Hierarchical Poisson with random intercepts allowed at the bill level*

	Parameter	SE
Perceived distance	−0.105	(0.030)
CMP distance	−0.059	(0.041)
Compromise distance	0.814	(0.344)
Minority cabinet	−1.007	(0.568)
Seat share	2.129	(0.306)
Junior minister	−0.003	(0.059)
Reviewer chair	−0.207	(0.236)
Minister chair	−0.332	(0.314)
Partner chair	−0.358	(0.237)
ln(cabinet size)	−1.031	(0.771)
ln(articles)	0.978	(0.096)
ln(days in review)	0.933	(0.131)
Plenary expiration	−1.619	(1.509)
Denmark	−4.001	(0.708)
Netherlands	0.152	(0.411)
Intercept	−8.041	(1.352)
Random intercept: var(bills)	9.528	(0.997)
N	4519	
log(likelihood)	−2661.435	

period have estimates near 1 (typical for exposure variables) and the more substantively interesting variables also have estimates in the "right direction." The more MPs a party has to share the burden of amending, the more amendments it submits. If the reviewing party's seat share increases from, say, 0.1 to 0.2, its predicted number of amendments increases by about 24 percent. This finding, though commonsensical, is novel and salient. Not only does it speak to informational costs of parliamentary scrutiny and amending in particular, but it also speaks to the proportionality of resources and influence more generally. That is, we know from qualitative examination of constitutional and chamber rules that parliamentary resources, particularly committee seats and staff, tend to be proportionally allocated and we tend to *presume* that this means parliamentary influence is also roughly proportional to seat share, at least within the governing coalition. However, we do not have much empirical evidence that is truly the case and the evidence that we do have, such as, Martin and Vanberg (2014), is indirect as we cannot parse the competing influences of size and salience. As a result, this finding is important to our understanding of the distribution of parliamentary influence.

Recall our rather detailed discussion earlier of how a cabinets' minority status should impact the degree to which we expect ministerial draft bills to be amended. In sum, a pivotal opposition party, regardless of ideological orientation vis-à-vis the cabinet, should reduce the number of amendments that we observe by incentivizing ministers to self-censor their policy proposals or constraining reviewing parties' ability to drag the policy toward themselves. This is precisely what the data reveal. Changing a cabinet's size from majority to minority reduces the number of proposed article changes by about 40 percent. This is one of the largest substantive effects in the model.

Just as interesting are the effects of dyadic CMP distance and compromise distance. The estimate on compromise distance is positive, substantively large, and statistically robust. The farther away the proposing minister from the coalition compromise, the more the reviewing party tends to amend. CMP distance, on the other hand, is statistically insignificant and signed negatively, which no theory would predict. However, the estimate on that covariate is among the least stable in the model when compared across specifications (note that compromise distance and voter perceived distance are *remarkably* stable across model specifications) and always quite close to zero. What does this mean, substantively? Taken together, the patterns of observed amendment behavior are substantially more consistent with a coalition-policing model of review behavior than with a self-interested model of review behavior. That is, to the extent that parties are motivated by policy concerns in their amendment behavior, there is very strong evidence that they are driven to safeguard the coalition compromise, while there is no evidence that they are driven by their own private policy concerns (i.e., parties are not simply using the review phase to try to drag policy proposals toward their own ideal point). This is a powerful confirmation of Martin and Vanberg's (2005, 2011) theoretical argument that their data do not allow. As noted earlier, because their data are collected and coded at the bill level, coalition-policing and self-interested amending are empirically inseparable. That is not the case with the data here, which provide compelling evidence for their model.

The final substantively interesting set of results regard the presence of a junior minister and identity of the committee chair. Having a junior minister in the department of the proposing minister has no discernible effect on amendment behavior in this sample. However, it should be noted that the reviewing party only has a junior minister in the proposing minister's department in about 7 percent of the observations here and these are heavily clustered in the Netherlands. The model also suggests that the identity of the committee chair is largely irrelevant to legislative scrutiny among cabinet partners. This comports with previous research finding no difference in scrutiny between committees chaired by the party of the proposing minister and committees chaired by their partner in government, but substantial increase in scrutiny when the committee is chaired by a member of the opposition (Fortunato, Martin, and Vanberg 2019). These results support the interpretation that the uptick in scrutiny under opposition chaired committees is evidence of opposition influence and that the chair's power *may* be exercised positively when held by opposition but is *almost certainly* exercised negatively when held by cabinet, protecting bills from opposition influence. This implies that committee chairpersons, in practice, act as more of a "backstop" than active police patrol in reference to the coalition bargain and that their "watchdog" function is a passive one

DISCUSSION

The hard constraints of collective cabinet responsibility are designed for the express purpose of maintaining (enforcing) a united front in the cabinet in spite of the diverse policy preferences of its members; in spite of their dissimilar bases of support; in spite of the intense pressures that parties feel to lash out publicly against the positions and proposals of their coalition partners. To publicly criticize one's coalition partner is to risk expulsion from cabinet. To complain that the terms of a private agreement have been violated by the proposal of one's coalition partner is to risk expulsion from cabinet. To publicly distance one's self from an undesirable compromise made law is to risk expulsion from cabinet. In light of voters' distaste for compromise and their willingness to punish the parties they have supported for it, the rules of collective cabinet responsibility are a leaden weight affixed to an overboard sailor. But political parties are resourceful actors.

In the face of all of these constraints, cabinet partners have found a potentially effective, albeit certainly inefficient workaround. Proposing ministers eschew compromise and propose (something closer to) their ideal policy. This ministerial drift allows the minister's party to signal their true policy preferences to the electorate, and to their supporters in particular, and also to demonstrate competence – to show the country that they will not be hamstrung by the conventions of coalition or restrained by their partners in cabinet. Their partners in cabinet, in turn, are provided the opportunity to air their grievances in legislative review. During the proposal's scrutiny, partners to the proposing minister are given the leeway to voice their own true policy preferences and to demonstrate their competence by reining in the proposing minister's drift. Each new amendment proposed serves as a public declaration of disagreement with their partner in government, but, importantly, one that does not violate collective responsibility.

This is not mere conjecture, there is evidence we may draw upon in the extant literature to see that there is at least some performative aspect to all of this – that at least some of the amendments offered are done so purely to massage the political discourse surrounding the cabinet. Of course, if this were not the case, we would not have discovered such strong evidence in the analysis above. Nonetheless, the case can be buttressed. Most saliently, Martin (2004) presents a theoretical and empirical analysis of government agenda setting. His analysis finds a strong relationship between the dissimilarity of preferences within a coalition in various policy areas and the timing of bills pertaining to those jurisdictions. For example, at the time of writing, a coalition between the Social Democratic Party and the Christian Democratic Union in Germany is likely to see eye-to-eye on matters of domestic labor market regulation, but is very unlikely to agree upon the generosity of welfare benefits. Martin (2004) suggests that this coalition will therefore prioritize labor market policy and deprioritize welfare policy. The argument here is that by delaying the initiation of welfare policy, the coalition is afforded more time for internal bargaining over the parameters of the policy. The more divisive the policy jurisdiction, the longer the coalition needs to negotiate over it, which implies that bills do not get submitted to parliament without a very clear picture of what the final policy will look like. In other words, the proposal itself comes at the end of an often long and hard fought negotiation that is to an extent relitigated for public consumption *after* the bill is proposed.

Work by Bräuninger and Debus (2009) provides complementary evidence by showing that, in the run up to election, governments submit less legislation and instead allow the submission of draft proposals from their own membership. By having private members of parliament, rather than ministers, submit legislation, the cabinet is removed from the picture, which means that (a) the content of those proposals reflects the "pure" ideological position of the proposer and (b) that the proposer's coalition partners are free to publicly harangue the proposal and its author.

Of course, these performative bills almost never survive to floor consideration. Related work by Bowler, Indridason, Bräuninger, and Debus (2016) details how governments substitute conflict amelioration devices for detailed declarations of compromise when the ideological distance between partners is vast. Rather than publicly announce their intention to compromise, cabinet partners instead publicly declare their intention to antagonize one another and build the parameters for that conflict into their coalition agreement. This all speaks to a kind of dramatization of the policy-making process that has largely gone unremarked upon in the coalition literature, but this masquerade can be important.

From the parties' strategic perspective, there is a sharp tradeoff here, but one that leans toward incentivizing this performative behavior. The gains from policy compromise are by no means constant sum, however, the costs most certainly are. That is, while all cabinet parties in government may collectively benefit from cooperation – and the theoretical bounds on these benefits are effectively limitless – all cabinet members are simultaneously in competition with the opposition *and one another* for votes. Because each vote secured by a party's partner in government is necessarily one less vote available to that party, virtually limitless gains from trade in policy compromise must be foregone to protect one's vote share. It not only understandable that parties devote such resources to signaling activity, it is eminently reasonable.

From a normative perspective, however, the case is more mixed. On the one hand, these performances perhaps allow cabinet members an avenue to mitigate the potential losses that coalition and all of its electoral constraints can force upon its participants. Even if these signals only reach the most interested political observers, the potential to preserve even a portion of one's vote share that would otherwise be surrendered to the costs of compromise is too tempting to resist. Perhaps, more appealingly from the normative perspective, however, is that this type of behavior provides strong evidence that parties are, in fact, listening to the electorate and responding to it. This is of course not the kind of responsiveness typically written about in political economic research. For example, the seminal works of Powell (2000, 2019) are devoted to understanding how institutional contexts condition the degree to which voters are likely to get the policy outcomes they desire. Related work by, for example, Soroka and Wlezien (2010) or Baumgartner and Jones (2010) is similarly focused on the relationship between the public's policy demands and government's policy outputs. Nonetheless, what we have found here *is* responsiveness. Cabinet parties are being attentive to the attitudes of the electorate and altering their behavior accordingly. Though this particular form (or forum) of responsiveness is new, it is in fact a version of what Mansbridge (2003) dubbed "anticipatory responsiveness." Parties are behaving in anticipation of voters' electoral reactions, which is informed by "deliberation," or real-time tracking of voters' perceptions of competence or brand stability, through the legislative period. Not only is the evidence for this attentiveness and alteration normatively appealing, it is also novel to the comparative research. This is some of the first documented empirical relationship between changing public attitudes and changing legislative behavior in coalitional systems.

On the other hand, these games are ultimately inefficient from the perspective of good governance. One of the cabinet's most valuable resources is time. Governments only have so many days in office to pursue their agenda and every minute that is absorbed into this process of brand and competence signaling to the electorate rather than being directed toward improving social welfare is a squandered opportunity to literally make the world a better place. But is this inefficiency worthwhile? Are parties truly able to stop the bleeding of support inflicted by coalition compromise? To begin to answer this question, let us first return to Nick Clegg's term as Deputy Prime Minister in the first Cameron cabinet and the eventual thrashing of the Liberal Democrats in the United Kingdom's 2015 parliamentary elections to learn what happens when parties forego the opportunity for differentiation.

APPENDIX

Descriptives for Amendment Model

Descriptive statistics for focal measures are given in Table 6.3, which shows a great deal of variability in the dependent variable as well as the key ideological covariates.

Table 6.3 *Descriptive statistics of key variables*

Variable	Mean	SD	Min	Max
Article changes	0.70	4.57	0.00	170.00
Voter distance	1.48	0.92	0.00	3.74
CMP distance	0.60	0.64	0.01	2.84
Compromise distance	0.25	0.30	0.01	1.80

Discussion of Central Model Construction

It is possible that certain *bills* are simply more likely to be amended than others for reasons that are not captured by the measured variables in the model. That is, because the level of observation is an individual party's response to a bill, and multiple parties may amend the same bill, there is potential for correlations across the rows of the data grouped on the bill. Indeed, the modal number of cabinet parties is 3 and *at least* two parties are observed amending about 80 percent of the bills in the sample. The model therefore allows random intercepts at the bill level. This level is not simply the most intuitive grouping structure in the data, diagnostics suggested by Fortunato and Stevenson (2013) suggest that the bills, rather than ministries or cabinets, are also the most *important* level to account for.

There is another issue apart from potential correlations across rows on the dependent variable resulting from unmeasured, group-level factors. The data are overdispersed with zeroes and their natural distribution violates (to be generous) Poisson assumptions of mean-variance equivalence. More importantly, the data generating process violates theoretical conditional independence assumptions. This means that, we do not have valid theoretical reason to believe that the latent propensity to amend requires the same amount of "effort" to move from two amendments to three amendments, as it does to move zero amendments to one amendment. Both the raw data and our qualitative understanding of the review process suggest that the real hurdle, the change in count for which the most effort is required, is the change from zero to one. *Given* that amendments will be offered at all, the difference in effort required to move from one to two, or from four to five should be roughly equivalent.

In these cases, researchers will often turn to a negative binomial specification (as in the Martin and Vanberg replication), or, less frequently, zero-inflated or hurdle models and these seem like a natural choice in this case. Our analysis will take a different tack, however. The bill-level random intercepts just discussed allow for efficient Poisson estimation. That is, diagnostics reveal that the random intercepts model out the overdispersion quite effectively and also that Poisson specifications produce better fit than the negative binomial when these random effects are allowed. Indeed, once bill-level random effects are estimated, the scaling parameter (θ) recovered from the negative binomial model is almost precisely 1. Typically, these are estimated in logged form and the parameter and standard error estimates are $\log(\theta) = -0.006$ (0.114). For the sake of comparison, estimating a negative binomial model *without* random effects yields an estimated dispersion parameter of $\log(\theta) = $

2.360 (0.059). This estimate is monstrous and implies a wild degree of overdispersion. In sum, these estimates tell us that the overdispersion has effectively been modeled out of the data by the bill-level random effects and that the specification presented in the main text is appropriate to the task.[9]

---

[9] It should be noted, however, that estimating zero-inflated or hurdle model specifications yield the same substantive results as the specification here. In fact, support for the central hypothesis is stronger under those specifications. The problem is that hierarchical modeling is onerous under those specifications and the random effects must therefore be omitted. The tradeoff is an increase in efficiency for a substantial decrease in model fit, or predictive power.

7

What Could Go Wrong?

We shall never know whether the position could have been retrieved politically by a different approach to coalition. But in the event it was not.

– Vince Cable (2017, 89)

In May 2010, the Conservatives and Liberal Democrats, respectively led by David Cameron and Nick Clegg, formed the United Kingdom's first coalition government since Churchill's "War Ministry," a coalition of the whole that shepherded the UK through the Second World War before resigning in 1945. The UK's first Deputy Prime Minister from a party other than the prime minister's in over sixty years, Clegg arrived at 10 Downing Street to a civil service unprepared to support him.

On that first day on Downing Street, there was no office waiting for me...the Civil Service buzzed around the building supporting the new PM and largely ignoring us. There wasn't even a phone. (Clegg 2016, 52)

Indeed, Clegg writes that of the roughly 200 civil servants employed in 10 Downing Street, only a single one was assigned to him. The absence of institutional support was a cruel complement to Clegg's individual lack of preparation. By his own account he was unprepared for government and it showed. Unlike his counterparts in the Conservative Party, he had never held a ministerial post or served as Shadow Minister. Unlike his counterparts on the continent – countries with long histories of coalition that have learned how to navigate it over the decades – he simply did not appreciate the difficulty of the fights ahead of him, both behind closed doors and especially in the open.

In the shadow of the economic mayhem wrought by the Great Recession and the European Debt Crisis that was in full throttle when

Cameron and Clegg formed their government, it was easy to forget that the Liberal Democratic platform, informed by the parliamentary expenses scandal broken in 2009, was largely dedicated to political reform – roughly 25 percent of their manifesto was dedicated to institutional changes to the political system. Innovating MP recall procedures and new constraints on MP tax allowances; changing the voting system and extending the franchise to citizens aged sixteen years; reducing the number of Commons MPs and converting the House of Lords to an elected branch; strengthening the parliament vis-à-vis the cabinet and instituting fixed parliamentary terms; introducing campaign finance restrictions and lobbying regulations; formalizing the UK constitution in text; and devolving competencies to local governments were all tenets of the Liberal Democratic platform (Liberal Democratic Party 2010). Though Clegg was able to secure the five-year fixed-term parliament from Cameron in the negotiation of the coalition's formation, most of these other goals quickly fell by the wayside as Cameron and Clegg set about tending to the economic crisis.

As a brief aside, who could blame Clegg for making the fixed-term parliament his first priority? Without the fixed term, Cameron would be at liberty to call for new elections whenever he liked, without a vote in the Commons, putting the Liberal Democrats at a tremendous bargaining disadvantage, living from one poll to the next. Clegg notes this himself in his memoirs concluding:

I was not prepared to have the rug pulled from under us halfway through the parliament just because it was to the electoral advantage of the Conservative Party (2016, 131).

Moving on, the manner in which the new government handled the crisis, as well as the all-consuming nature of the crisis itself, put Clegg and the Liberal Democrats in a vice. After drawing the fixed-term parliament concession from Cameron and the Conservatives, the Liberal Democrats were able to extract only one more opportunity for institutional change, the referendum on the so-called alternative vote, which political economists would commonly refer to as the single transferable vote or instant runoff voting (we will come back to the alternative vote referendum a bit later). But their contribution to the agenda effectively ended there – at least, that is what the popular press coverage would likely lead us to believe.

The Cameron–Clegg government's response to the crisis was austerity. We will leave aside debate on the prudence of austerity and stimulus in times of crisis in general and the specific case of the UK at this time.

What is important is that, although the Liberal Democrats broadly stood for more disciplined fiscal policy and lower government spending, they were forced to swallow some particularly unpleasant changes, most infamously the tuition fee debacle. The Liberal Democrats had taken the position that university tuition fees were "unfair," limiting the opportunities derived from higher education to the wealthy. This stance is prominently highlighted in the party's 2010 manifesto and Clegg was famously photographed holding a signed pledge card from the National Union of Students reading:

I pledge to vote against any increase in fees in the next parliament and to pressure the government to introduce a fairer alternative.

Clegg would not only break his promise not to vote for the fees, but would ultimately sign off on the introduction of legislation that would lead to a substantial increase in tuition fees, raising the cap from around £3,300 to £9,000.

Just imagine. Clegg had publicly signed a pledge to never vote in favor of a tuition increase. The Liberal Democrats had made a promise in their manifesto to pursue a policy of a £0 fee schedule. But Clegg and the Liberal Democrats, early in their term of office, allowed the submission, and subsequently voted for legislation that effectively tripled tuition fees. Clegg and the Liberal Democrats were savaged. There were literally violent protests in the streets of London (Lyall 2010). But still, while the protests were unfurling, Clegg was every bit the good soldier, honoring his commitment to the government and collective responsibility and proselytizing on behalf of the policy, which only made matters worse. Of course, we understand that collective responsibility is not a positive pact, mandating that all members go out and rally support on behalf of cabinet decisions, but a negative one, merely forbidding open criticism of the cabinet. This was a fool's errand, and, to his credit, Clegg is remarkably open in retrospect about how naïve he was in handling the whole matter:

I continued to try to explain the merits of the change in policy. As protesters were demonstrating on Whitehall in November 2010, I even went live on Jeremy Vine's BBC radio show and spoke to one of them, attempting to persuade the protesters of the logic of the policy. How wrong I was. I might as well have sought to persuade them that the moon is made of cheese (2016, 33).

It is about this time that Liberal Democratic popularity bottomed out, falling to single digits for the first time in nearly twenty years. All the while, Tory popularity was holding steady, or even *improving* from

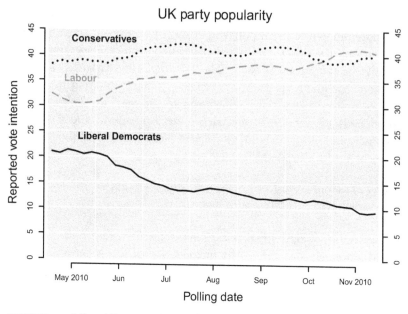

FIGURE 7.1 Liberal Democratic popularity loss over their first months in office

where they had been at the government's formation. This stark juxta-position of the popularity of the Conservatives and Liberal Democrats, shown in Figure 7.1, drives home the divide between collective cabinet responsibility and individual partisan fortunes. Policy is produced jointly, collectively, and all individual member parties are compelled to stand behind decisions made by the collective. But parties are held *individually* accountable for their behavior in government – they have made campaign promises individually, they have individual bases of support, and they will ultimately be individually rewarded or punished at the ballot box. Just because Clegg and Cameron must mutually consent to each policy decision does not mean that Liberal Democrats and Conservatives will share equally in the credit or blame. Not only is electoral support a constant sum, but responsibility attributions are not points, they are distributions. It is entirely possible for two parties to make a policy jointly, equally, but for one to be rewarded while the other is punished.

Nonetheless, Clegg seemed to walk into coalition believing in a range of possible outcomes from objectively "good" to objectively "bad," with credit and blame to be allocated accordingly – he did not understand the subjectivity of voters' perceptions. Further, his actions in the first year or two of government participation implied that he did not understand the electoral implications of compromise, of appearing to be rolled by his partner in government, of presenting the appearance that he was failing to honor his campaign commitments, let alone *actually failing to honor his campaign commitments*.

And we need not speculate about what Clegg did or did not understand. He is quite candid in his retrospective accounts and if we look over his public statements, we can see the evolution of his understanding of coalition compromise. For example, in September 2010, at the annual fall conference of the Liberal Democrats, Clegg's keynote speech was rife with enthusiastic promotion of his compromise with the Conservatives. Here he is, for example, on describing the coalition agreement:

The Coalition Programme... is not the Liberal Democrat manifesto. But it is not the Conservative manifesto either. It is our shared agenda. And I stand by it (2010).

And here he is describing his working relationship with Cameron and the Conservatives:

The truth is I never expected the Conservatives to embrace negotiation and compromise. But they did and it does them credit... we have become more than the sum of our parts (2010).

These statements feel embarrassingly naïve in hindsight. Even with the coalition still in its infancy – the conference came just four months after the formation of the government – the Liberal Democrats had already suffered precipitous popularity losses at this point and, still, it would take another year or so for Clegg to come to terms with the reality of his predicament and begin to figure out what his counterparts on the continent, tempered by decades of multiparty governance, have long known – the optics of coalition, the optics of compromise, and the optics of policy, and the policy-making *process*, matter substantially to the electorate.[1] Sometimes the *how* and public defense of the *why* are just as salient as the *what*. And, again, this is manifest in Clegg's public comments. For example, in his keynote speech at the annual conference of the Liberal Democratic party just one year later, Clegg is singing a very different tune:

---

[1] Some cynical commentators may argue that the optics of decisions are more important than their content. We will not go that far here, but Clegg does come right up to the edge of that sentiment at times.

Probably the most important lesson I have learned is this: No matter how hard you work on the details of a policy, it's no good if the perception is wrong (2011).

This is also evident in his description of how the Liberal Democrats were able to amend the *Health and Social Care Bill* proposed by the Conservative Minister of Health such that its central focus, reorganizing accountability for the provision of health care away from Whitehall and toward local commissions (which would fundamentally reshape electoral accountability for the National Health Service), was stripped from the legislation:

We were absolutely right to stop the NHS bill in its tracks. To ensure change on our terms. No arbitrary deadlines. No backdoor privatization. No threat to the basic principles at the heart of our NHS (2011).

Despite the change in public rhetoric, however, there was very little in the way of systematic changes in Liberal Democratic behavior until much later, if at all. As we will see in the empirical analysis to come, the Liberal Democrats never changed their behavior in the legislative review process and, if they systematically augmented their parliamentary rhetoric at all, it was not until 2014, nearly *fourth fifths* through the legislative session. This was, as the saying goes, too little, too late to stop the hemorrhaging of support, let alone recoup any of those losses. Of course, we know how this story ends. In 2015, the Liberal Democrats would go on to lose over 65 percent of their vote share and over 85 percent of their seats, while Cameron and the Conservatives, who were overwhelmingly viewed as having dominated the Liberal Democrats at nearly every turn, were able to gain a one percentage point in vote share, securing 108 percent of the seats they had won in 2010, and win an outright majority in parliament.

But knowing the destination does not make the journey any less informative. What we will do here is assess Liberal Democratic behavior in the parliament over the course of their term in cabinet. We will examine amendment documents, public committee proceedings, and the duration of legislative scrutiny through the cabinet's life and compare the Cameron–Clegg government to the single-party governments that preceded and succeeded it. While there has been some descriptive analysis of parliamentary procedure in the Commons published prior to this study, here we will estimate (what are to my reading of the literature) the first empirical models of legislative scrutiny in the UK's House of Commons.[2] These models will reveal that scrutiny processes varied little, if they varied at all, across the Brown government (preceding Cameron–Clegg), Cameron–Clegg coalition, and Cameron's single-party cabinet (succeeding Cameron-Clegg) – the data suggest that the Cameron–Clegg government was no more rigorous in its use of the legislative review than the single party governments that bookended it.

Following this is an analysis of parliamentary speeches given on the floor of the Commons, which tests for an evolution of Liberal Democratic strategy over the legislative term. These data reveal a startling level of consistency in the ideological content of the Liberal Democrats' parliamentary speeches vis-à-vis the Conservatives. While there is some directional (though not statistically discernible), suggestive evidence that the Liberal Democrats may have attempted to pull away from the Conservatives in their Commons rhetoric, these changes, if they truly came at all, came far too late.

Juxtapose Clegg's failure to differentiate with, for example, the behaviors we can see in the Netherland's first "Purple Coalition," a cabinet composed of the ideologically diverse Labour Party (PvdA), Liberal Party (VVD), and the Democratic Party (D66). The government formed in 1994 and survived two full terms before being defeated in 2002 by a new, insurgent populist party (the Pim Fortuyn list, named for its anti-Muslim and anti-immigrant leader) and the reemergence of the Christian Democratic Party (CDA). Though the Purple Coalition was soundly defeated in 2002, the ability of the member parties to preserve their brand through their first legislative period allowed them to perform quite well in the elections of 1998 and reform their union. How did they manage this? Of course, both of these cabinets are part of the analysis in Chapter 6, suggesting that they were responsive to their electorate in their parliamentary behaviors. Nonetheless, a brief, anecdotal recounting of some of the more overt displays of conflict provide a useful guide.

Shortly after forming their cabinet, the government organized a parliamentary investigation committee to assess the manner in which the Ministry of Justice was handling organized crime throughout the Netherlands. This committee, led by a member of the PvdA, proved to be such a public thorn in the side of the D66 Minister of Justice that the minister publicly threatened resignation in 1995 and had to be privately

---

[2] Descriptive work by Griffith (1974), and its spiritual successor Thompson (2012, 2015), is excellent and recommended for interested readers. Indeed, the coming discussion of process and procedures could not have composed without those excellent works.

persuaded by her fellow cabinet ministers to remain in government (Lucardie and Voerman 1996). In the next year, following accusations that the VVD Minister of Social Security and Employment had misrepresented a report on potential reforms to the welfare state, the D66 and PvdA were so incensed that they were able to successfully demand the deselection and replacement of the minister in question (Lucardie and Voerman 1997). In February 1997, in the midst of a porcine epidemic, the VVD Minister of Agriculture initiated a proposal to scale back the intensity of Dutch pig farming in an effort to improve the safety and sanitation of production. The proposal enraged the D66 who fought against the bill for ten months before ultimately allowing it to pass the parliament (Lucardie and Voerman 1998). Postmortems of the national elections in 1998 suggest that the failure of the D66 to successfully stand up to its larger partners in government may have caused a redistribution of some D66 seats to the VVD and PvdA. However, on balance, the fraught public conflict between the partners seems to have protected them from substantial losses, and, indeed, the cabinet as whole actually gained seats in the 1998 elections. We will not see such credible public conflict from the Cameron–Clegg government.

SCRUTINY IN THE HOUSE OF COMMONS

The UK's House of Commons has a weak committee system. There are *no* permanent committees to scrutinize legislation[3] – only ad hoc committees – and therefore no robust property rights, and no sustained committee service through which individual members may cultivate expertise. Further, because all committees are de jure ad hoc, each committee composer is granted substantial power to, for example, protect their legislation from any meaningful scrutiny, by stacking the committee with sympathetic members. These "Public Bill Committees," organized to scrutinize draft bills, are composed by the Committee of Selection, which may factor in the preferences of whips and even the proposing minister when choosing the committee membership. The hardest constraint on the Committee of Selection, outside of the maximum size of the committee (fifty, though the average is nineteen according to Thompson 2015), is that Public Bill Committees must "regard" the partisan composition of the

---

[3] There are permanent committees in the House of Commons, called "Select Committees." However, Select Committees do not scrutinize legislation, rather, they shadow executive departments for the purposes of (weak) general oversight and the vetting of appointees.

Commons (though this is not a true, hard constraint), and, that a new committee must be composed for each draft bill (this *is* a true, hard constraint). Finally, at least one cabinet minister and major party whip (nearly always the governing party) will serve on each committee. Most often, this means that the drafting minister has a hand in the scrutiny of their own legislation. Further more, the chair of each committee is de facto selected by majority whips who whip their members on committee to vote in favor of their preferred candidate.

Once the bill has been assigned and the committee has been formed, the committee lacks the authority to rewrite the legislation (a power that committees tend to possess in stronger systems) but it can amend the legislation. Of course, the composition of the committee (typically including the authoring minister and dominated by the House majority) tends to prevent drastic changes from being made. The committee also lacks subpoena power, meaning that it cannot *compel* members of the relevant bureaucracy to testify as to the bill's intentions or expected effects and it cannot subpoena documentation regarding the proposal's authoring which may help it to infer intention or expected effects. Given that the authoring minister tends to sit on the committee, it is somewhat ironic that the committee as an institution lacks the power to compel bureaucratic testimony. In practice, however, bureaucrats are somewhat regularly called to testify in committee, but, anecdotally, these are overwhelmingly at the request of the authoring minister. Of course, the cabinet's monopoly on information revelation is just one more indication that the cabinet tends to dominate the scrutiny of its legislation.

This informational asymmetry between committee membership and the cabinet is so vast that it was a point of amusement for Griffith (1974) in his description of the committees' workings and the behavior of the members of parliament that compose them. One particularly amusing anecdote came in the description of an opposition member who, after attempting to propose an amendment, admitted that he was asked to do so by a lobbyist and moreover that he, in fact, understood neither the legislation nor the change he was proposing to make to it, noting that he was without access to the relevant expertise. The member went so far as to ask for help from the majority:

I should be grateful if the Under-Secretary, who has had the advantage of all the legal advice of the Home Office would tell me whether that point, which I admit I put down without great faith in it, has any sense. (Griffith 1974, 91)

These limitations on committee powers and access to expertise are robust. However, they are only a portion of the constraints that House of Commons committees face in scrutinizing legislation. Ministers have profound authority to limit the scope of the committee's scrutiny. There are three parts to ministerial ability to inhibit scrutiny. First, each bill is subject to what Martin and Vanberg (2011, 44) call, "binding plenary debate" before the bill is assigned to committee, which "constrains deliberation and proposals for change." This means that the first and second readings determine the scope of the legislation and which aspects are open to scrutiny.[4] Officially, these constraints are imposed by the chamber whips, however, informally, they are effectively at the discretion of the initiating minister (Thompson and McNulty 2018). Second, each minister has the power to declare their proposal "urgent" and set an official "outdate" – the date by which the committee must report the bill back to the plenary – and therefore limit the duration of committee scrutiny. Finally, each minister possess "guillotine" powers – the right to force a take-it-or-leave-it vote on the bill, either as amended, or as initially proposed, which has the potential to render any changes the bill endured in committee moot. This gives the government a substantial "last mover" advantage. While this advantage does not *prevent* amendments, it does prevent them from mattering. Heller succinctly sums up the effect that this has on parties' behavior in legislative review, writing that "[t]hey might benefit from position taking, but . . . they can be punished in policy terms for breaking ranks" (2001, 795).

Zooming out, the institutional constraints on committee scrutiny mean that, in the competition for policy influence between the cabinet and the parliament, the parliament is always, at best, bringing a knife to a gunfight. Ministers are privileged by informational advantages that the parliament simply cannot compete with. There are no standing policy committees with regular membership or dedicated staff such that the expertise needed to compete with the government can be developed. If that was not bad enough, the procedural advantages that ministers enjoy may make any such expertise moot anyway.

What does this mean for the Cameron and Clegg government or our purposes here? On the one hand, the committees are ill-suited for matters of coalition policing. Where real disagreements between the Conservatives and Liberal Democrats manifest over an existing draft bill, the

---

4 Congressional scholars may recognize these limitations as similar to "germaneness" constraints of US Senate scrutiny.

reviewing party simply will not be able to force any real change to the proposal that the minister wishes to resist. There is no potential for real policy-motivated markup without the authoring minister submitting to it in advance (by consenting to a broad scope of scrutiny prior to committee referral) and again acquiescing to it after the fact (by not employing the guillotine). In the Commons, committees are simply incapable to adjudicate policy disagreements between ministers and their partners in government or the opposition.

On the other hand, committees may still serve as viable avenues for differentiation. All proposed amendments must be heard and voted on and are subsequently published into the official record – the same records that provide media outlets invaluable information in their coverage of the government and the House of Commons. Further more, each committee proceeding is public, recorded, and they are often broadcast on BBC stations or available to stream from the BBC website. This is to say that while committees may not provide an effective monitoring and policing forum, they may still provide an effective forum to differentiate, to signal disagreement and dissatisfaction with the policy proposals of one's partner in government. From the more qualitative discussion earlier, we already know that this differentiation was necessary, particularly for the Liberal Democrats, and we already know that Clegg and the Liberal Democrats resolved to differentiate. So let us find out whether or not these resolutions translated into actions.

There is only one cabinet in which we are truly interested here, and that is, of course, the Cameron–Clegg government. However, in order to contextualize behaviors observed within the Cameron–Clegg government, we will compare it to its predecessor and successor: Gordon Brown's single-party majority Labour cabinet, which governed from June 2007 until May 2010; and David Cameron's single-party majority Conservative cabinet, which governed from May 2015 until July 2016. Brown's government was somewhat shorter than a full term because he replaced Tony Blair, who resigned in the face of plummeting approval for his handling of the war in Iraq. Cameron's majority government was short lived because he resigned in the aftermath of the referendum on the UK's participation in the European Union, the so-called Brexit referendum. Nonetheless, these bookends provide a nice contrast to the coalition cabinet in terms of legislative scrutiny. If the Cameron–Clegg government was utilizing committee scrutiny as a means to differentiate, then this should be manifest in the activity of the committees in comparison to the single-party majority governments that abutted it. More specifically, we would expect that bills would face longer periods of scrutiny, as the Conservatives and Liberal Democrats would drag out the review process for grandstanding purposes. We should also, of course, observe more amendments being submitted by the Cameron–Clegg government in comparison to their single-party counterparts. Finally, as the proceedings themselves often provide high-profile opportunities for public antagonism of the bill's signatory and their party, we should expect that the typical number of proceedings will be greater during Cameron–Clegg coalition than their single-party counterparts.

After assessing differences between the Cameron–Clegg government and its predecessor and successor, we will move on to examining whether and how behaviors within the coalition evolved over time. More specifically, paying close attention to the scrutiny of Conservative bills, we will test for an evolution in how the Liberal Democrats approached the legislative review process. Did they convene more proceedings, submit more amendments, and spend more time scrutinizing Tory proposals as time went on and they became more familiar with the coalition game? Or, did they simply plod along the same course for the duration of their term in office?

Data and Analysis

To test for differences of legislative review behavior between the Cameron–Clegg coalition cabinet and their single-party counterparts, the Brown and Cameron II cabinets, we will need data on the handling of cabinet proposals for each of the three governments. To this end, all cabinet bills, along with information on their treatment in the House of Commons are gathered from the Parliamentary archives. For each legislative proposal, commonly referred to as "public bills," several characteristics are noted. First, the name of the drafting signatory, their party, and their ministerial department are recorded. Of course, only Labour ministers propose public bills during the Brown cabinet and only Conservative ministers propose bills during the Cameron II cabinet. However, we will wish to differentiate between the treatment of Conservative and Liberal Democratic proposals during the Cameron–Clegg government, so this information is necessary.

Next, the date of submission and the length of the initial proposal, in words, are recorded. Why record the length in words, rather than articles as we did in the preceding analysis of Belgium, Denmark, and the Netherlands? In short, the United Kingdom has a common law system of governance, like the United States, whereas most continental countries, including Belgium, Denmark, and the Netherlands, have civil law, or code law. Common law proposals tend to be substantially longer than their code law counterparts because the draft bills tend to be self-contained policy proposals rather than augmentations to the existing code. Moreover, the organization of legislative proposals in the United Kingdom is nowhere near as uniform as Belgium, Denmark, and the Netherlands, making the number of articles fairly arbitrary. On the contrary, articles are very important organizing tools in civil law legislation, as they are used to direct augmentations to the existing code.

After noting the bill's authorship information, date of initiation, and length, information regarding its scrutiny is recorded. As mentioned, counts of the number of amendments are recorded for each bill. Here, we record total amendments offered on each bill, rather than the number of articles changed. As noted, articles are substantially less meaningful organizational structures here. Once the amendment documents have been tallied, the number of House of Commons committee proceedings is counted. Because these proceedings are public, recorded, and often broadcast, and, because the observed number of proceedings vary so greatly (ranging from zero to twenty-two with a mean of about five), we will consider the possibility that differentiating behaviors that may be absent in the amendments themselves are manifest in the number of proceedings that a particular proposal is forced to endure.

The next stage in the review process, following all proceedings and the consideration of amendments in committee, is the "report stage." In this stage of the process, the bill is opened to debate on the floor of the Commons, allowing members outside of the committee to have their voice heard. Amendments may be suggested and attached to the bill if there is sufficient support. However, in practice, few changes are agreed to. In this process, just as in committee, the government holds powerful influence. What's more, not every bill is opened to report. In the total sample of 247 ministerial proposals, only 44 move to this stage. In the analysis later, we will examine whether or not this public, open debate stage is more common in the Cameron–Clegg government, giving the coalition partners opportunity to publicly air their grievances, than in single-party governments.

Following the open debate, all proposed changes are summarized in a formal report which is published to the parliamentary archives. These reports are important indicators of the bill's contentiousness and represent the culmination of an open debate on the floor of the Commons over the costs and benefits of the proposal. As such, their issuance and length are important indicators of demonstrated contention over the proposal and the degree to which the government is willing to publicly engage in debate. In expectation, we should observe more bills moving to the reporting stage and longer reports under Cameron–Clegg as compared to their single-party counterparts.

The final scrutiny indicator we will examine is the total duration of the proposal's review. This was the outcome variable in the first cross-national examination of legislative scrutiny in parliamentary democracies by Martin and Vanberg (2004). Martin and Vanberg argue that this serves as a reasonable proxy for the degree of scrutiny a bill receives as all aspects of the legislative review process require time to conduct. Several years later, the authors compared the length of the review process a bill endured to the number of amendments proposed to it and found that the central predictors were nearly identical (Martin and Vanberg 2011). Let us begin our analysis of legislative review in the House of Commons with this summary measure.

Figure 7.2 plots the distributions of scrutiny durations for Cameron–Clegg and their single-party counterparts, Brown and Cameron II. Note the seemingly "negative" values are not truly negative, they are simply an artifact of the density smoothing. The distributions are very similar, with the mean scrutiny duration under Cameron–Clegg (183) only four days longer than the mean under Brown and Cameron II (179). Further, the distributions are statistically indifferentiable – a difference of means test produces a t-statistic of only 0.243. In short, this uncontrolled comparison of durations suggests that there was no more legislative scrutiny during Cameron–Clegg than during their single-party government counterparts.

Although the means of the distributions are not distinct, they do have different appearances. In particular, Cameron–Clegg appears more diffuse than Brown and Cameron II. That is, the Brown and Cameron II distribution is single-peaked and densely clustered about the median. The Cameron–Clegg distribution, however, is a bit more spread from its median and veers toward bimodality with a cluster close to zero and another at about the one-year mark. An F-test comparing the variances of the two distributions concludes that the two are statistically distinct in their second moment and we are certain of the difference at the level $p = 0.034$. Why may this be?

There are several potential explanations, but two in particular have more prima facie credibility and are also more interesting in the context

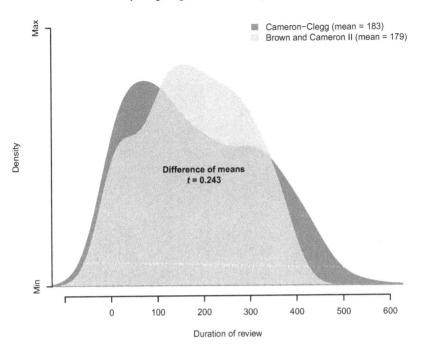

FIGURE 7.2 Comparing duration of review period across cabinets

of the broader arguments here. The first is that the parties changed their behavior over time – that they learned the coalition game and adapted their behaviors as the legislative term progressed. The second is that the differences are attributable to the partisanship of the authoring minister. Of course, there are also two possibilities here. The first is that the Liberal Democrats were able to drag out the review period of Conservative proposals for the purposes of differentiation. The second is that the Conservatives' purported domination of the Liberal Democrats extended to the review process.

To assess the first possibility, that the Cameron–Clegg government adapted its behavior over time, we can simply look at the scrutiny durations over the cabinet's term in office. This is plotted in Figure 7.3 and given alongside the review durations over the course of the Brown and Cameron II governments for the sake of comparison.

Figure 7.3 shows that the temporal patterns across the three cabinets are similar. Both Cameron–Clegg and Cameron II show sharp drop offs in review duration toward the end of their term, but this was for different

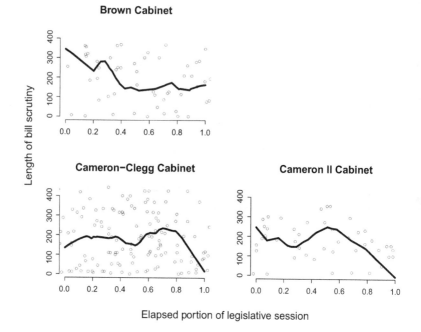

FIGURE 7.3 Comparing review durations over time across cabinets

reasons. For Cameron–Clegg, this reflects a "hurry-up offense" strategy where bills were being forced through parliament in the run-up to a very uncertain election in which both parties were expecting to lose seats. Indeed, nearly every election forecast predicted that both the Conservatives and Liberal Democrats would lose votes and the result would be a hung parliament. Of course, the Conservatives did quite well in the 2015 parliamentary elections to the surprise of most. The sharp drop off for Cameron II is a function of the Brexit referendum. Cameron, who was on the remain side of the campaign (though his party was divided), resigned after losing the referendum and most of his cabinet's bills were hastily aborted at his resignation.

In sum, Figure 7.3 shows us that we can reject the notion that the Cameron–Clegg government adapted its behavior over time as their coalition experience grew. Though there was a very slight up tick about three-quarters of the way through their term in office, this change is not statistically robust. These patterns suggest that, despite Clegg's resolutions to draw distinctions between the Liberal Democrats and the Conservatives, he was unable or unwilling to draw out the legislative review process for these purposes. Indeed, as we will see in more detail later, the data suggest that the within-cabinet variability in scrutiny behaviors are reflective of differences between Conservatives and Liberal Democrats rather than either or both parties learning to use the review process as a platform for differentiation over time and those interpartisan differences do not reflect well upon Clegg's leadership.

Let us now move forward to consider all of the measures of legislative scrutiny in a more rigorous fashion. Recall from the earlier discussion that we have counted the number of amendments proposed and the number of committee proceedings held for each bill. We also have data on whether or not the bill was referred to the reporting phase and, given its referral to reporting, how long the final report was. Finally, we can also examine the length of the total process of review in a more rigorous parametric model.

To assess the differences in review behavior across cabinets, each indicator of review is regressed on cabinet indicators controlling for the length of the original proposal in words – recall that this is a coarse measure of the breadth of policy change proposed in the legislation and also the potential opportunity for scrutiny. Each model also controls for the ministerial department of the proposal's signatory by allowing for random intercepts at this level. This is important, of course, as some policy areas are simply more complex or more prone to discord across parties and we want to model out potential correlations across rows of the data grouped on the policy area.

Our theoretical expectation is that, if Cameron and Clegg were using the review process to signal their parties' true preferences or their representational competence to their supporters, then we should observe greater review activity within their cabinet as compared to their single-party bookends. Therefore, our empirical expectation is that we should observe parameter estimates on the cabinet indicators in the following rank-ordering: Cameron–Clegg > Brown ~ Cameron II. More practically, since the Brown cabinet will serve as the omitted, baseline category, we should expect, in all models, a positive and significant parameter estimate on the Cameron–Clegg indicator, demonstrating a statistically significant increase in scrutiny activity in the Cameron–Clegg cabinet relative to the Brown cabinet. We should also expect that every Cameron–Clegg estimate is significantly greater than every parameter estimate on the Cameron II indicator, demonstrating a statistically significant increase in scrutiny activity in the Cameron–Clegg cabinet relative to the Cameron II cabinet.

Table 7.1 *Comparing legislative scrutiny across UK cabinets. Baseline is Brown government*

	Poisson		Bernoulli	Linear	
	Amendments	Proceedings	Reporting	Report length	Duration
Cameron–Clegg	0.817	0.011	−1.814	0.133	0.054
	(0.064)	(0.076)	(0.399)	(0.299)	(0.174)
Cameron II	0.840	−0.261	−3.004	−1.222	0.175
	(0.073)	(0.100)	(0.786)	(0.707)	(0.218)
log(Bill length)	0.378	0.396	0.331	0.055	0.297
	(0.015)	(0.023)	(0.126)	(0.118)	(0.041)
Constant	−1.868	−2.297	−3.353	9.993	2.089
	(0.178)	(0.248)	(1.252)	(1.217)	(0.432)
Random intercept:					
var(department)	0.249	0.062	0.061	0.219	0.245
Observations	238	238	238	44	238
log likelihood	−950.198	−558.517	−93.476	−59.667	−360.927

The model estimates are given in Table 7.1 where the type of model is noted above each column: Poisson for the amendments and proceedings; Bernoulli for referral to reporting stage; and Linear for the length of the ultimately issued report (given that the reporting stage was reached) in words logged and the total duration of the bill's scrutiny in days logged.

The first thing to note, across all but one model, is that the bill length is a strong positive correlate of the degree of scrutiny the proposal receives. It positively contributes to the expected number of amendments being proposed and proceedings being held. It is a strong positive predictor of the proposal being referred to the reporting stage. And, while it does not increase the expected length of the final report *given* that the bill will enter the reporting stage, it is the strongest predictor of the total duration of the bill's scrutiny. This is very important to note as it is the first nondescriptive examination of parliamentary scrutiny in the UK's House of Commons and, as such, it is very reassuring that at least some systematic correlates of scrutiny discovered in other parliamentary contexts are also present in the Commons. Likewise, if the length of the initial proposal was *uncorrelated* from the degree of scrutiny it faced, we would be forced to rethink the measure's usefulness in capturing the breadth of the changes to the status quo proposed in the draft bill. Fortunately, that is not the case.

Pivoting back to our central focus, examining the results of the amendments model, the Cameron–Clegg parameter is positive and significant, but smaller than the Cameron II estimate, indicating that, while Cameron–Clegg did propose more amendments than the Brown cabinet during their term in office, it was still less than the number proposed by the single-party majority government that succeeded them. As for the proceedings, a similar relationship is revealed with a near-zero estimate on the Cameron–Clegg indicator and a robust negative estimate on Cameron II. This tells us that Cameron–Clegg did hold more proceedings during their term in office than Cameron II, but no more than Brown. As noted earlier, the majority dominates the review process from the binding parameters on review determined in the second reading, to the composition of the committee, to the actual day-to-day procedures of committee assemblies and hearings. That is, the opposition is functionally irrelevant to the scrutiny process. Given this, what the data are telling us is that Cameron and Clegg did not use amendments to signal their dissatisfaction with one another's legislative proposals, nor did they convene more proceedings to publicly air their grievances. In other words, their behavior did not conform to expectations set by their continental counterparts, instead, they behaved indifferentiably from their domestic, single-party counterparts who *do not* have the same incentives to use these procedures to communicate with the electorate.

This regularity extends to the choice of sending the bill to the open debate of the reporting stage of review. The Cameron–Clegg government uses this procedure somewhat more often than Cameron II, but still significantly less than Brown. Further more, given bill's referral to open debate and scrutiny, the depth and breadth of debate and proposed alteration resulting from that process under Cameron–Clegg is indistinguishable from Brown. Finally, examining our summary measure of legislative scrutiny, the total duration of the bill's time under review, we see no appreciable differences between any of the governments. Over all five measures of legislative scrutiny our expected rank-ordering of Cameron–Clegg > Brown ~ Cameron II is never once recovered with any appreciable degree of statistical significance. In sum, Cameron and Clegg did not embrace the review process as a forum for differentiation.

Given that Cameron–Clegg did not behave differently from their single-party counterparts in the aggregate, it is worth considering whether or not the coalition adapted over time or, whether or not

Table 7.2 *Analyzing legislative scrutiny within Cameron–Clegg*

	Poisson		Bernoulli reporting	Linear	
	Amendments	Proceedings		Report length	Duration
Conservative proposal	−0.636 (0.343)	0.188 (0.637)	−6.282 (4.023)	−0.520 (4.087)	−1.836 (1.826)
log(days into legislative period)	−0.108 (0.047)	−0.036 (0.090)	−1.287 (0.609)	−0.033 (0.357)	−0.200 (0.261)
Conservative proposal × log(days)	0.058 (0.054)	−0.044 (0.099)	0.841 (0.649)	0.054 (0.698)	0.203 (0.281)
log(bill length)	0.386 (0.016)	0.430 (0.027)	0.303 (0.186)	0.177 (0.171)	0.254 (0.060)
Constant	−0.249 (0.342)	−2.357 (0.641)	3.953 (4.103)	9.276 (2.556)	4.053 (1.805)
Observations	136	136	136	17	136
log(likelihood)	−645.828	−321.050	−43.944	−22.294	−214.121

the Conservatives and Liberal Democrats behaved differently from one another. To do this, we will examine the same scrutiny outcomes once again: amendments, proceedings, referral to reporting stage, report length, and total duration. This time, however, we will constrain the sample to the Cameron–Clegg government and differentiate between the proposal's authoring party and the time at which the proposal was initiated. More specifically, each model will include a binary variable indicating that the bill has been proposed by the Conservatives, the (logged) number of says since the cabinet has been formed, as well as the interaction of these two variables. This will allow us to assess if Conservative and Liberal Democratic proposals face differing degrees of scrutiny in general, whether the typical degree of scrutiny changed over time as the partners in government (presumably) learned to better negotiate the travails of coalition governance, and whether or not the degree of change over time differed for the partners.

These model results are given in Table 7.2. The models estimated are the same as earlier, save the elimination of departmental random effects – there are simply too few observations to recover those estimates efficiently. As previously, in the cross-cabinet comparisons, the length of the initial proposal is a robust positive indicator of legislative scrutiny in all models, save the length of the final report for bills referred to that reporting stage. Again, this is encouraging as it tells us that our summary measure of proposal breadth is performing as expected *and* that there is commonality in the predictors of legislative scrutiny between the House of Commons and the lower houses of continental parliaments.

Looking over the parameter estimates on the Conservative proposal indicator, there is evidence that Conservative bills see fewer amendments, on average, than Liberal Democratic proposals. Given the findings from chapter 6, we should expect this difference in light of the size disparity between these two partners. Recall that we found size to be among the most important predictors of the number of amendments a party proposes. Given that the Conservatives held over five times the number of seats as the Liberal Democrats, and therefore had five times the available labor force to participate in the work of writing and proposing amendments, we should expect this result. Of course, this also means that Liberal Democrats were likely getting pushed around in the review process, just as they were perceived as getting pushed around in pre-proposal policy negotiations with the Conservatives. Even if Liberal Democratic policy proposals saw no more proceedings or reporting debates and endured no longer reports and durations of review than Conservative policy proposals, they did endure significantly more change.

More discouraging are the universally negative estimates on the calendar parameter. While only two of these estimates are statistically significant – the estimate in the amendments model and the estimate in the referral to reporting model – they still tell a powerful story: as the Cameron–Clegg government aged, it tends to scrutinize less, on average, rather than more, as we would expect if they were learning how to use the review period to send signals of differentiation and competence. If we examine the interactive effects between proposing party and the age of the cabinet, we find that the news is mixed, but negative on balance for the Liberal Democrats in particular. The results show that, to the extent that there was a negative correlation between the age of the cabinet and the degree of scrutiny endured by ministerial proposals, which was the case for amendments and for referral to the reporting stage, that correlation was *slightly* weaker on the Liberal Democratic side (meaning that the Liberal Democrats reduced their scrutiny less on average than the Conservatives over time). However, our certainty of those small differences is middling; weak in terms of amendments, but stronger in terms of report stage referral. That said, the fact that the Liberal Democrats engaged in precisely the opposite of the behavior they should have to a slightly smaller degree than their partners in cabinet is no great compliment. Even less so given Clegg's resolution to differentiate.

In sum, the data are fairly conclusive here that, in total, the Cameron–Clegg government did not utilize the review process for signaling ideological distinctiveness and representational competence. They offered no more amendments than their single-party majority counterparts Brown and Cameron II, nor did they call more proceedings, refer to reporting more often, draft longer reports, or subject proposals to longer review durations. Further, the data suggest that the Conservatives and Liberal Democrats did not learn to use this venue any more effectively over their time in government together. This goes for both the Conservatives *and* the Liberal Democrats who had privately and publicly committed to a campaign of "conspicuous differentiation."

Even though we can be confident in concluding that the Liberal Democrats (and Conservatives) were unsuccessful in utilizing the review phase to signal ideological distinctiveness and representational competence, we cannot conclude, however, that they were unsuccessful in utilizing the review phase for coalition policing. This is an important caveat, especially in light of the resounding criticism that Clegg has had to endure. Making that type of judgement would require an analysis specifically focused on the degree to which Clegg and the Liberal Democrats were able to rein in drifting Tory ministers and protect their own proposals from scrutiny. That analysis, which would require a fair amount of qualitative investigation of the life cycles (particularly the *content* of legislative amendments) of Conservative and Liberal Democratic proposals, is simply beyond the scope of our study here. Our charge was to test the empirical implications of the theoretical arguments discussed earlier: did Cameron and Clegg scrutinize more than their single-party majority counterparts; and, did Cameron and Clegg scrutinize more as their time in office progressed? The answer to both of these questions is a definitive "no."

SPEECH IN THE HOUSE OF COMMONS

Paramount to Clegg and the Liberal Democrats' ability to differentiate from the Conservatives, is their ability to reshape the media narrative regarding their similarity and difference *without* violating collective cabinet responsibility. We have just discussed how they may have employed legislative scrutiny to accomplish this. By amending the legislative proposals of their partners, a cabinet member may credibly signal their distaste for, and disagreement with, their cabinet partners' policies without violating collective responsibility – of course, the analysis showed, that they ultimately did not. However, as also discussed, the House of Commons is not particularly well equipped for that behavior. That is, the Commons has an exceptionally weak committee system in which individual members are unlikely to cultivate expertise and ministers are endowed with the power to bully committees, withdraw their proposals, force closed rule votes on their bills, and so on. These power asymmetries between the parliament and the cabinet make it quite difficult for partners of authoring ministers to propose changes to the legislation that would send sufficiently clear and strong signals of their distaste for the bill in order to demonstrate competence and ideological consistency to their supporters. This is a possible explanation for the results derived from the analysis of legislative scrutiny across the Brown, Cameron–Clegg, and Cameron II cabinets and *within* the Cameron–Clegg government over time.

Authoring ministers, however, are not endowed with such advantages in so-called topical debates in the House of Commons – debates over "a matter of regional, national or international importance" (House of Commons 2010, 31) – which do not have hard constraints on the content of speech set by the cabinet. Although the Speaker of the House of Commons (the chair of all parliamentary debates) technically has the power to limit speech time, the Standing Orders of the House guarantee the ministerial and leading opposition parties equal time in legislative debate, and allocate three minutes to the second largest opposition party for every five minutes allocated to ministerial/leading opposition parties (House of Commons 2010). However, the Standing Orders do not provide guidance for how to divide time among the smaller party factions, let alone within the government between coalition partners. In addition to this, other types of debate on legislative proposals, such as on their amendments or committee reports, or on their final vote timing, do not have statutory guidelines for the allocation speaking time allotted to cabinet and opposition. As such, in the aggregate, the speaker was effectively unconstrained in his ability to dole out speaking time in the Commons during the Cameron–Clegg government. In practice, however, the allocation of speaking time over this period was remarkably proportional to seat share, just as we would expect in the consensual parliaments on the continent. The allocation is given in Figure 7.4 in which each party is plotted according to its share of seats in the Commons and the share of words they spoke in Commons debate, omitting [Prime] Minister's Questions which are subject to different rules.

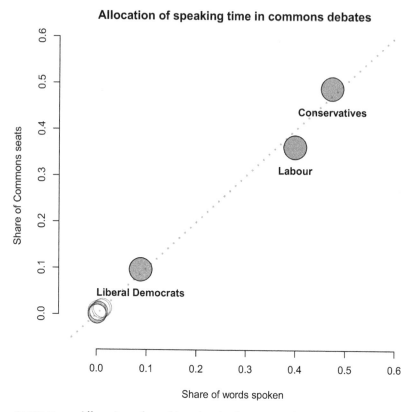

FIGURE 7.4 Allocation of speaking time in the House of Commons during the
Cameron–Clegg government

The figure highlights major parties – the coalition partners and
Labour, the leading opposition party – by labeling them and includes
a 45° line to denote a one-to-one relationship. Note that all of the
minor parties (including, at this point, the Scottish National Party, the
Democratic Unionist Party, and Plaid Cymru) are more or less precisely on the 45° line; however, it appears that the Speaker redirected
a fairly substantial amount of time away from Labour and redistributed
it, more or less proportionately, between the coalition partners. What is
salient here, however, is not the difference between cabinet and opposition parties, but the difference *within* the coalition. Even though the
Conservatives controlled 49 percent of the plenary debate time to the
10 percent controlled by the Liberal Democrats, these differences are not
precisely proportional to their seat shares – Conservatives spoke about
five words for every word spoken by the Liberal Democrats, whereas, in

a perfectly proportional world, the Conservatives' seat share would entitle them to about five and one-half words for every word spoken by the Liberal Democrats. In sum, while the Liberal Democrats are smaller, their freedom to express their preferences unmolested by ministers fearing policy loss in the review process and their overcompensation in speaking time relative to their seat share suggests that Commons debate may provide a better avenue for successful differentiation from the Tories. But, did Clegg and his co-partisans actually take advantage of this resource to wrest back control of their brand?

To answer this question, we will investigate the ideological content or expressed preferences contained in Commons speeches given by Conservatives and Liberal Democrats over the course of the coalition cabinet's time in office. Our first step here is to collect the text of the speeches. Fortunately, these are made publicly available online via Hansard – the official record of parliamentary debates in the United Kingdom. The documents containing the debates were downloaded from the Hansard archives website and then parsed into an easily manipulable text document organized into speaker-day rows of data. That is, the base document contained *all words*, spoken by *all MPs*, for *all days* of the Cameron–Clegg government (excepting ministerial questions, points of order, and other procedural discussion, which were stripped out). This base document is then parsed into an MP-day organization, such that one row of data contains all words spoken by a *particular MP* on a *particular day*, where the MP is identified by name and party.

As noted earlier, [Prime] Minister's Questions were redacted from the corpus, as these particular words are spoken under a different set of rules that were constructed to accommodate disagreement between government and opposition while fostering transparency between the cabinet, select committees that tend to mirror the cabinet's organization, and citizens of the United Kingdom (and also, perhaps, allow MPs to blow off a little steam). Further more, all interactions between the Speaker of the House and Members of the House (as entertaining as they may be) are stripped from the corpus, as are all mentions of MPs or ministers. In practice, ministerial references tend to be very high discrimination indicators that a particular party is speaking on a particular day. For example, members of opposition often refer to the authoring minister of the particular piece of legislation being debated and all speakers tend to reference the MP preceding them by regular pronouns adjoined by regular adjectives ("the right honorable gentleman" or "my great friend," etc.) – transitions in speaker almost always denote transitions in party control of the floor;

as such, speakers tend to unkindly refer to the members they follow. In estimation, these references tend to exaggerate differences between parties (as the ministerial party almost never refers to the minister, etc.) so they are withdrawn.[5]

Finally, all minor opposition parties are dropped from the corpus. This is done for two main reasons. First, our focus here is on how the Liberal Democrats evolve their speaking strategy to differentiate from the Conservatives (or not). While having reference text from an opposition party is beneficial to estimating the difference in expressed preferences between Tories and Lib Dems, having *all* opposition parties is unnecessary. This is convenient because, second, while a member of Labour speaks on every day in which debate is held, members of the minor opposition parties speak infrequently, which makes estimating a series of expressed preferences for them difficult. More to the point, because the model we will use to estimate expressed preferences estimates *relative* positions – that is uses differences in the words spoken by party A and party B to inform its estimates of party C – having an unstable constellation of parties entering the data would make for onerous comparison of recovered positions for a particular party over time.

Once these changes to the data have been made, rows are aggregated up to the party-day level, such that one row contains all words spoken by a particular party – Conservatives, Liberal Democrats, or Labour – on a given day of debate. From this refined corpus individual days are pulled out and analyzed separately following the recommendation of Lauderdale and Herzog (2016). That is, for each day of debate, we estimate a vector of ideal points, or, expressed preferences for the Conservatives, Liberal Democrats, and Labour from the words they have spoken in the Commons. The specific model estimated is Slapin and Proksch's (2008) "word fish" model, which assumes that the frequency with which words are spoken by a particular actor is a realization of a Poisson process driven by that actor's "position" in a unidimensional word space. [6]

---

[5] Note that leaving these references in the corpus does not alter the inferences we draw from the data. They only have the effect of separating the ministerial and non-ministerial parties on any given day, which, over the course of the parliamentary term, tends to exaggerate the difference between government and opposition parties and understate the difference between the cabinet partners. As we are only concerned with changes in the similarity and difference of expressed preferences within the governing coalition, these differences are irrelevant.

[6] The Slapin and Proksch (2008) model estimates discrimination parameters for each word in each corpus, which inform the researcher of how informative each word is in identifying the party positions. In most applications, these discrimination parameters can be very interesting. Here, however, because we analyze each day of debate in a separate

Distribution of recovered positions

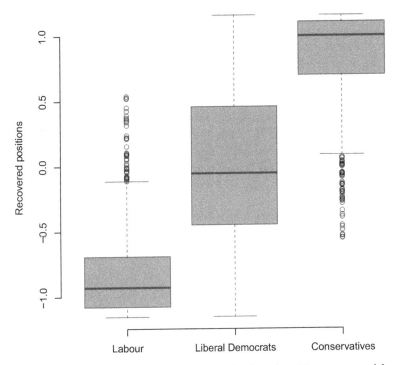

FIGURE 7.5 Assessing the distribution and order of positions recovered from the analysis of Commons speeches

These estimates allow us to systematically evaluate the degree of similarity and difference in the content of Conservative and Liberal Democratic Commons speeches, for every day of debate, over the entire course of their time in cabinet together. The expectation is that, as Clegg learns the danger of losing control of his brand by being perceived as too similar to the Conservatives, we should observe the Liberal Democrats pull away from the Conservatives and this should be manifest in the "ideal points" that we recover from their Commons debates.

These positions are summarized, over the entire term, in Figure 7.5. It is useful to have a look at the distribution of estimates for Conservative,

model, we have many, many discrimination parameters and their importance tends to vary by day, depending upon the proposal being debated. For example, "spending" may be a very informative word when policy regarding the National Health Service is being debated, but may lose most of its predictive power in budgeting debates. As such, we will omit analysis and discussion of these discrimination parameters here.

Liberal Democrats, and Labour, before examining the dynamics of Tory–Liberal Democratic interactions to validate the data, or, at least, make certain that the estimates are reasonable. If the model consistently yielded a rank-ordering of Conservatives > Labour > Liberal Democrats, we may suspect that the model was either misspecified, or, that the content of parliamentary debate is not driven by the ideological orientations of the parties, but perhaps some other political cleavage. As Figure 7.5 shows, this is not the case. The rank-ordering of the parties corresponds to our qualitative understanding of the ideological orientation of the parties where Labour is most left, Conservatives are most right, and the Liberal Democrats fit in between. The graphic also shows that the density of Liberal Democratic estimates is more diffuse – that

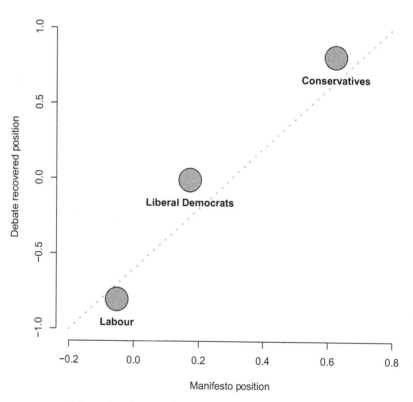

FIGURE 7.6 Assessing the correlation between speech-recovered positions and positions staked out in 2010 manifestos

there is more variability in the positioning content of Liberal Democratic speech than there is in the speeches of Labour and Conservatives. This, too, corresponds to our qualitative understanding of the parties, in particular the Liberal Democrats' typical preference for weaker centralization of authority within the party leadership and lesser discipline demands upon their rank-and-file. This is evident in the variability of the content of their speeches here, just as it is evident in, for example, the variability of their roll call voting behaviors in the Commons, as documented by Dewan and Spirling (2011).

The recovered estimates also correspond to our quantitative estimates of party brand, or platform position. This is shown in Figure 7.6, where the mean speech recovered positions are plotted against the left-right estimate of each party's 2010 manifesto (the manifesto positions are estimated, as in Chapter 6, following Lowe et al. 2011). This type of inter-measure comparison is a fairly common validation exercise in applied item response theory research (e.g., Slapin and Proksch 2008; Imai, Lo, and Olmsted 2016). What the figure shows us is that the average speech-derived positions are quite similar to the manifesto-derived positions, and that the two are strongly correlated. Indeed, the Pearson estimate is $\rho = 0.98$. Of course, there are only three observations when the speech positions are collapsed to their mean. But we are not concerned about the robustness of the correlation per se, rather the point here is merely to demonstrate the sensibility of the estimates on the whole, both qualitatively and quantitatively, before we analyze the manner in which the more fine-grained daily estimates change over time.

The temporal patterns of Conservative and Liberal Democratic speech are shown in Figure 7.7. In the figure, each circle corresponds to an estimated position for each day of Conservative speech and each cross corresponds to an estimated position for each day of Liberal Democratic speech. The lines are smoothed estimates of each party's position over time. Before getting into the detail of the patterns, there are two general observations to be made. The first is that there is a fairly high degree of variability *within* party over time. That is, Conservative and Liberal Democratic speeches vary widely in their ideological content from one day to the next. This is a function of several factors, most notably the content of the legislative agenda (*what* is being debated) and the speakers representing their party on any given day (*who* is doing the debating). Nonetheless, the second observation is that, over the long-term, there is a high degree of stability in the average position of both parties – the smoothed cardinal distance between Conservatives and Liberal

Ideological content of parliamentary speech

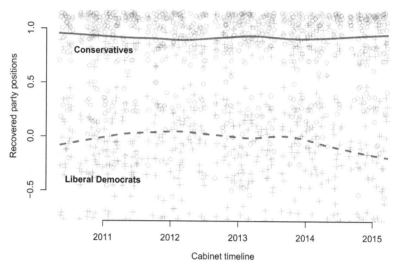

FIGURE 7.7 Differentiation in parliamentary speech. Ideological estimates derived from all speeches in the House of Commons by Conservatives and Liberal Democrats

Democrats is quite consistent over their term in office together. Of course, this is a not a good thing from the perspective of Clegg's attempts at brand management.

Recall that our expectation is that the Liberal Democrats should begin to pull away from the Conservatives fairly early on in the legislative session as their popularity begins to decline. Liberal Democratic support had begun slipping shortly after the formation of the cabinet and had already bottomed out into the single digits by late 2010. Shortly thereafter, by early to mid 2011, the conventional wisdom among political commentators was that the Liberal Democrats had been alienating their base through their continued role as cooperative partners to Cameron and the Conservatives. By Autumn of 2011, all of the signals of mass defection from the Liberal Democratic supporting coalition were present and Clegg was openly apologizing for his compromises and cooperative relationship with the Conservatives while simultaneously advocating for a campaign of ideological differentiation to take back control of the party brand. The context called for differentiation and the leadership endorsed differentiation, but did they actually deliver on their commitments?

Table 7.3 *Looking for differentiation in Commons speeches over time*

Covariate	Linear	Quadratic	Cubic
log(days into legislative period)	0.013	−0.202	0.200
	(0.021)	(0.133)	(0.467)
log(days into legislative period)^2		0.022	−0.078
		(0.014)	(0.113)
log(days into legislative period)^3			0.008
			(0.009)
Constant	1.097	1.574	1.109
	(0.119)	(0.315)	(0.607)
Observations	708	708	708
R^2	0.001	0.004	0.005

The data suggest that Clegg and the Liberal Democrats could not or would not deliver on their promise to differentiate on the floor of the Commons. Despite the Liberal Democrats' immediate popularity losses from the cabinet's formation sustaining through 2010 and 2011, their behavior remained unchanged. Despite Clegg's open calls for differentiation in Autumn 2011, they did not signal the distinctiveness of their brand in their parliamentary speeches nor did they appreciably increase their antagonism toward the Conservatives, even though there are allowances of such behavior through the duration of the review process in the rules of collective responsibility. There simply was no course correction in 2010 or 2011. In fact, the data suggest that, if there was a change at all, it appears that the Conservatives and the Liberal Democrats begin to *converge* upon one another in their Commons rhetoric from the coalition's formation until 2012. Indeed, if the Liberal Democrats ever began to use their parliamentary speeches in order to differentiate in earnest and pull away from their partners in government it did not happen until late in 2014, when the 2015 parliamentary elections were the horizon. But, given the very modest increase in separation it seems unlikely that this was a conscious choice. Indeed, tests for separation between the two time series reveal no statistically differentiable changes over the entire term in office.

This lack of change is formalized in the regression results presented in Table 7.3. Here, the absolute difference between the Liberal Democrats and the Conservatives recovered from the analysis of the speeches both parties made in the Commons each day of the legislative period is regressed upon a measure of the cabinet's age. In the first model, this difference is regressed on the logged number of days into the legislative period – the number of days in which parliamentary business was conducted (excluding ministerial question days). The parameter estimate in the linear model is positive, as we would hope, but it is small and the standard error is nearly twice as large as the coefficient. There is no robust relationship between time and the difference in expressed preferences between the Liberal Democrats and the Conservatives in the linear model. The quadratic model, which includes logged legislative days and that measure's squared term, also reveals no robust support. Although the positive estimate on the squared term approaches traditional levels of significance ($p = 0.102$), its effects never surpass the negative impact of the linear term. Finally, the cubic model is similarly discouraging. All parameter estimates are smaller than their standard errors and, even if each parameter was robust, they would not produce effects that reflect a sensible pivot toward differentiation following the announcement of the strategy. Further, the R^2 estimates on each models suggest that time simply does not provide significant explanatory power for the observed difference in the content of speeches given by Conservatives and Liberal Democrats on the floor of the House of Commons.

This is the real picture of Clegg's failure as Liberal Democratic leader. He understood the risk of losing control of his party's brand and he understood the need for ideological differentiation, even making public appeals for it in interviews and in speeches to his backbenchers and loyal supporters. And yet, the interpretation of the data *most* generous to Clegg and the Liberal Democrats – an interpretation that lacks statistical power – suggests that differentiation is not evident in Commons speeches until the government was nearly four years old with Liberal Democratic popularity holding steady at its nadir for almost the entire time. For four years, the Liberal Democrats were unwilling or unable to draw ideological distinctions from their partners in government in speeches given on the floor of parliament – one of the only venues they have in which they may draw such distinctions without breaking collective cabinet responsibility. Given the public record of Clegg's strategic direction to his party there can be only a few explanations for this delay (or failure).

The first is that Clegg and the Liberal Democrats never made the effort. That is, it is possible that Clegg simply did not recognize parliamentary debate as a useful forum for differentiation and brand management – that the Liberal Democrats were unaware of the potential impact of confrontational or antagonistic statements made to and about their partners in government. They may not have understood that their speeches can convey messages to the electorate, either directly, if the speech is sufficiently provocative to garner word-for-word news coverage, or indirectly, by reshaping the perceptions of elites, such as reporters and political commentators, who then, in turn, pass these signals on to the mass public.

Alternatively, the Liberal Democrats may have simply reserved their floor time for other purposes. Rather than using their speeches to communicate with their supporters and the wider electorate, they may have simply been focusing on winning hearts and minds *inside the chamber* itself, attempting to persuade members of other parties to join them in support or opposition of the issue at hand. In this case, the Liberal Democrats may have simply calculated that winning over support to their side of the issue was more valuable than whatever damage control fierce speeches pointed at the electorate may have accomplished. This is certainly plausible.

The third possible explanation is that Clegg simply failed to, or chose not to, impose discipline upon his members of parliament. This rings more true, given (a) what we know of the Liberal Democrats' preferences for relatively weak internal organization and (b) the very public nature of Clegg's calls for differentiation. In this event, it is likely that Liberal Democratic members of parliament used their speaking time selfishly, or at least with little regard for their leader's direction, choosing to communicate their own sincere or strategic individual preferences on the issue at hand, rather than coordinating on a concerted effort to manage the party's collective brand. This would certainly be compatible with our expectations for individual MP behavior within a party organization competing in a single-member district electoral system.

Unfortunately, Clegg's own accounts of the coalition's tenure in office do not provide much explanation for the patterns revealed here. But the patterns are, nonetheless, clear: if the Liberal Democrats began to intentionally focus their commons speeches on the effort of differentiation (and the data suggest that they never do), then they turned their attention to this matter entirely too feebly and entirely too late, long after seemingly permanent damage was done to their brand, long after the defection of large swaths of their supporting coalition in the electorate. This failure to differentiate runs parallel to the Liberal Democrats' behavior in the process of legislative review, where the level of scrutiny under Cameron–Clegg was indifferentiable from the levels of scrutiny under Brown and Cameron II. Likewise, Liberal Democratic behaviors showed no sign of adapting *over time* as the media narrative of their pragmatism, ideological flexibility, and openness to compromise – which was also often negatively portrayed as the Conservatives bending the Liberal Democrats to their will or the Liberal Democrats simply being inept negotiators – proliferated and their popularity eroded.

It may have been the cementing of this popular narrative that isolated the Conservatives from electoral losses (in addition to the degree in which the Conservatives were the benefactors of the atrophy in Liberal Democratic support). While Clegg and the Liberal Democrats were consistently portrayed as weak and all-too-willing to compromise, Cameron and the Conservatives were popularly portrayed as rolling over the Liberal Democrats, extracting concessions from them at almost every turn, and rarely, if ever, yielding concessions of their own. Over the course of their time in government together, Conservative popularity remained relatively stable, while Liberal Democratic popularity collapsed and never really recovered. The Conservatives were able to preserve their ideological brand and appear competent representatives of their supporters, while the Liberal Democrats' supporters felt alienated and became uncertain of what the party stood for. Of course, the 2015 elections would translate these reputations (earned or not) and supporter sentiments into outcomes: the Conservatives gained seats while the Liberal Democrats were slaughtered.

This case study makes the lesson from the preceding chapters clear: if parties do not take pains to protect their brand, the nature of coalition governance may erode their electoral support. We have uncovered systematic evidence that cabinet parties in Belgium, Denmark, and the Netherlands, three countries with long histories of coalition governance, use the legislative review period of the policy-making process to do just this. These cabinet parties submit legislative amendments to their partners' draft bills in order to signal their discontent with the proposal and in so doing demonstrate their competence and burnish their ideological brand. We have uncovered systematic evidence that the participants of the Cameron–Clegg government, completely inexperienced with multiparty governance, did not avail themselves of the fora for differentiation supplied by the legislative review period and the Liberal Democrats were crushed at the ballot box as a result. In the face of these findings, the natural next step in this course of study is to ask, was the fate of the Liberal Democrats sui generis or simply a single example of a systematic relationship between differentiation (or the lack thereof) and electoral performance? Further, if this relationship is systematic, just how many cabinet parties are able to avoid Clegg's fate?

8

Does It Ever Go Right?

What works in real life is people getting together with different perspectives and figuring out how to solve problems. Cooperation works. What works in politics is conflict.

– Bill Clinton (2011)

Over the course of the last five chapters, we have discussed the nature of gravity within coalition governance. Coalition partners must maintain a sufficiently strong centripetal force in order to simply coexist let alone govern. At the same time, they must maintain a sufficiently strong centrifugal force, keeping one another just at arms length, in order to avoid the appearance that they are selling out their supporters or otherwise sullying their carefully crafted policy brand.

Within the electorate, at the microlevel, we have learned that voters perceive compromise and cooperation as poor representation and these perceptions effect both the manner in which voters understand the policy positions of cabinet parties as well as the degree to which parties deserve credit for the accomplishments of the cabinet. As a result, cabinet parties perceived as overly accommodating – too apt to cooperate and too quick to compromise with their partners in government – are punished at the polls.

From there, we pivoted to the legislature and derived expectations for cabinet party behaviors, within the confines of collective cabinet responsibility, in response to how their electorate perceived them. In the case of Belgium, Denmark, and the Netherlands – three countries well acquainted with the cycle of coalition – we found that cabinet partners behaved as expected. On average, when perceived as being too compromising, or too cooperative, when the integrity of their ideological brands was in danger of being marred by coalition, the parties became antagonistic toward one another, amending each other's legislation in order to send competency and differentiating signals to their supporters. In the case of the Cameron–Clegg government in the United Kingdom, on the other hand – a country with no experience with coalition in the post-war era – we found that the cabinet partners in general and the Liberal Democrats in particular, failed to respond to the electorate. And, at least partially as a result of alienating their base, the Liberal Democrats were obliterated in the following elections.

In sum, we have strong evidence of how voters react to coalition compromise at the microlevel: they do not care for it and are prone to punishing it. We have strong evidence that, at least in advanced parliamentary democracies that are well acquainted with coalition, parties are sensitive to this risk of punishment and attempt to mitigate via differentiation in the policy-making process. Further more, we have episodic evidence that failure to respect the risks of coalition compromise and cooperation can lead to catastrophic results. What we have yet to determine is whether these effects are systematic and persist over a range of parliamentary democracies. Is coalition compromise – the accommodative, cooperative behaviors, or, the centripetal forces required to make multiparty governance work – systematically punished at the macro level if not properly counterbalanced? This question is the very heart of the book's core argument and this is the question we will begin to answer here.

SIGNALING THROUGH NOISE

Thus far we have discussed two central for a for differentiation within the confines of collective cabinet responsibility. We have discussed the parliamentary scrutiny of cabinet proposals, the marking up and amending of one's partner's legislation to emphasize points of difference, signal one's true policy preferences, and demonstrated representative competence. We have also discussed parliamentary debate in which one may communicate, explicitly, one's dissatisfaction with the proposals of a partner in governance, one's policy preferences, and one's achievement's in government. But there may be other avenues for differentiation. These may perhaps be less, or less systematic behaviors, but this does not mean that these avenues should be dismissed. For example, Sagarzazu and Klüver (2017) have argued that parties may use direct communication, in the form of official press releases, to signal their supporters. Their central argument, which is related to our focus here, is that parties have different priorities at different times. When elections are proximate, cabinet partners must emphasize their differences in order to court electoral support. However, when elections are distant, government parties are more free to coordinate on shared goals. More specifically, Sagarzazu and Klüver (2017) argue that *type* of policies government parties discuss in their direct communications should be systematically correlated with the electoral cycle – that cabinet partners emphasize similar policy types in the heart of the legislative term, but their emphases become dissimilar in the shadow of election.

Of course, press releases are unlikely to have real, *direct* policy implications (though they may be able to influence the agenda) and they are unlikely to entice real-time responses from one's partner in government. Nonetheless, such communication may carry salient policy information that can be important to the establishment and maintenance of party brands. For example, in addition to the study just cited, Grimmer (2013) analyzes the content of press releases and finds that United States Senators from parties that are unpopular in their home state use their press releases to emphasize their role in particularistic, or distributive policy victories. Well-aligned senators, on the other hand, tend to focus more on signaling their ideological bona fides. All of this is to say that these studies reveal alternative potential avenues for differentiation – that other avenues do, in fact, exist, and our strategy must take this into account.

But before we begin thinking about what this may or may not mean for our measurement and estimation approaches, we should return to the discussion in earlier chapters about what are and are not reasonable levels of attention, or reasonable behaviors more generally, to expect from voters, and contemplate how this should affect parties' approach to differentiation. In short, is it reasonable to expect voters to observe *any* political interaction, parliamentary (debate, legislative markup, etc.) or otherwise (bargaining ultimata, media interviews, etc.) *directly*? It seems clear that, in the overwhelming majority of cases, the answer to this question is a resounding, "no." Voters simply have too much on their plate in their own day-to-day lives to be plausibly expected to absorb the minutiae of the political process in any real detail. Indeed, if we are honest with ourselves, as students of politics – the most interested of the most interested citizens – even we observe only a vanishingly small number of political interactions directly. Instead, the most interested of us get our political data from media accounts of political interactions, while the moderately interested may absorb just a small subset of these accounts, and the disinterested may absorb little or no news reports directly, but only get a "feel" for the goings on through social interactions or inadvertent or indirect exposure to political reporting. This "inadvertent or indirect exposure" may be, for example, noticing some headlines while walking past a news stand, observing a chyron running on a news station on a gym television while jogging on a treadmill, or catching the last minute or so of a news broadcast while tuning into the station for a different program, and so on.

What this means for our purposes here is that even the most rabid "political junkies" and the least engaged citizens alike are more apt to get whatever political information they receive via news reporting, rather than direct observation of political procedure. The mediation incentivizes cabinet parties to take a comprehensive approach to differentiation – pursuing the goal via multiple avenues, including those that may not have direct policy consequences or are more "informal" – and also to attempt to massage the media narrative directly, perhaps by talking to reporters off the record, choosing to frame certain interactions in particular ways, and so on. Thus, while direct, policy-oriented differentiation is likely to bear the most fruit as these behaviors are more meaningful and politically salient than others, we certainly do not want to preclude other, less policy-oriented, or less formal routes to differentiation from our analysis. In other words, while analyzing parliamentary speech and the legislative scrutiny of cabinet proposals are likely to be the best strategies for *detecting* differentiation, these may not be the best strategies for determining the *effectiveness* of differentiation – focusing on these strategies alone would simply discard too much potentially meaningful information.

The approach that we will take, then, is not to derive our measure directly from some set of observable political interactions, rather, we will derive our measure from a more inclusive analysis of political media coverage. This has several advantages, but a few in particular are worth noting. First, there are robust efficiency gains. Rather than enumerating a set of observable political interactions and then collecting the raw data before designing, implementing, and validating a coding scheme for each, and then, of course designing, implementing, and validating a method of aggregation for all of the interaction types into a single measure of differentiation, a media-based approach allows us to rely on a single (though quite large) data source, coding scheme, and so on. Further, this single data source bears the advantage of having already aggregated the universe of observable political interactions into a single type of data. That is, the media collectively decide which interactions are more or less salient for their consumers and design the mix of their coverage of all of these interactions accordingly. In this way, the salience of each type of different interaction is "baked in" to the measure already.[1] Indeed, as Benoit and Laver have written:

> ... political discourse is rather like a giant feral factor analysis. The concepts that emerge – liberal versus conservative, left versus right – emerge because people over the years have found them simple and effective ways to communicate their perceptions of similarity and difference (2012, 198).

This intuition extends to both the *type* of events that receive coverage and the *relative weighting* of all event types in the distribution of media coverage of political interaction. In other words, the kind of events that receive coverage and the degree to which they are covered reflects the collective wisdom of political elites wishing to communicate salient points of similarity and difference between political actors. Finally, because media reports are colored by the observations and dispositions of reporters, it is likely that the type of behavior that would be unobservable to political scientists in the official record may be manifest in descriptions of the interactions. That is, background comments by party leaders, the body language and physical positioning of cabinet partners vis-à-vis one another at press conferences, or the tone, rather than the text, of spoken words may all, in the long term, contribute to the interpretation of other more explicit actions taken by members of the coalition, which will, in turn, condition press coverage of the those events.

This media-based approach is even more useful here as we are not concerned with government priorities or productivity, as in other research using media-based measures of government activity (e.g., Mayhew 1991; Jones and Baumgartner 2005), but rather voters' *perceptions* of the characteristics of members of government. This leads to the second focal advantage of this approach: we will be measuring the distribution of information that voters are actually sampling from, rather than measuring some subset of that distribution's potential antecedents. Of course, this is a substantially more direct measure of the extent to which cabinet

---

[1] This is not dissimilar from previous analyses that have relied on media choices to determine what is or is not relevant or important, or to otherwise synthesize broad and wide-ranging political interactions. Most notably, Mayhew (1991) relies on coverage of the US Congress by leading newspapers to build a listing of important legislation for his analysis of the effects of divided government on legislative productivity. Similarly, research on the construction of political agendas by Jones and Baumgartner (2005) and Baumgartner and Jones (2010) has turned to media for estimates of policy salience or voter attentiveness to a particular issue.

members are capable of generating a record of conflict or antagonism to counterbalance a narrative dominated by the compromise and cooperation necessary to make multiparty governance work. Empirically, our expectation is that the more a party is able to coax its media narrative away from cooperation and toward conflict, the more it is able to guard against degradations of its ideological brand or perceptions of representational incompetence and, therefore, against electoralpenalties.

Measuring the Signal

How are we to decompose the vast trough of media accounts of political interactions into a concise, unidimensional measure of conflict and cooperation between cabinet partners? One approach would be to crawl through the universe (or a subset) of media accounts of statements made and actions taken by political parties and, using analytical tools previously developed for estimating ideal points from political texts (e.g., Slapin and Proksch 2008; Lauderdale and Herzog 2016), attempt to extract an estimate of an "antagonism-agreement" continuum in lieu of the typical left-right estimates. That is, rather than construct a corpus for each party containing all of its parliamentary speeches or electoral manifestos, we would construct a corpus of media attributions or descriptions of its actions and statements toward its partners in government or other parties in the legislature. A similar approach has recently been taken using parliamentary speech data (Proksch et al. 2019).

A second approach would be to gather up all of the *dyadic* interactions *between* parties – for example, when some party *A* publicly disparages the legislative proposal of some party *B*, or when the leader of party *A* compliments the leader of party *B*, and so on – and consider these interactions as positive or negative responses to an underlying, latent dimension of conflict or cooperation between the two parties. As this approach is rooted in binaries, it should feel more familiar than most approaches. Though the universe of stimuli are not common to all actors – that is, not all actors have the opportunity to offer affirmative or negative responses to all stimuli as they do in, for example, the scaling of roll call data in the US Congress or United Nations (e.g., Poole 2005; Voeten 2000) – scaling this type of binary data to recover latent dimensions of compatibility or cooperativeness has been common in political economic research for some time, in particular in the subfield of international relations (e.g., Goldstein 1992; Signorino and Ritter 1999). We will take a similar approach, here. The central idea is to scour media coverage of political interactions between all parties in a given system at a given time (here, one year at a time within a given country), code these interactions as either positive (cooperative) or negative (conflictual), and compile them for all party dyads, which will then allow us to estimate the degree to which two parties were cooperative, on one side of spectrum, or in conflict, on the other side of the spectrum.

Relying on data from the Integrated Crisis Early Warning System project (Boschee et al. 2015), Weschle (2018) has recently performed nearly all of the required heavy-lifting to recover just these types of estimates for a large number of party dyads over a large number of country-years; spanning thirteen countries from the period of 2001–2014. Weschle details the specifics of the estimation in his article and on-line appendix in some detail, and it is certainly worth reading both documents, but for our purposes, what matters is that the estimates recovered are dyadic measures of cooperation and conflict between pairs of parties.[2]

Weschle (2018) validates these estimates by comparing them to changes in the dyadic similarity in the parties' policy pronouncements

---

[2] We begin here with a ratio of positive to negative interactions $y_{ij} = ln(\frac{+int_{ij}}{-int_{ij}})$, where i and j index parties and $+int$ and $-int$ sum positive and negative interactions for all unique party dyads in a particular system. These dyadic scores can then be used to construct an agreement score matrix, detailing the similarity of party i's interactions with all parties to all parties j's interactions to all parties. That is, in a three-party (A, B, C) system, the matrix would be 3×3, where cell AB would give the agreement between party A's and party B's interactions with each other and their individual interactions with party C. This agreement-score matrix can then be eigenvalue decomposed to recover "placements" on a common, unidimensional conflict-cooperation dimension for all party dyads. This type of decomposition, which is part of several correspondence-based scaling models, most notably NOMINATE (Poole and Rosenthal 2000) and its progeny is explained rather succinctly by Poole (2005). The fundamental intuition behind Weschle's work is the same, with the caveat that he allows the estimation of error components, or random effects, at the level of the individual parties and the dyads to regularize the estimates to the overall level of routinized conflict engaged in by any particular party. That is, because all dyads are estimated simultaneously, if we imagine some particularly antagonistic party, that is always thumbing the eyes of their counterparts in the parliament, we would want to allow the model to account for this overly aggressive behavior on the part of this party, rather than letting it bias the recovered estimates of all party dyads. Also, because these relationships are, by assumption, symmetric – meaning that the direction of an attack from party A to party B is coded simply as a conflictual interaction between party dyad AB – the model must build this, let us call it, assumed reciprocity, in to estimation.

and whether or not the parties are allied in coalition or allied in opposition. The analysis finds that the estimates correspond somewhat to differences in parties' pronounced dissimilarity on a nationalism-multiculturalism dimension, but also that the estimates correspond not at all to differences in parties' pronounced general, left-right placements. The real difference is an intercept shift where coalition dyads rate as more cooperative than dyads allied in opposition or dyads composed of mixed government and opposition parties. These findings are generally sensible and correspond to previous research on the electorate's *perceptions* of the similarity of party dyads, particularly Fortunato and Stevenson (2013) who find that voters perceive coalesced dyads to be more similar than dyads allied in opposition or dyads composed of mixed government and opposition parties, all else being equal. These differences are given in Figure 8.1, which reveal that the relationship between manifesto differences and the media-derived estimates of cooperativeness is effectively flat and what really matters is the overall difference in estimated cooperativeness between cabinet dyads and non-coalesced dyads.

These differences are important; not only do they reflect the primacy of government participation in determining the tone of media coverage, but also the relative insignificance of platform positioning to estimated levels of conflict or cooperation – that the most salient determinant of patterns of cooperation and conflict is the structure of governing coalition. This lack of responsiveness (both within governing dyads and across dyad types) runs contrary to models of policymaking or party behavior built entirely upon policy incentives, which would predict a stark, negative relationship between media-derived estimates of cooperativeness and declared preference dissimilarity. These models would suggest that conflict and cooperation in the policy-making process are entirely a function of policy disagreement. But the data do not reflect this. Despite substantial variability in the observed level of intracabinet cooperativeness, the data reflect a type of stasis in the level of cooperativeness *relative* to the corresponding degree of declared preference dissimilarity.[3] Why may this be? One potential explanation is that this stasis reflects an equilibrium level of antagonism – that government partners conspicuously counterbalance cooperative activities, such as striking a policy compromise, with conflictual activities, such as shouting at one another on the floor of parliament.

---

[3] It is very important to note that there is, in fact, a *substantial* degree of variability in the media-derived estimates of cooperativeness for cabinet dyads. The point being made here is that, quite simply, none of this variability is explained by differences in manifesto positioning.

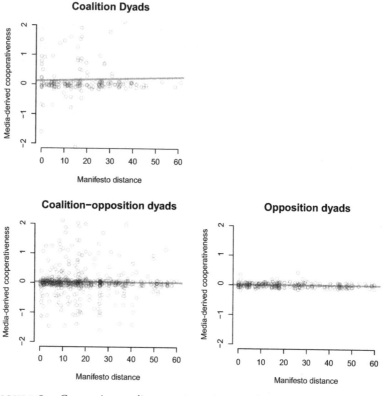

FIGURE 8.1 Comparing media narrative estimates of cooperation to manifesto declared dissimilarity

Of course, the revealed stability of media-derived intracabinet cooperativeness relative to manifesto dissimilarity shown in Figure 8.1 may also just be telling us that the estimates have no real information in them and are simply all noise and no signal. To examine this possibility, we can take an additional step in validating the estimates to make certain that they are appropriate for our purposes. That is, in order for the measure to be informative in answering our central question of whether cabinet parties can mitigate coalition compromise penalties by antagonizing their partners in government in the legislative review process, through parliamentary speech, legislative scrutiny, or otherwise, the measure must successfully capture these types of behaviors. In other words, if the measure does not reflect antagonism through legislative review or parliamentary speech, then we may conclude that (a) the measure is, as phrased earlier, all noise and no signal, (b) the measure is insufficiently sensitive to these specific types of behaviors, or, worse, (c) these behaviors do not affect the media narrative on political interactions and therefore cannot effectively mitigate compromise penalties. In each case, comparing the cooperation measure to electoral returns (and the remainder of this book) would be moot.

Fortunately, we have information on both legislative review and parliamentary speech on hand, and, importantly, there is some overlap between these data and the media-derived measures of coalition cooperation. More specifically, we have eight complete dyad-years of amendment behavior overlapping the media measure in the Netherlands and four complete dyad-years of parliamentary speech behavior overlapping the media measure in the United Kingdom.

We begin by comparing media-derived cooperation to patterns of legislative amending in the Netherlands. The dependent variable of interest here is the media-derived estimates of cooperation-conflict between a pair of cabinet partners. The dyad-years for which we have overlapping coverage in our amendment data are the Christen Democratisch Appèl (CDA) – Volkspartij voor Vrijheid en Democratie (VVD) 2003, 2004, 2005, 2011; CDA – Partij van de Arbeid (PvdA) 2007, 2008, 2009; and PvdA – VVD 2013.

One reason that there are only eight dyad-years to compare across the measures in the Netherlands is that there are several dyads with insufficient legislative activity to recover efficient estimates of their legislative review antagonism in a particular year. A second reason is the country-year nature of the media measure. Because the measure sums all media reports in a given calendar year, there are many observations that are "spoiled" by aggregating coalesced and non-coalesced interactions between dyads. These constraints also preclude us from comparing any estimates from Belgium and Denmark, the other two countries in which we analyzed legislative scrutiny in Chapter 6. There are too few country-years in which these countries were governed by a single cabinet that produced sufficient legislation to recover efficient dyad-year estimates of scrutiny behavior.

To derive dyad-level estimates of antagonism in the legislative review process, a version of the main statistical model in Chapter 6 (given in Table 6.2) is estimated using only the Dutch observations. The other central difference is that our model here includes fixed-effects estimates for each of the listed dyad-years in lieu of the country fixed effects specified in the pooled model we analyzed earlier in this book. These dyad-year estimates capture the deviation in the legislative review behavior for those

Table 8.1 *Comparing review behavior to*
media narrative dissimilarity

Legislative review conflict	−0.262
	(0.039)
Constant	0.035
	(0.044)
Observations	8
R^2	0.882

dyads in those years relative to all other dyad years in the Netherlands over our sample period. Positive estimates indicate more antagonistic or conflictual behavior and negative estimates indicate more cooperative or compromising behavior. Therefore, the expectation is that comparing these amendment behavior estimates to the media-derived cooperation estimates will reveal a negative correlation if the media estimates are capturing legislative review behaviors, or, if legislative review behaviors are part of a broader suite of differentiating tactics which, in the aggregate, are successful in altering the media narrative on the cabinet's interpartisan interactions.

This comparison of conflict in the legislative review process to our overall, media-derived estimate of the cooperation of the cabinet partners is given in Table 8.1. Here, the media cooperativeness measure is regressed on the legislative review conflict estimate in a simple ordinary least squares model. The results show a negative and quite robust relationship between the two measures. Further, the model fit is exceptionally high,[4] suggesting that a majority of the variability in the media-derived cooperation measure can be described with estimates of antagonism from observable behaviors in the legislative review process. This is precisely what we hoped to find in this validation exercise – media-derived estimates of partisan cooperation or antagonism correspond to actions taken during the parliamentary scrutiny of cabinet proposals. These results suggest that the Weschle (2018) estimates are appropriate for our tests.

Let us now assess the similarity between media narrative measures of cooperativeness and estimates derived from speeches given on the floor of the House of Commons. Again, the dependent variable is the dyadic

---

[4] In the interest of transparency, it should be noted that both the size of the negative correlation and the model fit are in part driven by the outlying nature of Balkenende III cabinet, which was much more conflictual than the other cabinets in the sample. Nonetheless, the negative relationship prevails after dropping these observations.

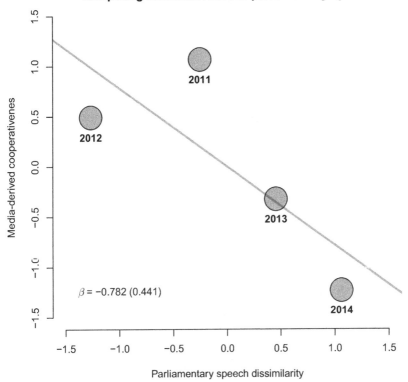

FIGURE 8.2 Comparing media narrative estimates of cooperation to parliamentary speech estimates of dissimilarity

estimates of cooperation yielded by the Weschle (2018) model, this time for the Conservatives and the Liberal Democrats in the United Kingdom for 2011–2014, the four full calendar years of their government. The independent variable is the average ideological distance between Conservatives and Liberal Democrats derived from the scaling of their daily parliamentary speeches – the same values described in Chapter 7 and depicted in Figure 7.7. As there are only four observations to compare, we will forego interpreting a statistical model and instead simply examine the relationship graphically. Figure 8.2 plots the media scores against the parliamentary speech scores, both of which have been rescaled to be standard normal.

Figure 8.2 shows a strong, negative relationship between the two measures, as the level of ideological dissimilarity between the parties as expressed in parliamentary speeches increases, so too does the degree of conflict between the two parties as reported by the media.

What is particularly powerful about this comparison is that, as you may recall, the level of change in the expressed dissimilarity between Conservatives and Liberal Democrats over their time in cabinet together was small and did not match the pattern predicted by our theoretical arguments (hence the savaging of the Liberal Democrats' seat share in the 2015 elections). In other words, the data suggest that the media measure is sufficiently responsive to parliamentary behavior, that it is correlated to the subtle changes in patterns of expressed similarity and difference we recovered in our analysis of Commons speeches.

Of course, we simply do not have enough observations to make any statements regarding our certainty over this relationship. Nonetheless, the results are quite encouraging and provide further evidence of the promise of using Weschle's (2018) measure of cooperation for testing our central hypothesis here: that media-derived cooperativeness is *negatively* correlated with the electoral performance of members of incumbent coalition cabinets, or, that differentiating from one's partners in government by building a robust record of antagonization is electorally fruitful.

ARE ELECTORAL LOSSES MITIGATED?

The central claim that we are wanting to test in this chapter is that parties can mitigate the electoral losses imposed on them by coalition compromise by strategically differentiating from their partners in government. This differentiation can happen in debates on the floor of parliament where parties are free to express their dissent on the legislative proposals of their partners in cabinet. It can happen in the legislative review process where reviewing parties are free to markup and amend the draft bills of their coalition partners, making clear and explicit distinctions between themselves and their partners on the concrete policy matters before them. It can also happen outside of these venues, say, on background discussion with journalists, the issuance of party press releases, and so on. Import-antly, however the differentiating behaviors are executed, they must be successful in breaking through the cacophony of political interactions to influence the media narrative regarding the incumbent. Without media conveyance of these behaviors, parties can only hope to reach a very small minority of exceptionally interested voters.

We have already discussed how we will measure a cabinet party's ability to differentiate from its partners in government, we will use the media-derived, dyadic measures of cooperativeness between coalition parties estimated by Weschle (2018). These dyadic measures can be used to create party-level estimates of coalition cooperation for each incumbent party rather simply. In the case where there are only two parties in cabinet, no augmentation is necessary and the estimates will be identical for each of the two members of government. When there are more than two parties in cabinet, we simply take the average of all dyadic scores for each individual cabinet party.

Before calculating the individual party-level estimates of coalition cooperation, however, the root dyadic measures are rescaled. We simply subtract the standardized dyadic estimates from the incumbent dyad values to normalize all incumbents to the overall level of cooperation. Then, the cabinet dyad measures are used to calculate the individual cabinet party scores.

With our variable of interest in hand, we can move on to assessing the effect of cabinet cooperation on electoral performance. We use data on cabinet composition and electoral performance from the Parliament and Government Composition Database (Döring and Manow 2011).[5] The electoral returns from this database, or, rather, the *change* in electoral performance from one election to the next for incumbent parties, will serve as the dependent variable in the statistical models below. To these data, we add some economic measures in order to account for general performance voting. Using data taken from the International Monetary Fund World Economic Outlook Database (International Monetary Fund 2017), we calculate the change in gross domestic product growth in percentage points and the level of unemployment over the last year of the incumbent's term in office leading into elections – these have become the standard measures for performance voting models (e.g., Powell and Whitten 1993; Becher and Donnelly 2013).

Once the data have been aggregated, there are, all told, sixty-two complete, election-year observations for members of incumbent coalition

---

[5] There are a few mistakes in Döring and Manow's (2011) cabinet composition data (France seems to be the most troublesome country, which is understandable given the instability of its party system), so the data are checked against national government and parliamentary websites before estimation.

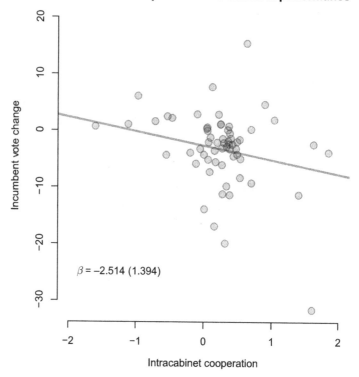

FIGURE 8.3 Coalition cooperation and electoral performance

cabinets. The sample spans thirty-four different parties, competing in twenty-seven elections held in ten countries: Austria, Belgium, Denmark, Finland, France, Germany, Greece, Italy, the Netherlands, and Portugal.[6] Figure 8.3 plots these data where the *x*-axis corresponds to the media-derived cooperativeness of cabinet parties and the *y*-axis corresponds to the change in those parties' vote share. These data are fitted with a simple linear model and the slope (with standard error) is conveyed in the lower left-hand corner. The fitted line on the plot shows that there is a strong negative correlation between cabinet cooperativeness and electoral performance. However, the distribution of the raw data points also show

---

[6] Unfortunately, Weschle (2018) data stop just shy of the UK's 2015 parliamentary elections, and, as a result, we do not include the Cameron and Clegg government in our final analysis. That said, reconsidering the entirety of the last chapter and the actual results of the election, we can probably guess how those observations would have contributed to these model results.

Table 8.2 *Effect of coalition cooperation on electoral performance*

Coalition cooperation	−2.514	−2.398	−2.519	−2.396
	(1.394)	(1.366)	(1.406)	(1.379)
Unemployment		−0.828		−0.829
		(0.437)		(0.442)
Change in GDP			0.040	−0.013
			(0.412)	(0.405)
Constant	−2.652	−9.840	−2.644	−9.852
	(0.894)	(3.896)	(0.906)	(3.946)
Observations	62	62	62	62
R^2	0.051	0.106	0.052	0.106

that the relationship is imperfect – that there must be other salient factors at play in determining electoral performance. Of course, this is to be expected given the deep and well-known literature on performance voting in advanced, industrial democracies (e.g., Powell and Whitten 1993; Duch and Stevenson 2008). In light of this, we will resist drawing any conclusions before considering a model that takes economic performance into account.

Table 8.2 presents a set of models that regress the electoral performance of individual incumbent cabinet members on the focal variable – the degree to which these incumbent parties have established a reputation for cooperation (positive values) or conflict (negative values) with their partners in government as manifest in media coverage of their behavior – as well as two measures of economic performance: change in productivity and the overall level of unemployment.

In each of the models, the estimate on the focal variable is negative, substantively large, and statistically significant to traditional levels. This relationship persists even when accounting for economic performance as manifest in the level of unemployment and changes in productivity. Further, the magnitude of the estimated effect is quite stable across each of the models – in general, across the four models, a first difference *increase* in the cooperativeness of a party correlates to a loss of 1.447–1.522 percentage points in the popular vote. This is very comparable to the loss we would expect given a first difference increase (1.887) in unemployment – a loss of about 1.563 percentage points of the popular vote. These are not small losses. Plurality winners, and therefore the conferment of formateur privileges, are often determined by less than 2 percentage points, and routinely determined by substantially less. Indeed, three of the four Dutch parliamentary elections held in our sample (between 2003 and 2012) were determined by significantly less than two points. Likewise, three of the four Danish elections held in our sample (between 2001 and 2011) were also decided by less than two points. All of this is to say that these effects are consequential not only to the distribution of seat shares across parliamentary parties, but are of a sufficient magnitude to routinely reshape the composition of governments.

Given that these analyses are, in a manner of speaking, macrolevel replications of the microlevel modeling in Chapter 5 (using the nine panel surveys administered across six parliamentary democracies), we can be quite certain of the *direction* of the relationship. More specifically, we have found across two sets of analyses, using different data to model the relationship at different levels, with different measurements of the focal variables, that building a reputation for compromise and cooperation in multiparty government – rather than a reputation for strong stands and antagonism – can be quite harmful to the electoral fortunes of incumbent parties.

All told, the evidence presents a compelling case for the central argument. Voters dislike coalition compromise and are willing to punish it. Cabinet parties, in turn, have substantial motivation to flout compromise and antagonize their partners in government in order to mitigate the potential losses resulting from coalition compromise. The analysis conducted here suggests that this is, indeed, a successful strategy. We have learned that there is a very close correspondence between differentiating actions taken in parliament, either in process of scrutinizing legislation or in speeches given on the floor, and media messaging regarding the level of conflict of cooperation between cabinet partners. Further more, we also have learned that the more the media portray cabinet parties as pugnacious or antagonistic, the better those parties fare in the following election, or, referring back to the Bill Clinton (2011) quote that opens the chapter: "What works in politics is conflict."

ARE THE EFFECTS OF COOPERATION CONTAGIOUS?

Is it possible that the harm of establishing a reputation for compromise and cooperation, rather than a reputation for strong stands and antagonism, can spillover to other competitive fora? That is, parties do not merely compete in national contests for control for the central government. There are municipal and provincial elections in which they compete for policy-making power, as well as contests for control of the European Parliament. And, indeed, there are many studies suggesting that these elections are, at least in part, determined by the reputation of the party or parties controlling the central government. For example, Mughan (1986) and Curtice and Payne (1991) present compelling evidence that local "by-elections" in the United Kingdom are strongly influenced by voters' relationship with the party controlling 10 Downing Street and the House of Commons. Likewise, research on provincial parliamentary elections in Canada by Scarrow (1960) and Erikson and Filippov (2001), as well as studies of provincial parliamentary, or *Landtag*, elections in Germany by Lohmann, Brady, and Rivers (1997) and Kedar (2006, 2009), also reveal that regional votes are cast with an eye toward the central government, most often meant to counterbalance or moderate its policy choices. And, of course, the "second-order" theory of European elections – that they serve as a referendum on the domestic central government and little or nothing else – has been a subject of a great deal of research, notably from Reif and Schmitt (1980) and continuing through Hobolt and Wittrock (2011).

Given the strong empirical case that the performance or behavior of parties controlling the central government spills over into sub-national and supranational electoral results, we would be remiss to pass up the opportunity to evaluate whether the reputations for compromise or conflict established by cabinet partners in the central government also spillover into subnational or supranational competitions. Here we will look for spillover by analyzing German Landtag elections over the period for which we have the data on coalition cooperation as derived from media reports.

Why assess the impact of national party reputations in the Länder-level elections? First, the period for which we have Weschle's (2018) data covers three European elections over the ten countries listed earlier that are regularly governed by coalition cabinets – thirty elections in total. Within the German Federation, there is coverage for *at least* three elections over the sixteen Landtag, bringing the total number of elections to fifty. Perhaps more importantly, concentrating on the subnational parliaments of a single country holds constant not only electoral rules and the general political economic environment, but also the party system itself. This creates a much cleaner test case.

Further more, while European elections are commonly viewed as unimportant and struggle to reach participation rates in the low 40 percent area, Ladtag elections are commonly viewed as quite salient and see turnout figures typically ranging from the low 60 percent region to the mid 70 percent region. That is to say, Landtag elections are important enough that we should see more systematic behaviors manifest in the vote totals than in the European elections. Also, participation in Landtag elections is sufficiently broad that we are less likely to be capturing the behavior of a substantially different population than the participants of national elections, whereas comparing national to European electorates reveals that the European electorate is disproportionately more interested and informed than typical national electorates (Schmitt and Mannheimer 1991).

Finally, while looking for spillover within a single country allows the opportunity to analyze the electoral performance of parties composing of only a handful of central government cabinets – five in this case – these cabinets each span several years and Weschle's (2018) data are estimated annually. Thus, while we have the behaviors of just five cabinets to consider, we observe these cabinets at fourteen different points in time. This is salient because the electoral rotations of the sixteen Landtage are asynchronous with the national parliament and each other – some mandate elections every five years, some every four years, and all have the potential for early elections to interrupt those maximal constitutional interelectoral periods – and, as a result, there is at least one Landtag election for every year we have media-derived measurements of coalition compromise. This institutional structure makes the Federal Republic of Germany an excellent test laboratory for comparative research as has been argued previously by Kedar (2009), Fortunato, König, and Proksch (2013), Willumsen, Stecker, and Goetz (2018), and others.

Analysis of Landtag Electoral Results

To test for spillover effects of central government coalition cooperation into subnational electoral performance, we compare the performance of all parties competing in Landtag elections to their established reputations for coalition cooperation in the national government. If detrimental effects of coalition compromise spillover into subnational electoral performance, then higher levels of cooperation should be associated with poorer electoral performance.

There are two primary ways to conduct this analysis. The first is to only examine the performance of Lander parties whose national counterparts are participating in cabinet, for example, all Lander Christian Democratic parties while the Christian Democratic Union is a member of cabinet at the federal level. The second is to include all parties and assign those whose national counterpart is *not* participating in cabinet at the federal level a coalition cooperation score of 0, creating an implied interaction between coalition cooperation and participation in cabinet at the federal level – that is, only those parties whose national counterpart is participating in cabinet at the federal level may have non-zero values of coalition compromise. As it turns out, both approaches yield the same substantive results, so we will only assess the second approach here.

The dependent variable in the analysis is the change in vote share for all parties competing in all Landtag elections between 2001 and 2014. The covariate of interest is, as earlier, media-derived estimates of coalition cooperation for national government members of cabinet, which are imputed to their subnational counterparts. For example, in 2006, Germany was governed by a coalition of the CDU/CSU and the SPD at the national level. In this year, there were elections in five Länder (Baden-Wurttemberg, Berlin, Mecklenburg-Vorpommern, Rhineland-Palatinate, and Saxony-Anhalt). Thus, in each Landtag election, the CDU and SPD are assigned the value of coalition cooperation derived from analysis of media coverage of the national cabinet participants. All of the other parties in those elections are assigned a value of zero on this covariate. This national coalition cooperation measure is regressed on Landtag election performance, where a negative and statistically significant parameter estimate would imply spillover of the compromise penalty.

The results of this analysis are given in Table 8.3. The different specifications are meant to account for party performance or competence in different ways. One model allows for punishment of Landtag incumbent cabinet members by interacting land unemployment with land incumbent status. Another allows for punishment of federal incumbent cabinet members by interacting federal unemployment with federal incumbent status. The final allows for both. Across all models, the estimate on coalition cooperation is quite small (ranging between about one-fourth and one-twentieth the absolute size of estimates in Table 8.2) and statistically insignificant. These results imply no spillover of federal-level coalition compromise into Länder electoral results.

Before accepting these results at face value and moving on, it is worth scrutinizing the model construction and estimates on the other parameters to assess the degree to which they imply a well-specified (or reasonably specified) analysis of electoral performance. For example, previous research suggests that national incumbents tend to pay a penalty in Landtag elections (e.g., Lohmann, Brady, and Rivers 1997; Kedar 2006, 2009). Do we see evidence for this penalty in our analysis? The answer is yes, but the evidence is weak. In both models accounting for

Table 8.3 *Looking for diffusion of compromise penalties in Landtag elections*

Coalition cooperation	0.693	0.634	0.125	0.227
	(0.447)	(0.430)	(0.436)	(0.427)
Land incumbent		−1.388		0.882
		(1.926)		(1.980)
Land unemployment		0.031		0.052
		(0.098)		(0.106)
Land incumbent × land unemployment		−0.283		−0.355
		(0.170)		(0.170)
Federal incumbent			−5.091	−4.985
			(4.169)	(4.274)
Federal unemployment			−0.218	−0.141
			(0.250)	(0.275)
Federal incumbent × federal unemployment			−0.002	0.105
			(0.478)	(0.484)
Constant	−0.155	0.922	3.365	2.735
	(0.374)	(1.117)	(2.237)	(2.187)
Observations	278	278	278	278
R^2	0.009	0.129	0.148	0.204

federal incumbency, the estimate on the federal incumbency parameter is negative, as we would expect. However, this parameter falls short of traditional significance thresholds. On the other hand, the analysis here includes less than half the number of elections included, for example, in Kedar (2006), so it is possible that the issue may be power rather than specification. The estimates do provide evidence for accountability voting, however, as Lohmann, Brady, and Rivers (1997) have also found. That is, the interaction of land unemployment with land incumbency reveals a strong negative relationship, just as we would predict if Landtag voters were taking the incumbent cabinet to task for poor performance, or rewarding them for good performance. Thus, we conclude that the model is reasonably well specified given the similarities between the results uncovered here and the results uncovered in previous research. We may also conclude, therefore, that there is no evidence of spillover in the compromise penalty assessed to national cabinet participants for their subnational counterparts, at least over this fourteen-year period in Germany. Coalition compromise endangers the party contingents that engage in it, but there is no evidence that these penalties will ring out to party groups competing in elections at other levels of government.

DISCUSSION

The central thrust of this chapter is simple: all of the arguments and analyses made to this point – the microlevel analysis of voters' reaction to coalition compromise in their perceptions of the policy stands and representative competence of cabinet parties, the panel study of voters' propensity to punish compromise, the cross-national analysis of party differentiation in the legislative review process, and the rather exhaustive case study of the Cameron–Clegg government's parliamentary scrutiny of cabinet proposals and speeches made on the floor of parliament – when taken together, imply that parties who are better able to cultivate an image of principled, uncompromising policy stands, or even outright antagonism of their partners in government, should outperform their counterparts who have appeared too compromising when elections are called.

Using new measures of the level of conflict or cooperation parties engage in derived from the ongoing media narrative of political inter-actions, we discovered that a record of conflict, rather than compromise, bore electoral benefits, even when taking into account economic cir-cumstances. Though subsequent analysis suggests that the degree to which parties establish a record of conflict or compromise in national government does not spillover into the electoral performance of their subnational arms (at least in Germany), the central finding is, of course, strong evidence for the overarching argument of this book. But, it is fair to ask what this finding means in the broader scheme of things. What does this say, not about the electoral incentives for parties, but, rather, about our expectations for the type of behaviors in which gov-erning coalitions engage, their willingness or ability to devote the lion's share of their time and effort to good governance, and the prospects for meaningful policy change?

As we discussed in the concluding section of Chapter 6, there must be some performative element to the behavior of governing parties – politics demands this. But it is possible that we have perhaps underestimated the extent to which the electoral demands for performative differentiation, or exaggerated conflict with in the coalition, may be driving behavioral choices. That is, we have understood for some time now that parties face tradeoffs in pursuit of policy, office, and electoral goals. This was most notably theorized in seminal work by Strøm (1990a). And further research has suggested that these tradeoffs are occasionally *direct*, mean-ing, as we have argued here, that the pursuit of expedient or efficient coalition governance can often mean that "party leaders may need to dilute their policy commitments and thus antagonize their supporters" (Müller and Strøm 1999, 9). However, though we have long believed it was theoretically possible that policy goals may necessarily come at an electoral cost, it is likely that we underestimated the prevalence of this occurrence, and that we have likewise underestimated the policy costs of vote-seeking behaviors. Our findings here put these tradeoffs in starker relief because, unlike previous research, we have drawn an explicit link between the differentiation from cabinet partners and electoral welfare – we have illustrated that eschewing policy goals by publicly antagonizing one's allies in coalition is, in itself, a powerful and effective vote-seeking behavior.

What this means, of course, is that each coalition policy choice (whether it truly is a compromise or may merely be credibly characterized as such) must be weighed against the damage that it may potentially inflict to the policy brands and reputation for representational competence of each cabinet party. This goes beyond evaluating what is preferred by one's supporters and what is not. Beyond evaluating whether or not the policy is a meaningful improvement from the status quo. Beyond one's expectations for the health of the coalition alliance in the event of the policy's failure. Parties' must infer the probability and potential extent of brand erosion imposed by the policy (and the coverage of its design, passage, and implementation by the media), whether the observable implications of the policy bear sufficient benefit to counterbalance these potential brand costs, and whether there is ample opportunity in the legislative term to mitigate or repair the brand damage by antagonizing their partners in cabinet.

This not only makes discrete policy choices more difficult, but substantially complicates the allocation of time and resources. How much of a party's committee contingent's time and energy should be allocated to reining in belligerent ministerial proposals with careful, policy-oriented amendments and how much time should be given over to exaggerating small differences for the benefits of appearance? How many words of parliamentary speech should be devoted to winning hearts and minds over to one's policy position and how many should be given over to grandstanding? These are elemental decisions upon which cabinet parties must stake their seat shares. And who will absorb the costs if such decisions are made poorly? Perhaps the leadership may face recall, but, more directly, it is the backbenchers whose seats are at stake. This makes more dire the complicated relationship between the leadership, who tend to benefit from compromise, and the rank-and-file, who are often thought of as having more "pure" policy stances (e.g., Martin and Vanberg 2011). Not only do leaderships have incentive to trade on the principles of backbenchers, but they may also in fact be gambling with their very seats in parliament when so doing. As a result, an examination of the relationship between party-level leadership selection mechanisms, the rules governing parties' electoral list construction, and the propensity to compromise with one's partners in government seems a promising avenue for future research.

These types of hard choices and their implications may warrant a rethinking of our expectations for policy responsiveness and important policy change. Of course, the behaviors that we have uncovered do provide evidence that parties are attentive to the electorate – that they are sensitive to the attitudes of voters and that they augment their behavior in responses to changes in these attitudes. However, the nature of this responsiveness may imply the tendency for parties to tradeoff policy actions in favor of vote-seeking actions. In other words, that the type of electoral mandates that Powell (2000) writes are characteristic of majoritarian governing institutions may be even more rare, in practice, in proportional systems than we previously may have suspected. This is because parties not only have to bargain over policy with their partners in government, but do so while still allowing time and energy for performative differentiation.

On balance, these concerns add an element of policy-making inefficiency, in excess of what has previously been discussed, for example, in the veto players literature (Tsebelis 1995, 2002), that should constrain the overall level of policy change under coalition government and therefore the overall level of policy responsiveness in coalition government. This is of course less of a problem for rather broad policy areas within which the median voter's preferences are unlikely to change with any rapidity, or, for policy areas within which the preferences of the median voter are often spanned by governing coalitions. However, in the event that shocks perturb the distribution of the electorate's policy preferences necessitating a policy change (or, making salient heretofore dormant divisions across members of the governing coalition), the need for cabinet members to manage their individual brands while simultaneously searching for common ground with their partners in government make coalition cabinets even more poorly suited to respond to changing demands of the electorate than we may have previously suspected.

9

Pushing Forward

Over the course of the previous chapters, we have learned quite a bit about the pressures placed on cabinet parties by their supporters' expectations for dominance, how parties attempt to cope with these pressures, and the potential costs of failing to do so competently. The typical voter in a multiparty parliamentary system, like all humans, can be pathologically optimistic. This is manifest in high hopes for preferred political outcomes. Hopes that their preferred party, when entering into a coalition cabinet, will be able to impose its will upon its partners and the parliament, securing each and every one of the policies it promised to its supporters unmolested by coalition compromise. These high hopes – despite the political reality of a set of electoral and policy-making institutions that make compromise unavoidable – make voters prone to disappointment when inevitable policy concessions are made by their preferred party. This disappointment, which leads to perceptions of representational incompetence and weak ideological positions, ultimately results in electoral penalties and these penalties are powerful motivating forces for cabinet behavior. Voters' propensity to punish compromise and cooperation incentivizes cabinet parties to antagonize one another – to markup each other's legislation in order to signal their resolve and true policy preferences, to squabble in parliamentary speeches, to embellish small points of difference in public interactions – in order to avoid or mitigate electoral losses. The better a party is at signaling conflict with its partners in coalition, *even when true policy conflict is absent*, the fewer votes it can expect to lose at the following election.

Rather than recap the finer points of the theoretical arguments and empirical analyses presented earlier in this book, let us turn our attention to identifying how what we have learned here may reshape our understanding of previous research and, perhaps more importantly, think about what the implications of this study are for future research. Are familiar tensions mitigated or exacerbated by the dynamics discussed here? Are new tensions made manifest?

One obvious starting point for striking out on new research is to continue running down the relationships uncovered in the preceding chapters to gain a more nuanced understanding of them. For instance, when voters update their perceptions of the policy stands of governing parties in response to coalition compromise, are these *durable* changes, or, do they dissipate with time? Are these changes self-contained, or, do they have a contagion effect for related party groups? That is, for example, under federalism, would we expect perceptions of provincial party contingents to change in response to coalition dynamics in the national parliament, or vice versa? Or, if one member of a relatively tight-knit party family joins a coalition, does its behavior cause spillover into perceptions of other parties in its family? The analysis in the previous chapter suggests that federal contagion is unlikely in Germany; however, that test was far from perfect, and there are many federal countries (Austria, Brazil, Canada, India, etc.) where national reputations may spillover into subnational elections (or vice versa) still to be investigated. Further, there is also potential for systematic spillover into European Parliamentary elections.

Similarly straightforward would be to reconsider previous research in the face of the arguments and empirical relationships presented here. We will begin with consideration of party competition, focusing on responses in the electorate, before pivoting to consideration of how partisan behaviors in the legislature are affected by voters, focusing first on the two central questions of coalition governance: formation and durability.

Party Competition

One of the most central take aways from this book for future research is the degree to which actions taken in the legislative process are salient aspects of partisan competition. Of course, this is not an entirely new finding. Recent research on party competition in parliamentary democracies where coalition is the norm has been in a process of transitioning away from the study of how partisan *promises* (i.e., election manifestos) influence competition to the study of how partisan *actions* (i.e., the formation of governments or policy outputs, etc.) influence competition. We have discussed several of these papers analyzing the effect of coalition formation already. Beginning with Fortunato and Stevenson (2013) and Lupu (2013), scholars of party competition have been studying how cabinet participation influences the manner in which voters perceive political parties producing interest extensions (Adams, Ezrow, and Wlezien 2016) and refinements of the central result (Falcó-Gimeno and Muñoz 2017). On the one hand, tying the observable behaviors of parties in government to voters' perceptions of them is novel to literature focused on parliamentary systems. On the other hand, for our Americanist counterparts, this is old hat. For over fifty years, beginning in earnest with Schoenbebger (1969) and Erikson (1971), scholars of American politics have been analyzing the impact of Congressional roll call voting on electoral returns and the appetite for this kind of research has not declined, with notable recent examples including Canes-Wrone, Brady, and Cogan (2002), Carson et al. (2010), and Fortunato and Monroe (2020).

More recent research on parliamentary systems has continued to analyze observable parties behaviors, examining actual outcomes. Bernardi and Adams (2019) present compelling evidence that voters weight policy outcomes more heavily than campaign rhetoric, at least when it comes to social spending and Adams, Weschle, and Wlezien (2020) argue that general patterns of conflict and cooperation filter down to voters via the media and influence the manner in which voters perceive them. Of course, that argument, and evidence for it, is foundational to this book. But what of more specific behaviors, events, or interactions? How may they influence the manner in which parties are perceived or supported? How may parties respond to these changes, or expected changes?

Recent work by Fortunato, Silva, and Williams (2020) provides some guidance for structuring this agenda by urging scholars to consider actions or events on three dimensions. First, the probability that a voter will observe the event either directly or indirectly should be reasonably high. Cabinet formation, for example, is perhaps the single most visible political event in most countries, the outcome of which is repeated over and over again throughout the legislative period each and every time the partisan composition of the government is mentioned. Second, the events must be credible indications of parties' preferences, motivations, competence, and so on. For example, Fernandez-Vazquez (2018, 2019) argues that some pronouncements are quite likely to be viewed by the electorate as cheap talk and therefore ignored, while others are more likely to be viewed as credible and accepted, conditioned on the characteristics of the party and the competitive environment. Third, the actions must be salient to voters. They must, in one form or another, *matter*. Recall that this is very similar to our discussion in Chapters 3 and 6 regarding the selection of fora for differentiation – the degree to which elites and the mass public can expected to care about an action determines, in part, whether parties find that action a suitable means of communication with the electorate. The same holds here in determining which actions will inform the manner in which voters perceive and choose to support parties.

So, which actions or events provide suitable fits to these parameters for the future study of how voters understand and choose from their menu of partisan alternatives? It is certainly hoped that readers are convinced that legislative review and parliamentary debate are two such actions, at least in countries where these fora are (a) open, (b) salient, and (c) individualized as discussed in Chapter 3. Given that the review process was analyzed in just four countries and parliamentary debate in just one country, there is plenty of soil here to till. The most intuitive direction to take this research, however, is simply to consider the record of policy production.

Each cabinet proposes, passes, and executes policy and, in so doing, produces a clear record of action. These records – and by this we are simply meaning an accounting of all of the legislative proposals that a cabinet managed to pass into law – are, at present, criminally understudied. But they need not be. In the not-so-distant past, we were more or less incapable of exploiting these records apart from analyzing their most basic parameters. We have counted the number of ratified laws to learn how the formal separation of powers, or power sharing across parties or branches of government, conditions the efficiency of lawmaking (e.g., Tsebelis 1995, 2002). We have summed the number of words in each law to estimate a proxy for implementory discretion in order to study how legislative capacity enables, and dissimilar preferences across the legislative and executive incentivizes, the construction of more specific legislation (e.g., Huber, Shipan, and Pfahler 2001; Huber and Shipan 2002). It goes without saying that these theoretical and empirical contributions represent a substantial advance in legislative research. Nonetheless, we now possess the tools necessary to begin extracting more from these raw data.

We may estimate the extent to which any given law represents the policy interests of individual members of cabinet by comparing the text of the law to the text of their campaign manifestos, their official press releases, their public speeches, and so on. This would allow enterprising researchers leverage in estimating the distribution of influence across parties, or the "weight" that each party's ideal point contributes to each law, dynamically, over the course of the legislative period.[1] This would provide what is essentially a measure of bargaining prowess that could be compared to levels of voter support, the stickiness of voters' perceptions of parties' brands, and so on. It would also provide a dynamic measure of the ideological direction, or content of policy change. Assessing whether or not voters are receptive or responsive to such content would be a substantial step forward in understanding the nature of, or real potential for, democratic accountability.

Not only are these central questions interesting and important, but they are likely to lead to an avalanche of follow-up studies. If voters *are not* attentive to the content of policy production or the distribution of partisan influence, why not? Is the media not accurately relaying this information in its coverage of government, choosing instead to focus on other aspects of the political process or simply losing the fine gradations of difference from one outcome to the next. Could it be, instead, that the information is being accurately distributed to voters, but they are simply unable or unwilling to absorb it in sufficient detail to react systematically to it? If this is the case, are the signals being crowded out by other political information, or is it simply too incremental to be of interest, or, is there so much such information that voters become overwhelmed and "check out?"

If voters *are* attentive to the content of policy production or the distribution of partisan influence, then how do they respond? How do the observable characteristics of voters condition their reception of, and response to, this information? Are parties punished for bargaining losses more when the result is moving policy further away from their core supporters? Given that parties are better positioned to anticipate the timing of policy outcomes, do they redistribute their communicative resources and strategies in advance of outcomes they anticipate will be disliked, or are they more conservative in their strategy and wait until they see

---

[1] Of course, legislative proposals must conform to certain stylistic parameters and overwhelmingly use a legalistic voice that make these kinds of comparisons onerous. But comparison is still possible.

the reaction? There are countless potential avenues for new research on responsiveness and accountability.

Coalition Formation

How does the attentiveness of voters condition the nature of coalition formation? Martin and Vanberg (2020) have already taken up this question by incorporating lessons from the international relations literature on bargaining over conflict into a model of coalition formation. That is, the authors posit that potential coalition participants face potential "audience costs" (e.g., Fearon 1994; Tomz 2007) and are therefore constrained by the demands of their supporters. Martin and Vanberg argue that the different types of assets that coalition members must divide are differentially observable by the electorate with, specifically, the number of ministerial portfolios being the most easily observable asset. The empirical regularity that portfolio shares tend to be nearly identical to seat shares arises because parties can claim that these are equitable outcomes, even if these proportional outcomes do not perfectly correspond with the real distribution of bargaining power within the proto-coalition reflecting pivotality, outside coalition alternatives, institutional advantages (like formateur status or privileges of reversion rules), and so on. This equitable allocation of easily observable resources according to easily observable bargaining weights gives participants cover to divide less easily observable payoffs in a manner that better reflects the true, less easily observable bargaining power of participants. The notion that voters are attuned to the process of coalition bargaining, but have reasonable limitations in their ability to observe and scrutinize the process, reshapes, at an elemental level, our understanding of what outcomes are possible or probable.

Noteworthy of this research is the model of the reasonable voter. That is, that the authors accept the reality that voters are not all-knowing super computers – as is occasionally posited by (predominantly formal theoretical) models of voter or party behavior – and that voters are not know-nothings, incapable of even basic surveillance of political interaction – as is occasionally posited by (predominantly Americanist) models of voter or party behavior, or, *implied* by models of party behavior that omit voters altogether. Favoring the *reasonable voter*, rather than the perfectly *rational voter* (with all the attendant dogmatic presumptions that moniker connotes), or the *irrational voter*, is a central contribution of this book, as well as Martin and Vanberg (2020), and will be quite important to pushing the field forward in our future endeavors. Discussions similar to those we had in Chapters 6 and 8 about what voters can and cannot be reasonably expected to know or care about, discussions that have been quite rare in political research to this point, should absolutely become common.

Moving past Martin and Vanberg (2020), how may we expect the centripetal and centrifugal pressures of coalition governance to reshape bargaining over formation? Certainly, what we have learned here provides a more solid empirical backing for our presumptions regarding external support parties, particularly those with niche or extremist policy preferences. Strøm's (1990b) argued that minority cabinets arise when potential coalition partners believe that the potential electoral costs of participation outweigh the likely policy gains, and, the ability to influence policy with regularity as an informal external support party makes resisting formal participation more attractive. Our findings here support Strøm's arguments by providing robust evidence that those presumed electoral costs are real and drive partisan behavior.

Classically, we have considered these expected costs of government participation in terms of simple policy differences with one's partners in cabinet, but this is unlikely to be the only factor. That is, there must be observable characteristics of parties that would lead us to expect greater or lesser penalties for government participation that may influence our expectations for which constellations of parties may coalesce and, when and where we should expect to observe minority cabinets. For example, it is well documented that niche parties (exempting Greens) and so-called anti-system parties rarely join coalition cabinets (Martin and Stevenson 2001) and we think of this regularity as emanating from the formateur's desire to avoid the potential headaches that these parties may bring to cabinet with them. Just as plausible, given Strøm's arguments and our greater understanding of niche parties (e.g., Meguid 2005), is that these parties avoid coalition participation because it would be too costly to their brand, even if their policy preferences are generally compatible with the formateur.[2] That is, it is not that *policy differences* create

---

[2] This is more common than we may expect. Notable examples include The first Rutte cabinet in the Netherlands in 2010 that received external support from the Party for Freedom, a right party that is generally compatible with Rutte's People's Party for Freedom and Democracy but whose extreme anti-immigration brand could not endure government participation.

insurmountable hurdles to co-governance, but that *brand differences* create insurmountable costs to co-governance.

Just as likely is that institutional differences that lead to greater or lesser opportunity for differentiation within coalition governments over their term in office together may reshape the constellations of parties that may consent to co-governance. For example, in Norway, one of the cases in Strøm's (1990b), legislative scrutiny and change are attributed to party groups, the legislative review process produces a "majority report" and a "minority report," which (by design or not) obscures the contributions made to the review process by *individual* parties. In other words, this scrutiny structure creates a hurdle to differentiation, which may make some parties more tentative about coalescing. More generally, we want to learn, in the presence of an attentive public (albeit, one with limited resources for surveillance), how does variation in the rules governing legislative scrutiny and debate, or, variation in the scope and strength of rules governing collective responsibility, reshape parties' abilities to signal competence and resolve to their supporters and how may this, in turn, reshape parties' abilities to consent to co-governance with minimal electoral risk? However, at present, we lack a detailed accounting of such institutions and therefore cannot begin to understand whether and how they may impact patterns of government participation.

Given that a government has been formed, participants often draw up contracts to govern cabinet behaviors. Previous research by, for example, Müller and Strøm (2000), Timmermans (2003), or Bowler, Bräuninger, Debus, and Indridason (2016), present theoretical arguments about the content of formalized coalition agreements, typically in terms of limiting agency or constructing conflict resolution devices. These are inherently policy-motivated arguments, but their empirical implications may also be understood through the lenses of a watchful electorate.[3] That is, ideological dissimilarity has been found to predict the inclusion of conflict resolution devices and we have believed this to be the case because this dissimilarity would ultimately lead to difficulties in striking a policy compromise. Therefore, as preferences become dissimilar, policy tensions rise, and dispute becomes more likely. Bowler, Bräuninger, Debus, and Indridason (2016) write that these devices allow cabinet partners to kick the can down the road on divisive issues and prioritize issues over which the

---

[3] Even Eichorst (2014), who makes an explicitly electoral argument, must derive policy-driven empirical implications to test it.

coalition partners agree, quite similar to the argument made by Martin (2004) about the implications of internal policing for the structure of the legislative agenda.

These findings come into sharper focus when we consider that these agreements are (most often) public and that voters may observe them. When we remind ourselves that voters may evaluate the terms of the bargain struck in these agreements, it makes sense that compacts between ideologically diverse parties focus on conflict resolution devices rather than specific policy goals – why advertise to your supporters the ways in which you intend to sell them out? It is better to signal to the electorate that you anticipate such heated discord that you must agree to a set of ground rules for the brawl. Indeed, given that voters dislike compromise and that parties seem to understand and respond to this, it is reasonable to ask why it is that agreements containing the parameters for compromise are *ever* made public at all?

One possibility is that the parties are so profoundly distrustful of one another that they must use the agreement as a public commitment device in order to overcome their skepticism of each other's intentions. However, coalition is a repeated game, and this repetition may make the expected long-term punishment (or reciprocity) for failing to honor one's *private* commitments great enough that it may, in and of itself, be sufficient to enforce preferred behaviors in the absence of a *public* commitment device.

Another possibility is that the compromise contract serves as a credible commitment not from one coalition partner to another, but from the government to the market. That is, there is a well-documented relationship between political uncertainty and tumultuous markets. This is manifest in economic growth (Alesina et al. 1996), exchange rate fluctuations (Moore and Mukherjee 2006), governments' ability to borrow (Fortunato and Turner 2018), and so on. It is possible that, just as preferential trade agreements may allow countries to credibly commit to asset security in the presence of tumultuous political factors (e.g., Büthe and Milner 2008), coalition agreements may allow governments to credibly commit to a regulatory environment, or a more general political economic landscape, in the presence of electoral incentives that create crosspressures on coalition participants. That is, coalition agreements may credibly signal an intent to *specific policy outcomes* in order to assuage market concerns over inherently unpredictable bargaining environments where parties are incentivized toward intransigence and unreasonable demands.

Coalition Durability

Should our findings also influence our understanding of, and expectations for, government durability? This is somewhat less clear than the question of formation. As discussed at some length in Chapter 2, conflict has long been a part of our conceptual understanding of coalition stability and, whether that conflict arises due to policy disagreements, personal disputes, or shocks to the political system seems purposefully irrelevant to our existing models. That is, our theoretical models of cabinet durability are almost exclusively intentionally vague about the roots of coalition conflict and more specific about the observable characteristics of cabinets that may make them better suited to weather that conflict.

The interesting revelation here is not about our expectations for how capable coalitions are to withstand conflict, rather, whether or not we believe what is *observable* is indicative of *true* conflict. More specifically, given what we have learned about the electoral benefits of signaling coalition conflict, we may conclude that the squabbles we observe are not necessarily a manifestation of the kind of real policy disagreement over which we suspect partners may be tempted to dissolve the cabinet. Rather, the conflict that we observe may imply a healthy cabinet, one that is sufficiently antagonistic outwardly to allow for internally harmonious policy-making negotiation and progress. In other words, what we have learned here may not change our fundamental understanding of the nature of coalition conflict and its effects on cabinet durability, but it most certainly should influence our approach to the *empirical* study of coalition conflict and its effects on cabinet durability.

This is especially the case in light of recent advances by Weschle (2018) in measuring expressed conflict in political interactions. It would be surprising if this book made its way to press before some enterprising scholar attempted to use measures based on Weschle's approach to estimate a dynamic model of government stability and, should the results of that model imply a null or even negative relationship between expressed conflict and the probability of dissolution, we should not be surprised. Indeed, attempting to derive theoretical expectations for the relationship between *true* internal discord, *expressed* public conflict, and cabinet stability, would require a new model of coalition behavior in which the government participants are capable of sending coordinated *and* individual signals to a reasonably attentive electorate in order to attempt to control their internal and external gravity, maximizing gains from trade on the one hand and minimizing electoral damage on the other.

This is related to another potentially interesting thread for coalition stability. Our findings imply that government durability is endogenous to government efficiency – the scope and depth of policy change and the pace with which that change is realized. More specifically, given that voters are negatively responsive to coalition compromise, it is possible that the efficiency with which the cabinet makes policy is negatively related to its stability. This may manifest in at least two ways. First, consider a coalition cabinet, like the Cameron–Clegg government, in which one partner is widely perceived as dominating the other in policy negotiation and the pace of policy change is relatively rapid. In this case, as the legislative period progresses and policies are made, the support of the dominated party would wither in kind, potentially creating an environment in which it would be advantageous for the dominating party to dissolve the cabinet and move to elections in order to capitalize upon its partner's weakness and improve its position in parliament. This arises as a special case of the Lupia and Strøm (1995) and Diermeier and Stevenson (2000) model of government durability, where the cabinet actions (which are not a moving part of the original model) reshape expected seat shares in each period.

Second, consider a more evenly paired coalition, in which two parties are widely perceived as being equally successful in policy negotiations. Under these circumstances, as the legislative period progresses and policies are made, the support of both parties would wither in kind, potentially creating an environment in which it would be advantageous for both parties to dissolve the cabinet and move to elections in order to "stop the bleeding" – to curtail their expected vote losses before they become too dire. We have already discussed that this general relationship – that policy change can exacerbate electoral losses – is also implied by the median gap model of electoral change (Stevenson 2002), but the mechanism is different and, as such, the specifics of the implications are different as well. It is likely that a rigorous theoretical and empirical examination of this broader relationship would open new and interesting avenues of inquiry and may help us better understand, not only the relationship between policy change and government stability, but the downstream effects of this relationship on, for example, party system volatility and fragmentation.

New Questions

Of course, efficiency is an interesting outcome in and of itself, in addition to being a potential predictor of government longevity. It is normatively desirable that governments are willing and able to change the policy landscape, particularly if this capacity is used to "rapidly and comprehensively alter policy in response to shifts in public sentiment" or respond to crises (Fortunato and Turner 2018, 624). Tsebelis (2002) argued quite convincingly that coalition cabinets, relative to their single-party counterparts, are less capable of efficiently altering policy because internal bargaining processes are more complex and more time consuming to negotiate, if they can be overcome at all. But let us take another step and think of how our understanding of efficiency evolves as the industry standard of coalition governance changes.

In the world of ministerial dominance, the primary hinderance to policy change is the composition of the cabinet (Laver and Shepsle 1990). Cabinet formation is more costly with two members than one, and more costly still with three members than two (Diermeier and Van Roozendaal 1998; Martin and Vanberg 2003). These transaction costs and the additional constraints of each member party's indifference curve on the legislative agenda slow policy change relative to single-party cabinets.

The coalition compromise model adds legislative review to the drag already imposed by cabinet composition (Martin and Vanberg 2005). Instead of allowing ministerial discretion within the indifference arc of the member parties (relative to the status quo) via the allocation of ministerial portfolios, the coalition is often enforcing a grand bargain through parliamentary scrutiny of draft bills, further slowing policy change relative to single-party cabinets and increasing our expectations for delay in larger coalitions relative to smaller coalitions (in terms of parties) and ideologically heterogenous governments relative to ideologically homogenous governments. Over the course of the preceding chapters, we have added the necessity for differentiation to the mix, once again slowing expected policy change relative to single-party cabinets and perhaps also (but not necessarily) for large relative to small and heterogenous relative to homogenous governments.

This efficiency gap, according to Powell (2000) and others, is part of a principal trade-off between coalition and single-party governance in which the capacity for rapid policy change, clear accountability, and simpler deselection are exchanged for greater policy congruence, inclusive deliberation, and minority protection. What has not been part of this trade-off is the need for differentiation and how it may consume already scarce resources. Are the benefits of multiparty governance really worthwhile if electoral pressures force its participants to fritter away time, labor, and other valuable assets on performative discord? More pressingly, in the event of a crisis, are coalition partners able to put aside their private interests in brand maintenance, come together, and do what is best for the country, or, do they find themselves compelled to dawdle and needle one another, even under those dire circumstances? Qualitative and theoretical accounts of the government responses to the debt crises in Cyprus, Greece, Ireland, Portugal, and Spain – both in the directly afflicted countries and in other European Union member states – provide mixed evidence that government participants are, indeed, willing to do so (e.g., Walter 2016; Schneider and Slantchev 2018). Note that these studies are not focused on this question per se and so we must push forward to engage it head on: under what conditions will parties choose not to indulge their private electoral interests?

Leaving behind the idea of crisis and *need* for immediate action, it is worth asking whether the incentives to engage in performative antagonism divert attention away from seemingly less salient operations of government that may have interesting consequences. First, we would want to know, if parties are devoting attention and resources toward differentiation, from where is this attention being diverted? Are parties sacrificing efforts needed to help new ministers assert and maintain control over their departments, resulting in a type of agency drift in policy implementation that scholars have typically presumed was reserved for presidential systems where bureaucratic and legislative control is divided between separately survivable entities? It is possible that this kind of diversion of resources may result in inefficiency or cost overruns – effects similar to what Huber (1998) theorized we could expect in response to ministerial instability. Are more antagonistic coalitions less able to compel quality performance and preferred outcomes from their civil service because they are pouring their efforts into differentiation?

Relatedly, it may be the case that differentiation, particularly differentiation in the legislative review process, distracts from the actual business of legislative scrutiny. There is a degree of amusing irony to the notion that parties become so consumed with *signaling* their true preferences for policy outcomes that they may become distracted from using the means afforded to them to put force behind their demands and actually curtail ministerial drift. In other words, it is possible that parties become so distracted by signaling ideological resolve that they allow avoidably distasteful policy proposals to slip by? Of course, this is presuming a level of variability in the policy implications of legislative effort, whether it is intended for differentiation or drift constraint, that the preceding chapters did not engage with. This, too, is worthy of future research, in addition to the broader question of whether policy outcomes adhere more tightly to coalition compromise when reviewing parties are less distracted by the need or desire for differentiation.

More generally, there are observable implications of wasteful practices by governing parties. Coalitions obsessed with brand management should be less likely to submit their budgets in a timely fashion. They may similarly be too busy antagonizing one another to make the kind of important bureaucratic appointments necessary to properly staff departments. Or, they may simply make fewer attempts to reshape policy, which would be evident in the content of the legislative agenda. There are countless outcomes that could potentially be studied in order to better understand the impact of brand maintenance efforts on the quality of governance.

It should be noted that although these questions are new to coalition scholars, they are classics in the American literature. Indeed, it was over four decades ago when Mayhew (1974) pointed out that congressional representatives preferred easily observable, individual brand building activities, to the potentially more meaningful, in policy terms, business of legislative or partisan service. In other words, Mayhew taught us that there is a trade-off between electoral incentives and policy incentives. Later, Cain, Ferejohn, and Fiorina (1987) took this idea and ran with it, chasing down its implications for stalemate and inefficiency in the policy-making process and the drive toward particularistic, rather than programmatic policymaking. What *is* novel here, is that scholars have assumed that centralized electoral institutions that redistributed agency from individual members toward party leaders would overcome these tensions. Although that certainly seems to be the case for the incentives toward particularistic, rather than programmatic policymaking, we have just learned fairly conclusively that the redirection of electoral agency from individual members to party leadership does not eliminate the drive for position-taking behaviors. Electorally induced inefficiency prevails in perfectly disciplined party systems if those parties must coalesce to govern.

Getting back to the matter at hand, given the potential diversion of attention away from the mechanics of policymaking and executive oversight, an interesting course of study may be to attempt to identify situations in which the eyes of the electorate are off the governing coalition for one reason or another, or, the governing coalition has reason to believe that its decision-making will not be scrutinized come election time. Of course, it is difficult to dream up events or processes that would yield such conditions, but certainly such conditions must exist, if not in total, then in part.

One possibility is to compare the behavior of traditionally formed coalition governments to so-called caretaker governments – the cabinets that take the reins of the state, typically after the dissolution of a traditionally formed cabinet, to shepherd the country into the next election. Elections do not happen instantaneously after coalition dissolutions and someone must run the country in the interim. In the words of Laver and Shepsle (1996, 46): "Put very crudely, somebody has to remain in office to sign the checks – someone has to have a finger on the trigger." Despite controlling the function of government while in office, these coalitions are typically presumed to bear little or no electoral responsibility, so much so that our performance voting models overwhelmingly just ignore these cabinets and treat the dissolved coalition that they have taken over for as the incumbent.

In policymaking studies, these cabinets are treated similarly, often simply discarded from the sample. Indeed, this is the case in our own analysis of legislative scrutiny in Chapter 6. But these cabinets provide a rare opportunity to study the effect of electoral concern on governance. How does the behavior of caretaker cabinets, plausibly unconstrained by the scrutiny of a watchful electorate, differ from the behavior of traditionally formed cabinets who will be held to a higher level of accountability by their supporters? Are caretakers better able to invest in, for example, bureaucratic efficiency than their counterparts? Or, do caretakers simply shirk, knowing that any good they are able to do is likely to go unrewarded? We simply do not know, but there is opportunity to learn. While half of the caretaker governments serve less than four months (according to Seki and Williams 2014), nearly one-fifth serve six months or more. This is a significant amount of time for caretakers to make a mark on the workings of government. Even if it is difficult to measure *direct* government activity over a period of a few months, there are observable implications of the government's function which may be measured in small intervals. If the Ministry of Energy began to shirk during periods of caretaker rule, then we may be able to observe higher levels of carbon output from power plants, short-term spikes in electricity costs, or increases in production-related accidents. If the Ministry of Food and

Agriculture began to shirk, then we may observe increases in reports of food-borne illness, complaints of over fishing, or violations to European Union appellation protections. The observable implications of good governance surround us.

These are all questions of immediate impact, but the far-sighted implications may be even more important. That is, large policy investments, or, the types of grand reform that are needed from time to time to acclimate to a changing political economic world and maximize (expected) long-term productivity, most often *require* compromise. For example, infrastructural investments may entail too little spending for the more left party, or too much spending for the more right party, or, the depth of private market partnership may be too deep for the more left party, or not deep enough for the more right party. These kinds of sweeping changes tend to also be high-profile political events with dense coverage of not only the details of the package of policy changes, but also the process of bargaining over them. This, in turn, raises the stakes for parties engaged in the bargaining process.

Gerhardt Schöder's "Agenda 2010" policy changes in Germany are one such sweeping reform project. This was a collection of policies that sought to make the labor sector more flexible and the provision of unemployment benefits less costly. The package reduced unemployment insurance duration and "forced" the unemployed into open positions, regardless if they were overqualified or formerly overcompensated for them, once they had been searching unsuccessfully for a certain period of time. The policy changes also flattened out unemployment benefits such that they were no longer tethered to former compensation and reformed public employment services provision (Camerra-Rowe 2004). These reforms were largely viewed by experts as prudent and necessary for Germany to thrive in the modern labor market while sustaining fiscal discipline, but were nonetheless largely discordant with the policy brand of Schöder's Social Democratic Party. As a result, Schöder and the SPD paid dearly for these reforms at the polls (Schwander and Manow 2017).

Fortunately for Germany, these reforms are viewed, in retrospect, as successful and critical to the country's stable and sustained productivity. Unfortunately for the Social Democrats, they were kicked out of office long before they would have been able to reap the rewards of these ambitious policies. Anecdotal evidence of this type abounds. A forward-looking political party identifies a large problem. It works carefully to craft prudent and well-reasoned solutions to that problem. If the solution tarnishes the party's brand, voters punish it for putting the far-sighted needs of the country ahead of the short-sighted needs of the party to protect its image. If we may overgeneralize the issue: it is an unfortunate fact of life for right parties that not every problem can be headed off by austerity, just as it is an unfortunate fact of life for left parties that not every problem can be headed off by stimulus. But, of course, we cannot directly observe the counterfactual. We cannot perfectly identify instances in which a governing party identifies the opportunity for long-term planning if they do not act upon it, so we cannot accurately identify the costs of action to the party or the cost of inaction to the country.

But these measurement hurdles are not insurmountable. With the help of rigorous theoretical modeling and innovative empirical modeling, these kinds of unobservable quantities may, indeed, be estimable. On this, we may look to our colleagues interested in interstate conflict for suggestions. This may seem odd, but the parallels are strong. After all, what have we been modeling in the preceding chapters here if not the presence and implications of audience costs? Just as conflict scholars wish to know how the *type* of supporting coalition they have and the institutional parameters for leadership selection and deselection influence decision-making in international disputes by shaping leaders' expectations for future domestic punishment (e.g., Weeks 2012; Crisman-Cox and Gibilisco 2018), we are interested in learning the degree to which coalition participants' expectations for electoral punishment shape their decisions in domestic bargaining and action. And similar challenges apply. Expectations for punishment are inherently unobservable as are counterfactual choices. Cabinet parties' desire to act in the public good, or their tolerance for sanctioning risk when advancing policies discordant with their brand are critical, yet unobservable components to the choice function.

We may consider these components analogous to "resolve," a state's willingness or ability to endure casualties and asset losses in a conflict. Just as a coalition party's tolerance for electoral losses may enable it to make bold policy choices, a state's tolerance for casualties may enable it to be bold in conflict bargaining. Recently, Crisman-Cox (2019) presented an innovative estimation strategy for this inherently unobservable quantity. It is likely that importing these lessons into coalition bargaining (beyond the formation of the cabinet) may help us better understand what types of parties are capable of bold, sweeping, far-sighted policy innovation (and when) and what types of parties may be sufficiently frightened of electoral reprisal that they find themselves shackled to their brand and therefore incapable of acting in the long-term interests of the country.

Of course, we need not fully understand or estimate coalition parties' tolerance for electoral risk to begin to assess the implications of gravity management — the counterbalancing of centripetal and centrifugal forces the coalition parties must engage in to prevent cabinet dissolution or an electoral thrashing — for their choices in government. Understanding that there are trade-offs between short-term electoral incentives and the long-term investments required for good governance is sufficient to begin to think through the economic implications. Do markets punish states with coalition cabinets for their reticence to act or the uncertainty of their actions with lower credit ratings or weaker foreign investment flows, or, does this reticence make for a de facto stickier status quo and therefore the type of less variable future political economic environments that credit markets and investors prefer? Do these relationships induce compounding effects that further inhibit or encourage long-term growth?

To take this one step further, we may ask: under what conditions will voters trade-off programmatic rigidity for managerial competence? Or, does voters' constant desire for "wins" – or, refusal to compromise, demand for ideological purity, and so on – come at a cost of accountability? Would voters be able to select *better* leadership if they were able to divorce themselves from their innate desire to punish parties for doing the specific thing[4] that they overwhelmingly claim to support in the abstract? There has been some research, particularly in the American case, attempting to disentangle how various candidate/party attributes are weighted in the average voter's utility function, including observable characteristics highly likely to correlate to competence (e.g., Hainmueller, Hopkins, and, Yamamoto 2014). But we cannot jump straight to the empirical puzzle for coalitional voters quite yet, unfortunately.

Given the relative complexity of voting in coalitional systems, where past performance (including bargaining competence) must be weighed against *expected* future policy pursuits – the calculation of which requires forecasting likely coalition arrangements and attaching likely weighted policy positions to these forecasted governments – a more expansive and inclusive treatment of the voting calculus is long overdue. That is, the study of voting in complex multiparty systems has been cleaved by a theoretical divide into two fairly distinct camps: the prospective voting

4 Compromise, of course.

side, which seeks to understand how voters cope with the complexities of post-electoral bargaining over government composition (e.g., Kedar 2005; Duch, May, and Armstrong 2010); and the retrospective voting side, which seeks to understand how voters cope with the complexities of multiparty policymaking, which can obfuscate responsibility for policy outcomes (e.g., Powell and Whitten 1993; Fortunato et al. 2020). Of course, these camps have proceeded in relative isolation by necessity – these are hard problems to solve and we have only recently begun to directly engage with the idea that voters are reasonable and capable of coping with these complexities (even if imperfectly). However, moving forward, we must find a way to marry these theoretical approaches into a unified model of vote choice under multiparty governance in order to understand how voters are making these decisions and what relative weight they place on overall performance, ideological proximity, and *representational* competence, or, an unyielding approach to compromise. Understanding how voters' demand for ideological purity undermines their ability to select competent leadership who pursue policy goals that are preferred by the median citizen is critical to our ability to answer simple, yet pivotal, normative questions of democratic function.

Hold the Thread

There is a substantial drawback to all of this new modeling, however. To be frank: it is a messy endeavor and failing to step back and reconcile new work with old becomes easy. In other words, it is clear that a great deal of the theoretical work – on both the behavior of parties and the behavior of voters – simplified out the equation operations and interactions that we now understand to be vital components of the democratic process (e.g., government formation, multiparty policy bargaining, differential responsibility attribution, etc). Nonetheless, these models were parsimonious. They were effective. We learned from them and we have had to *un*learn a surprisingly small amount of what we thought we knew. With each new wrinkle and new complication comes new insights and new questions, but also potentially new constraints and new limitations and, although it is a difficult balance to strike, it is important to continue to strive for simplicity, generalizability, and *continuity* wherever possible. This does not necessarily mean limiting the number of moving parts in our models, but it does mean thinking through which moving parts are necessary and what are, or are not, reasonable constraints to place upon them.

For example, earlier, we characterized the coalition compromise model (Martin and Vanberg 2005) as a complication of the ministerial autonomy model (Laver and Shepsle 1996) to make a point about the evolution of our expectations for policy-making efficiency, which may have led some to conclude that the two were completely distinct, or that coalition compromise describes a smaller (or a necessarily more complicated) world than ministerial autonomy. But it is important to bear in mind that ministerial autonomy arises out of the coalition compromise model as a special case when policing costs are prohibitive. As such, coalition compromise allows us to understand a broader swath of policy-making behaviors through the addition of the policing wrinkle – the new parameter served to *increase* applicability. In other words, we did not have to abandon ministerial autonomy and everything that it helped us learn about multiparty governance in order to make our way to coalition compromise; we simply had to work through the parameter space to rediscover it, and, indeed, there *are* many cases where the institutional contexts in which governments operate create policymaking environments that are closer to ministerial dominance than coalition compromise.[5]

All of this is to say that, although it is fair to conclude that we have learned something new here about the implications of coalition policymaking for voter behavior and the way in which cabinet partners interact with one another in response to those voter behaviors, this does not erase what we have learned previously, it simply recontextualizes past lessons into a more nuanced yet simultaneously broader world of political interaction. This means that our progress need not be strictly additive – but that each new advance presents the opportunity to revisit past research and learn something new from it. Just as Laver and Shepsle (1996) allowed us to learn about the role of party positioning ("strong parties") in coalition bargaining that helped us to better understand the regularity of minority governments to complement what we were taught by Strøm's (1990b), Martin and Vanberg (2011) allowed us to learn about the role of policing institutions in coalition policymaking that helped us to better understand the regularities of qualitative portfolio allocation to complement what we were taught by Laver

---

[5] It should go without saying that, without ministerial dominance (Laver and Shepsle 1990, 1996) – and the work that it was built upon (e.g., Riker 1962; Shepsle 1979) – there would be no coalition compromise model (Martin and Vanberg 2011) and, without coalition compromise, we would not be having this discussion about coalitions' internal and external gravity and their implications for cabinet, voter, and market behaviors.

and Shepsle (1996). Here, we have discussed the necessity for compromise and cooperation in multiparty governance and the threat that this imposes upon the electoral fortunes of cabinet participants. We learned that voters dislike compromise and punish it at the ballot box, but also that the damage to party brands caused by compromise may have even longer lasting effects. This motivates parties to protect their brands by antagonizing their partners in coalition and creating a reputation for conflictual behavior that can, in fact, ameliorate potential electoral losses resulting from coalition participation. Hopefully, there are elements to the preceding chapters that will shed new light on previous findings to help move the field forward in understanding the cycle of governance – electoral behaviors, the formation of cabinets, policy-making processes, voter reactions, party adjustments, government dissolutions, and the real political economic implications of all of these actions on markets and the lived experience of citizens – as well as motivate new questions to answer.

Bibliography

Adams, James, Michael Clark, Lawrence Ezrow and Garrett Glasgow. 2006. "Are niche parties fundamentally different from mainstream parties? The causes and the electoral consequences of Western European parties' policy shifts, 1976–1998." *American Journal of Political Science* 50(3): 513–529.

Adams, James, Lawrence Ezrow, Samuel Merrill and Zeynep Somer-Topcu. 2013. "Does collective responsibility for performance alter party strategies? Policy-seeking parties in proportional systems." *British Journal of Political Science* 43(1): 1–23.

Adams, James, Lawrence Ezrow, and Zeynep Somer-Topcu. 2011. "Is anybody listening? Evidence that voters do not respond to European parties, policy statements during elections." *American Journal of Political Science* 55(2): 370–382.

Adams, James, Lawrence Ezrow, and Zeynep Somer-Topcu. 2014. "Do voters respond to party manifestos or to a wider information environment? An analysis of mass-elite linkages on European integration." *American Journal of Political Science* 58(4): 967–978.

Adams, James, Lawrence Ezrow and Christopher Wlezien. 2016. "The company you keep: How voters infer party positions on European integration from governing coalition arrangements." *American Journal of Political Science* 60(4): 811–823.

Adams, James and Zeynep Somer-Topcu. 2009. "Moderate now, win votes later: The electoral consequences of parties, policy shifts in 25 postwar democracies." *The Journal of Politics* 71(2): 678–692.

Adams, Jim, Simon Weschle, and Christopher Wlezien. 2020. "Elite Interactions and Voters' Perceptions of Parties' Policy Positions." *Forthcoming. American Journal of Political Science*

Alesina, Alberto and Howard Rosenthal. 1995. *Partisan Politics, Divided Government, and the Economy.* Cambridge University Press.

Alesina, Alberto, Sule Özler, Nouriel Roubini and Phillip Swagel. 1996. "Political instability and economic growth." *Journal of Economic Growth* 1(2): 189–211.

Andersen, Ellen Ø. 2016. "Gmo-afgrøder skal godkendes i Folketinget." *Politiken* May 21, 2016.

Anderson, Christopher J., André Blais, Shaun Bowler, Todd Donovan and Ola Listhaug. 2005. *Loser's Consent: Elections and Democratic Legitimacy*. New York: Oxford University Press.

Anderson, Christopher J. and Andrew J. LoTempio. 2002. "Winning, losing and political trust in America." *British Journal of Political Science* 32(2): 335–351.

Anderson, Christopher J. and Christine A. Guillory. 1997. "Political institutions and satisfaction with democracy: A cross-national analysis of consensus and majoritarian systems." *American Political Science Review* 91(1): 66–81.

Ansolabehere, Stephen, James M. Snyder Jr., Aaron B. Strauss and Michael M. Ting. 2005. "Voting weights and formateur advantages in the formation of coalition governments." *American Journal of Political Science* 49(3): 550–563.

Austen-Smith, David and Jeffrey Banks. 1990. "Stable governments and the allocation of policy portfolios." *American Political Science Review* 84(3): 891–906.

Babad, Elisha and Yosi Katz. 1991. "Wishful thinking – against all odds." *Journal of Applied Social Psychology* 21(23): 1921–1938.

Bargsted, Matias A. and Orit Kedar. 2009. "Coalition-targeted Duvergerian voting: How expectations affect voter choice under proportional representation." *American Journal of Political Science* 53(2): 307–323.

Baron, David P. 1991. "A spatial bargaining theory of government formation in parliamentary systems." *American Political Science Review* 85(1): 137–164.

Baron, David P. 1998. "Comparative dynamics of parliamentary governments." *American Political Science Review* 92(3): 593–609.

Bartels, Larry M. 1996. "Uninformed votes: Information effects in presidential elections." *American Journal of Political Science* 40(1): 194–230.

Baumgartner, Frank R. and Bryan D. Jones. 2010. *Agendas and Instability in American Politics*. Chicago: University of Chicago Press.

Bawn, Kathleen and Zeynep Somer-Topcu. 2012. "Government versus opposition at the polls: How governing status affects the impact of policy positions." *American Journal of Political Science* 56(2): 433–446.

Becher, Michael and Flemming Juul Christiansen. 2015. "Dissolution threats and legislative bargaining." *American Journal of Political Science* 59(3): 641–655.

Becher, Michael and Michael Donnelly. 2013. "Economic performance, individual evaluations, and the vote: Investigating the causal mechanism." *The Journal of Politics* 75(4): 968–979.

Beck, Nathaniel and Jonathan N. Katz. 2007. "Random coefficient models for time-series-cross"-section data: Monte Carlo experiments." *Political Analysis* 15(2): 182–195.

Benoit, Kenneth and Michael Laver. 2012. "The dimensionality of political space: Epistemological and methodological considerations." *European Union Politics* 13(2): 194–218.

Bernardi, Luca and James Adams. 2019. "Does government support respond to governments? Social welfare rhetoric or their spending? An analysis of government support in Britain, Spain and the United States." *British Journal of Political Science* 49(4): 1407–1429.

Bille, Lars. 2013. "Denmark." *European Journal of Political Research: Political Data Yearbook* 52(1): 56–60.

Boschee, Elizabeth, Jennifer Lautenschlager, Sean O'Brien, Steve Shellman, James Starz and Michael Ward. 2015. "ICEWS Coded Event Data."

Boseley, Sarah. 2011. "NHS bill 'will let Andrew Lansley wash his hands of health service'." *The Guardian* August 30.

Bowler, Shaun, Indridi H. Indridason, Thomas Bräuninger and Marc Debus. 2016. "Let's just agree to disagree: Dispute resolution mechanisms in coalition agreements." *The Journal of Politics* 78(4): 1264–1278.

Bowler, Shaun, Justin Freebourn, Jana Grittersova and Indridi H. Indridason. 2019. "Bonds, Bargaining Duration, and Political Uncertainty." *Manuscript: University of California, Riverside.*

Bräuninger, Thomas and Marc Debus. 2009. "Legislative agenda-setting in parliamentary democracies." *European Journal of Political Research* 48(6): 804–839.

Browne, Eric C., John P. Frendreis and Dennis W. Gleiber. 1984. "An 'Events' approach to the problem of cabinet stability." *Comparative Political Studies* 17: 167–197.

Bryson, Bill. 2003. *A Short History of Nearly Everything.* New York: Broadway Books.

Büthe, Tim and Helen V. Milner. 2008. "The politics of foreign direct investment into developing countries: Increasing FDI through international trade agreements?" *American Journal of Political Science* 52(4): 741–762.

Cable, Vince. 2017. "A Lib Dem perspective on centre-left politics post-2015." *The Political Quarterly* 88(1): 87–96.

Cain, Bruce, John Ferejohn and Morris Fiorina. 1987. *The Personal Vote: Constituency Service and Electoral Independence.* Cambridge, MA: Harvard University Press.

Camerra-Rowe, Pamela. 2004. "Agenda 2010: Redefining German social democracy." *German Politics and Society* 22(1): 1–30.

Campbell, Angus. 1960. "Surge and decline: A study of electoral change." *Public Opinion Quarterly* 24(3): 397–418.

Canes-Wrone, Brandice, David W. Brady and John F. Cogan. 2002. "Out of step, out of office: Electoral accountability and House members' voting." *American Political Science Review* 96(1): 127–140.

Card, David and Gordon B. Dahl. 2011. "Family violence and football: The effect of unexpected emotional cues on violent behavior." *The Quarterly Journal of Economics* 126(1): 103–143.

Carroll, Royce and Gary W. Cox. 2007. "The logic of Gamson's Law: Pre-election coalitions and portfolio allocations." *American Journal of Political Science* 51(2): 300–313.

Carroll, Royce and Gary W. Cox. 2012. "Shadowing ministers: Monitoring partners in coalition governments." *Comparative Political Studies* 45(2): 220–236.

Carson, Jamie L., Gregory Koger, Matthew J. Lebo and Everett Young. 2010. "The electoral costs of party loyalty in Congress." *American Journal of Political Science* 54(3): 598–616.

Chiba, Daina, Lanny W. Martin and Randolph T. Stevenson. 2015. "A copula approach to the problem of selection bias in models of government survival." *Political Analysis* 23(1): 42–58.

Clegg, Nick. 2010. "Nick Clegg's speech to Liberal Democrat Conference." *Liberal Democrats Conference, September 20, 2010*. Liverpool.

Clegg, Nick. 2011. "Nick Clegg's speech to Liberal Democrat Conference." *Liberal Democrats Conference, September 21, 2011*. Birmingham.

Clegg, Nick. 2013. "Extracts of Nick Clegg's Speech on Governing Until 2015." *UK Liberal Democrats, May 22, 2013*.

Clegg, Nick. 2016. *Politics: Between the Extremes*. New York: Random House.

Clinton, Bill. 2011. "Interview with Jon Stewart". In *The Daily Show with Jon Stewart*. Vol. Season 17, Episode 18. New York: Comedy Central.

Converse, Philip E. 1966. "The concept of a normal vote." *Elections and the Political Order* 9: 39.

Cox, Gary W. 1985. "Electoral equilibrium under approval voting." *American Journal of Political Science* 29(1): 112–118.

Cox, Gary W. 1990. "Centripetal and centrifugal incentives in electoral systems." *American Journal of Political Science* 34(4): 903–935.

Cox, Gary W. and Mathew D. McCubbins. 2005. *Setting the Agenda: Responsible Party Government in the US House of Representatives*. New York: Cambridge University Press.

Crisman-Cox, Casey. 2019. "Democracy, Reputation for Resolve, and Civil Conflict." *Manuscript: Texas A&M University*.

Crisman-Cox, Casey and Michael Gibilisco. 2018. "Audience costs and the dynamics of war and peace." *American Journal of Political Science* 62(3): 566–580.

Curtice, John and Clive Payne. 1991. "Local elections as national referendums in Great Britain." *Electoral Studies* 10(1): 3–17.

De Swaan, Abram. 1973. *Coalition Theories and Government Formation*. Amsterdam: Elsevier.

DeJoy, David M. 1989. "The optimism bias and traffic accident risk perception." *Accident Analysis & Prevention* 21(4): 333–340.

Dewan, Torun and Arthur Spirling. 2011. "Strategic opposition and government cohesion in Westminster democracies." *American Political Science Review* 105(2): 337–358.

Diermeier, Daniel, Hülya Eraslan and Antonio Merlo. 2003. "A structural model of government formation." *Econometrica* 71(1): 27–70.

Diermeier, Daniel and Peter Van Roozendaal. 1998. "The duration of cabinet formation processes in western multi-party democracies." *British Journal of Political Science* 28(4): 609–626.

Diermeier, Daniel and Randolph T. Stevenson. 2000. "Cabinet terminations and critical events." *American Political Science Review* 94(3): 627–640.

Diermeier, Daniel and Randolph T. Stevenson. 1999. "Cabinet survival and competing risks." *American Journal of Political Science* 43(4): 1051–1068.

Döring, Herbert. 2001. "Parliamentary agenda control and legislative outcomes in Western Europe." *Legislative Studies Quarterly* 26(1): 145–165.

Döring, Herbert, ed. 1995. *Parliaments and Majority Rule in Western Europe*. New York: St. Martin's Press.

Döring, Holger and Philip Manow. 2011. "Parliament and government composition database (ParlGov): A short introduction." *White Paper* pp. 1–12.

Downs, Anthony. 1957. *An Economic Theory of Democracy*. New York: Harper and Row.

Duch, Raymond M., Jeff May and David A. Armstrong. 2010. "Coalition-directed voting in multiparty democracies." *American Political Science Review* 104(04): 698–719.

Duch, Raymond M. and Randolph T. Stevenson. 2008. *The Economic Vote: How Political and Economic Institutions Condition Election Results*. Cambridge: Cambridge University Press.

Economist. 2011a. "Gallows humour: The good and bad reasons for the Lib Dems' strange optimism." *September 24, 2011* p. 70.

Economist. 2011b. "A Long, Unhappy Marriage." *September 24, 2011* pp. 67–68.

Economist. 2012. "Dutch Surprise: Voters may get what they least expected: a stable two-party coalition." *September 15, 2012* p. 34.

Edmans, Alex, Diego Garcia and Øyvind Norli. 2007. "Sports sentiment and stock returns." *The Journal of Finance* 62(4): 1967–1998.

Eichorst, Jason. 2014. "Explaining variation in coalition agreements: The electoral and policy motivations for drafting agreements." *European Journal of Political Research* 53(1): 98–115.

Eren, Ozkan and Naci Mocan. 2018. "Emotional judges and unlucky juveniles." *American Economic Journal: Applied Economics* 10(3): 171–205.

Erikson, Robert S. 1971. "The electoral impact of congressional roll call voting." *American Political Science Review* 65(4): 1018–1032.

Erikson, Robert S. and Mikhail G. Filippov. 2001. "Electoral balancing in federal and sub-national elections: the case of Canada." *Constitutional Political Economy* 12(4): 313–331.

Ezrow, Lawrence. 2008. "Research note: On the inverse relationship between votes and proximity for niche parties." *European Journal of Political Research* 47(2): 206–220.

Falcó-Gimeno, Albert and Jordi Muñoz. 2017. "Show me your friends: a survey experiment on the effect of coalition signals." The Journal of Politics 79(4): 1454–1459.

Falcó-Gimeno, Albert and Pablo Fernandez-Vazquez. 2020. "Choices that matter: Coalition formation and parties' ideological reputations." *Political Science Research and Methods* 8(2): 285–300.

Fearon, James D. 1994. "Domestic political audiences and the escalation of international disputes." *American Political Science Review* 88(3): 577–592.

Fernandez-Vazquez, Pablo. 2018. "Voter discounting of party campaign manifestos: An analysis of mainstream and niche parties in Western Europe, 1971–2011." *Party Politics* 26: 471–483

Fernandez-Vazquez, Pablo. 2019. "The credibility of party policy rhetoric survey experimental evidence." *The Journal of Politics* 81(1): 309–314.

Fernandez-Vazquez, Pablo and Zeynep Somer-Topcu. 2019. "The informational role of party leader changes on voter perceptions of party positions." *British Journal of Political Science* 49(3): 977–999.

Fiorina, Morris P. 1981. "Retrospective voting in American national elections.".

Fortunato, David. 2019a. "The electoral implications of coalition policy-making." *British Journal of Political Science* 49: 59–80.

Fortunato, David. 2019b. "Legislative review and party differentiation in coalition governments." *American Political Science Review* 113(1): 242–247.

Fortunato, David and Ian R. Turner. 2018. "Legislative capacity and credit risk." *American Journal of Political Science* 62(3): 623–636.

Fortunato, David and James Adams. 2015. "How voters' perceptions of junior coalition partners depend on the prime minister's position." *European Journal of Political Research* 54(3): 601–621.

Fortunato, David, Lanny W. Martin and Georg Vanberg. 2019. "Committee chairs and legislative review in parliamentary democracies." *British Journal of Political Science* 49(2): 785–797.

Fortunato, David and Matt W. Loftis. 2018. "Cabinet durability and fiscal discipline." *American Political Science Review.* 112(4): 939–953.

Fortunato, David and Nathan W. Monroe. 2020. "Agenda control and electoral success in the US House." *British Journal of Political Science* pp. 1–11.

Fortunato, David, Nick C. N. Lin, Randolph T. Stevenson and Mathias Tromborg. 2020. "Attributing Policy Influence under Multiparty Governance." *American Political Science Review. Forthcoming.*

Fortunato, David and Randolph T. Stevenson. 2013. "Perceptions of partisan ideologies: The effect of coalition participation." *American Journal of Political Science* 57(2): 459–477.

Fortunato, David and Randolph T. Stevenson. 2018. "Heuristics and Coalition Expectations." Manuscript. Rice University.

Fortunato, David, Thiago Silva and Laron K. Williams. 2020. Strategies for Studying Voters? Perceptions of Party Brands. In 8th Annual Conference of the European Political Science Association (EPSA), Vienna, Austria.

Fortunato, David, Thomas König and Sven-Oliver Proksch. 2013. "Government agenda-setting and bicameral conflict resolution." *Political Research Quarterly* 66(4): 938–951.

Franklin, Mark N. and Thomas T. Mackie. 1984. "Reassessing the importance of size and ideology for the formation of governing coalitions in parliamentary democracies." *American Journal of Political Science* 28(4): 671–692.

Gamson, William A. 1961. "A theory of coalition formation." *American Sociological Review* 26(3): 373–382.

Glasgow, Garrett, Matt Golder and Sona N. Golder. 2011. "Who 'wins'? Determining the party of the prime minister." *American Journal of Political Science* 55(4): 937–954.

Goldstein, Joshua S. 1992. "A conflict-cooperation scale for WEIS events data." *Journal of Conflict Resolution* 36(2): 369–385.

Griffith, John Aneurin Grey. 1974. *Parliamentary Scrutiny of Government Bills.* London: Allen and Unwin for PEP and the Study of Parliament Group.

Grimmer, Justin. 2013. "Appropriators not position takers: The distorting effects of electoral incentives on congressional representation." *American Journal of Political Science* 57(3): 624–642.

Grofman, Bernard. 1985. "The neglected role of the status quo in models of issue voting." *The Journal of Politics* 47(01): 229–237.

Hainmueller, Jens, Daniel J. Hopkins and Teppei Yamamoto. 2014. "Causal inference in conjoint analysis: Understanding multidimensional choices via stated preference experiments." *Political Analysis* 22(1): 1–30.

Hanmer, Michael J. and Kerem Ozan Kalkan. 2013. "Behind the curve: Clarifying the best approach to calculating predicted probabilities and marginal effects from limited dependent variable models." *American Journal of Political Science* 57(1): 263–277.

Harbridge, Laurel and Neil Malhotra. 2011. "Electoral incentives and partisan conflict in congress: Evidence from survey experiments." *American Journal of Political Science* 55(3): 494–510.

Harbridge, Laurel, Neil Malhotra and Brian F Harrison. 2014. "Public Preferences for Bipartisanship in the Policymaking Process." *Legislative Studies Quarterly* 39(3): 327–355.

Healy, Andrew J., Neil Malhotra and Cecilia Hyunjung Mo. 2010. "Irrelevant events affect voters' evaluations of government performance." *Proceedings of the National Academy of Sciences* 107(29): 12804–12809.

Heller, William B. 2001. "Making policy stick: Why the government gets what it wants in multiparty parliaments." *American Journal of Political Science* 45(4): 780–798.

Helweg-Larsen, Marie and James A. Shepperd. 2001. "Do moderators of the optimistic bias affect personal or target risk estimates? A review of the literature." *Personality and Social Psychology Review* 5(1): 74–95.

Hibbing, John R. and Elizabeth Theiss-Morse. 2002. *Stealth Democracy: Americans' Beliefs about How Government Should Work*. New York: Cambridge University Press.

Hobolt, Sara Binzer and Jill Wittrock. 2011. "The second-order election model revisited: An experimental test of vote choices in European Parliament elections." *Electoral Studies* 30(1): 29–40.

Hobolt, Sara, James Tilley and Susan Banducci. 2013. "Clarity of responsibility: How government cohesion conditions performance voting." *European Journal of Political Research* 52(2): 164–187.

Honaker, James, Gary King, Matthew Blackwell et al. 2011. "Amelia II: A program for missing data." *Journal of Statistical Software* 45(7): 1–47.

House of Commons. 2010. *Standing Orders of the House of Commons: Public Business*. London, The Stationary Office.

Huber, John D. 1996. "The vote of confidence in parliamentary democracies." *American Political Science Review* 90(2): 269–282.

Huber, John D. 1998. "How does cabinet instability affect political performance? Portfolio volatility and health care cost containment in parliamentary democracies." *American Political Science Review* 92(3): 577–591.

Huber, John D. and Charles R. Shipan. 2002. *Deliberate Discretion: The Institutional Foundations of Bureaucratic Autonomy*. Cambridge: Cambridge University Press.

Huber, John D., Charles R. Shipan and Madelaine Pfahler. 2001. "Legislatures and statutory control of bureaucracy." *American Journal of Political Science* 45(2): 330–345.

Imai, Kosuke, James Lo and Jonathan Olmsted. 2016. "Fast estimation of ideal points with massive data." *American Political Science Review* 110(4): 631–656.

Indridason, Indridi H. and Christopher Kam. 2008. "Cabinet reshuffles and ministerial drift." *British Journal of Political Science* 38(04): 621–656.

International Monetary Fund. 2017. "World Economic Outlook Database.".

Jones, Bryan D and Frank R Baumgartner. 2005. *The Politics of Attention: How Government Prioritizes Problems*. Chicago: University of Chicago Press.

Kahneman, Daniel and Amos Tversky. 1977. Intuitive prediction: Biases and corrective procedures. Technical report, Decisions and Designs Inc. Mclean Va.

Kam, Christopher J. 2009. *Party Discipline and Parliamentary Politics*. New York: Cambridge University Press.

Kayser, Mark Andreas and Michael Peress. 2012. "Benchmarking across borders: electoral accountability and the necessity of comparison." *American Political Science Review* 106(03): 661–684.

Kedar, Orit. 2005. "When moderate voters prefer extreme parties: Policy balancing in parliamentary elections." *American Political Science Review* 99(2): 185–199.

Kedar, Orit. 2006. "How voters work around institutions: Policy balancing in staggered elections." *Electoral Studies* 25(3): 509–527.

Kedar, Orit. 2009. *Voting for Policy, not Parties: How Voters Compensate for Power Sharing*. New York: Cambridge University Press.

Key, Valdimer Orlando et al. 1955. "Politics, parties, and pressure groups." New York: Crowell.

Key, Valdimer Orlando et al. 1966. *The Responsible Electorate*. Cambridge, MA: Belknap Press of Harvard University Press.

Kim, Dong-Hun and Gerhard Loewenberg. 2005. "Committees in coalition governments." *Comparative Political Studies* 38(9): 1104–1129.

King, Gary, James E. Alt, Nancy E. Burns and Michael Laver. 1990. "A Unified Model of Cabinet Dissolution in Parliamentary Democracies." *American Journal of Political Science* 34(3): 846–71.

King, Gary, James Honaker, Anne Joseph and Kenneth Scheve. 2001. "Analyzing incomplete political science data: An alternative algorithm for multiple imputation." *American Political Science Review* 95(1): 49–70.

Lauderdale, Benjamin E. and Alexander Herzog. 2016. "Measuring political positions from legislative speech." *Political Analysis* 24(3): 374–394.

Laver, Michael and Kenneth A. Shepsle. 1990. "Coalitions and cabinet government." *American Political Science Review* 84(3): 873–890.

Laver, Michael and Kenneth A. Shepsle. 1998. "Events, equilibria, and government survival." *American Journal of Political Science* 42(1): 28–54.

Laver, Michael and Kenneth Shepsle. 1996. *Making and Breaking Governments: Cabinets and Legislatures in Parliamentary Democracies*. Cambridge: Cambridge University Press.

Laver, Michael and Kenneth Shepsle, eds. 1994. *Cabinet Ministers and Parliamentary Government*. Cambridge: Cambridge University Press.

Lewis-Beck, Michael S. 1988. "Economics and the American voter: Past, present, future." *Political Behavior* 10(1): 5–21.

Lewis, Jeffrey B. and Drew A. Linzer. 2005. "Estimating regression models in which the dependent variable is based on estimates." *Political Analysis* 13(4): 345–364.

Liberal Democratic Party. 2010. "Change that works for you." *Building a Fairer Britain.*

Lipsmeyer, Christine S. and Heather Nicole Pierce. 2011. "The eyes that bind: Junior ministers as oversight mechanisms in coalition governments." *The Journal of Politics* 73(04): 1152–1164.

Loewenstein, George F., Leigh Thompson and Max H. Bazerman. 1989. "Social utility and decision making in interpersonal contexts." *Journal of Personality and Social Psychology* 57(3): 426.

Lohmann, Susanne, David W. Brady and Douglas Rivers. 1997. "Party identification, retrospective voting, and moderating elections in a federal system: West Germany, 1961-1989." *Comparative Political Studies* 30(4): 420–449.

Lowe, Will, Kenneth Benoit, Slava Mikhaylov and Michael Laver. 2011. "Scaling policy preferences from coded political texts." *Legislative Studies Quarterly* 36(1): 123–155.

Lucardie, Paul and Gerrit Voerman. 1996. "The Netherlands." *European Journal of Political Research* 30: 415–419.

Lucardie, Paul and Gerrit Voerman. 1997. "The Netherlands." *European Journal of Political Research* 32: 447–449.

Lucardie, Paul and Gerrit Voerman. 1998. "The Netherlands." *European Journal of Political Research* 34: 471–473.

Luebbert, Gregory. 1986. *Comparative Democracy: Policy Making and Governing Coalitions in Europe and Israel*. New York: Columbia University Press.

Lund, Kenneth. 2013. "Folketinget har vedtaget omstridt offentlighedslov." *Politiken* Jun 4, 2013.

Lupia, Arthur and Kaare Strøm. 1995. "Coalition Termination and the Strategic Timing of Parliamentary Elections." *American Political Science Review* 89(3): 648–665.

Lupu, Noam. 2013. "Party brands and partisanship: Theory with evidence from a survey experiment in Argentina." *American Journal of Political Science* 57(1): 49–64.

Luskin, Robert C. 1987. "Measuring political sophistication." *American Journal of Political Science* 31(4): 856–899.

Lyall, Sarah. 2010. "Protests Over Rise in Tuition Take Violent Turn in London." *New York Times* p. A6.

Mair, Peter and Ingrid Van Biezen. 2001. "Party membership in twenty European democracies, 1980-2000." *Party Politics* 7(1): 5–21.

Mansbridge, Jane. 2003. "Rethinking representation." *American Political Science Review* 97(4): 515–528.

Martin, Lanny W. 2004. "The government agenda in parliamentary democracies." *American Journal of Political Science* 48(3): 445–461.

Martin, Lanny W. and Georg Vanberg. 2003. "Wasting time? The impact of ideology and size on delay in coalition formation." *British Journal of Political Science* 33: 323–332.

Martin, Lanny W. and Georg Vanberg. 2004. "Policing the Bargain: Coalition government and parliamentary scrutiny." *American Journal of Political Science* 48(1): 13–27.

Martin, Lanny W. and Georg Vanberg. 2005. "Coalition policymaking and legislative review." *American Political Science Review* 99: 93–106.

Martin, Lanny W. and Georg Vanberg. 2008. "Coalition government and political communication." *Political Research Quarterly* 61: 502–516.

Martin, Lanny W. and Georg Vanberg. 2011. *Parliaments and Coalitions: The Role of Legislative Institutions in Multiparty Governance.* Oxford University Press.

Martin, Lanny W. and Georg Vanberg. 2014. "Parties and Policymaking in Multiparty Governments: The Legislative Median, Ministerial Autonomy, and the Coalition Compromise." *American Journal of Political Science* 58(4): 979–996.

Martin, Lanny W. and Georg Vanberg. 2020. "What You See is Not Always What You Get: Bargaining Before an Audience Under Multiparty Government." Forthcoming. *American Political Science Review.*

Martin, Lanny W. and Randolph T. Stevenson. 2001. "Government formation in parliamentary democracies." *American Journal of Political Science* 45(1): 33–50.

Martin, Lanny W. and Randolph T. Stevenson. 2010. "The Conditional Impact of Incumbency on Government Formation in Parliamentary Democracies." *American Political Science Review*, 104(3), 503–518.

Mattson, Ingvar and Kaare Strøm. 1995. Parliamentary Committees. In *Parliaments and Majority Rule in Western Europe*, ed. Herbert Döring. New York: St. Martin's Press.

Mayhew, David R. 1974. *Congress: The Electoral Connection.* New Haven: Yale University Press.

Mayhew, David R. 1991. *Divided We Govern.* New Haven: Yale University Press.

McFadden, Daniel L. 1973. Conditional Logit Analysis of Qualitative Choice Behaviour. In *Frontiers in Econometrics*, ed. P. Zarembka. New York: Academic Press.

Meguid, Bonnie M. 2005. "Competition between unequals: The role of mainstream party strategy in niche party success." *American Political Science Review* 99(03): 347–359.

Merlo, Antonio. 1997. "Bargaining over governments in a stochastic environment." *Journal of Political Economy* 105(1): 101–131.

Miller, Warren E. 1991. "Party identification, realignment, and party voting: Back to the basics." *American Political Science Review* 85(2): 557–568.

Moore, Will H. and Bumba Mukherjee. 2006. "Coalition government formation and foreign exchange markets: Theory and evidence from Europe." *International Studies Quarterly* 50(1): 93–118.

Morelli, Massimo. 1999. "Demand competition and policy compromise in legislative bargaining." *American Political Science Review* 93(4): 809–820.

Mueller, John E. 1970. "Presidential popularity from Truman to Johnson." *American Political Science Review* 64(1): 18–34.

Mueller, John E. 1973. *War, Presidents, and Public Opinion*. New York: Wiley New York.

Mughan, Anthony. 1986. "Toward a political explanation of government vote losses in midterm by-elections." *American Political Science Review* 80(3): 761–775.

Müller, Wolfgang C. and Kaare Strøm. 1999. *Policy, Office, or Votes? How Political Parties in Western Europe Make Hard Decisions*. Cambridge: Cambridge University Press.

Müller, Wolfgang C. and Kaare Strøm. 2003. *Coalition Governments in Western Europe*. New York: Oxford University Press.

Müller, Wolfgang C. and Kaare Strøm, eds. 2000. *Coalition Governments in Western Europe*. Oxford: Oxford University Press.

Nannestad, Peter and Martin Paldam. 2002. "The Cost of Ruling". In *Economic Voting*, ed. Han Dorussen and Michaell Taylor. New York: Routledge pp. 17–44.

Naurin, Elin, Terry J. Royed and Robert Thomson. 2019. *Party Mandates and Democracy: Making, Breaking, and Keeping Election Pledges in Twelve Countries*. New Comparative Politics.

Paldam, Martin. 1986. "The distribution of election results and the two explanations of the cost of ruling." *European Journal of Political Economy* 2(1): 5–24.

Paldam, Martin and Peter Skott. 1995. "A rational-voter explanation of the cost of ruling." *Public Choice* 83(1–2): 159–172.

Poguntke, Thomas. 2011. "Germany." *European Journal of Political Research: Political Data Yearbook* 50(7–8): 980–984.

Poole, Keith T. 2005. *Spatial Models of Parliamentary Voting*. New York: Cambridge University Press.

Poole, Keith T. and Howard Rosenthal. 2000. *Congress: A Political-economic History of Roll Call Voting*. New York: Oxford University Press on Demand.

Powell, G. Bingham. 2000. *Elections as Instruments of Democracy: Majoritarian and Proportional Views*. New Haven: Yale University Press.

Powell, G. Bingham. 2019. *Ideological Representation—Achieved and Astray: Elections, Institutions and the Breakdown of Ideological Congruence In Parliamentary Democracies*. New York: Cambridge University Press.

Powell, G. Bingham and Guy D. Whitten. 1993. "A cross-national analysis of economic voting: taking account of the political context." *American Journal of Political Science* 37(2): 391–414.

Prior, Markus. 2005. "News vs. entertainment: How increasing media choice widens gaps in political knowledge and turnout." *American Journal of Political Science* 49(3): 577–592.

Proksch, Sven-Oliver, Will Lowe, Jens Wäckerle and Stuart Soroka. 2019. "Multilingual sentiment analysis: A new approach to measuring conflict in legislative speeches." *Legislative Studies Quarterly* 44(1): 97–131.

Puri, Manju and David T. Robinson. 2007. "Optimism and economic choice." *Journal of Financial Economics* 86(1): 71–99.

Ramirez, Mark D. 2009. "The dynamics of partisan conflict on congressional approval." *American Journal of Political Science* 53(3): 681–694.

Redlawsk, David P. 2002. "Hot cognition or cool consideration? Testing the effects of motivated reasoning on political decision making." *The Journal of Politics* 64(4): 1021–1044.

Reif, Karlheinz and Hermann Schmitt. 1980. "Nine second-order national elections – a conceptual framework for the analysis of European Election results." *European Journal of Political Research* 8(1): 3–44.

Riker, William. 1962. *The Theory of Political Coalitions*. New Haven: Yale University Press.

Rubin, Donald B. 2004. *Multiple Imputation for Nonresponse in Surveys*. Vol. 81, Hoboken, NJ: John Wiley & Sons.

Russo, Federico and Matti Wiberg. 2010. "Parliamentary questioning in 17 European parliaments: Some steps towards comparison." *The Journal of Legislative Studies* 16(2): 215–232.

Sagarzazu, Iñaki and Heike Klüver. 2017. "Coalition governments and party competition: Political communication strategies of coalition parties." *Political Science Research and Methods* 5(2): 333–349.

Scarrow, Howard A. 1960. "Federal-provincial voting patterns in Canada." *Canadian Journal of Economics and Political Science/Revue canadienne de economiques et science politique* 26(2): 289–298.

Scheve, Kenneth and Michael Tomz. 1999. "Electoral surprise and the midterm loss in US congressional elections." *British Journal of Political Science* 29(03): 507–521.

Schmitt, Hermann and Renato Mannheimer. 1991. "About voting and non-voting in the European elections of June 1989." *European Journal of Political Research* 19(1): 31–54.

Schneider, Christina J. and Branislav L. Slantchev. 2018. "The domestic politics of international cooperation: Germany and the European debt crisis." *International Organization* 72(1): 1–31.

Schoenbebger, Robert A. 1969. "Campaign strategy and party loyalty: the electoral relevance of candidate decision-making in the 1964 congressional elections." *American Political Science Review* 63(2): 515–520.

Schofield, Norman and Michael Laver. 1985. "Bargaining theory and portfolio payoffs in European coalition governments 1945–83." *British Journal of Political Science* 15(2): 143–164.

Schumacher, Gijs, Marc Van de Wardt, Barbara Vis and Michael Baggesen Klitgaard. 2015. "How aspiration to office conditions the impact of government participation on party platform change." *American Journal of Political Science* 59(4): 1040–1054.

Schwander, Hanna and Philip Manow. 2017. "'Modernize and Die'? German social democracy and the electoral consequences of the Agenda 2010." *Socio-Economic Review* 15(1): 117–134.

Seki, Katsunori and Laron K. Williams. 2014. "Updating the party government data set." *Electoral Studies* 34: 270–279.

Shepsle, Kenneth A. 1979. "Institutional arrangements and equilibrium in multidimensional voting models." *American Journal of Political Science* 23(1): 27–59.

Shively, W. Phillips. 1972. "Party identification, party choice, and voting stability: the Weimar case." *American Political Science Review* 66(4): 1203–1225.

Signorino, Curtis S. and Jeffrey M. Ritter. 1999. "Tau-b or not tau-b: Measuring the similarity of foreign policy positions." *International Studies Quarterly* 43(1): 115–144.

Slapin, Jonathan B., Justin H. Kirkland, Joseph A. Lazzaro, Patrick A. Leslie and Tom O'Grady. 2018. "Ideology, grandstanding, and strategic party disloyalty in the British Parliament." *American Political Science Review* 112(1): 15–30.

Slapin, Jonathan B. and Sven-Oliver Proksch. 2008. "A scaling model for estimating time-series party positions from texts." *American Journal of Political Science* 52(3): 705–722.

Somer-Topcu, Zeynep. 2009. "Timely decisions: The effects of past national elections on party policy change." *The Journal of Politics* 71(01): 238–248.

Soroka, Stuart N. and Christopher Wlezien. 2010. *Degrees of Democracy: Politics, Public Opinion, and Policy*. New York: Cambridge University Press.

Spoon, Jae-Jae and Heike Klüver. 2017. "Does anybody notice? How policy positions of coalition parties are perceived by voters." *European Journal of Political Research* 56(1): 115–132.

Stevenson, Randolph T. 2002. "The cost of ruling, cabinet duration, and the "median-gap" model." *Public Choice* 113(1-2): 157–178.

Strøm, Kaare. 1990a. "A behavioral theory of competitive political parties." *American Journal of Political Science* 34(2): 565–98.

Strøm, Kaare. 1990b. *Minority Government and Majority Rule*. Cambridge: Cambridge University Press.

Strøm, Kaare. 1998. "Parliamentary committees in European democracies." *The Journal of Legislative Studies* 4(1): 21–59.

Strøm, Kaare, Ian Budge and Michael Laver. 1994. "Constraints on government formation in parliamentary democracies." *American Journal of Political Science* 38(2): 303–335.

Strøm, Kaare and Wolfgang C. Müller. 1999. "The keys to togetherness: Coalition agreements in parliamentary democracies." *The Journal of Legislative Studies* 5(3-4): 255–282.

Strøm, Kaare, Wolfgang Müller and Torbjörn Bergman, eds. 2008. *Cabinets and Coalition Bargaining: The Democratic Life Cycle in Western Europe*. Oxford: Oxford University Press.

Taber, Charles S. and Milton Lodge. 2006. "Motivated skepticism in the evaluation of political beliefs." *American Journal of Political Science* 50(3): 755–769.

Tajfel, Henri, Michael G. Billig, Robert P. Bundy and Claude Flament. 1971. "Social categorization and intergroup behaviour." *European Journal of Social Psychology* 1(2): 149–178.

Tavits, Margit. 2008. "The role of parties' past behavior in coalition formation." *American Political Science Review* 102(04): 495–507.

The Cabinet Office. 2010. *Ministerial Code*. The UK Civil Service.

Thies, Michael F. 2001. "Keeping tabs on partners: The logic of delegation in coalition governments." *American Journal of Political Science* 45(3): 580–598.

Thompson, Leigh, Kathleen L. Valley and Roderick M. Kramer. 1995. "The bittersweet feeling of success: An examination of social perception in negotiation." *Journal of Experimental Social Psychology* 31(6): 467–492.

Thompson, Louise. 2012. "More of the same or a period of change? The impact of bill committees in the twenty-first century House of Commons." *Parliamentary Affairs* 66(3): 459–479.

Thompson, Louise. 2015. *Making British Law: Committees in Action*. New York: Springer.

Thompson, Louise and Tony McNulty. 2018. "Committee Scrutiny of Legislation". In *Exploring Parliament*, ed. Cristina Leston-Bandeira and Louise Thompson. Oxford: Oxford University Press pp. 90–99.

Thomson, Robert, Terry Royed, Elin Naurin, Joaquín Artés, Rory Costello, Laurenz Ennser-Jedenastik, Mark Ferguson, Petia Kostadinova, Catherine Moury, François Pétry et al. 2017. "The fulfillment of parties? election pledges: A comparative study on the impact of power sharing." *American Journal of Political Science* 61(3): 527–542.

Timmermans, Arco I. 2003. *High Politics in the Low Countries: An Empirical Study of Coalition Agreements in Belgium and the Netherlands*. Burlington, VT: Ashgate Publishing.

Tomz, Michael. 2007. "Domestic audience costs in international relations: An experimental approach." *International Organization* 61(4): 821–840.

Tomz, Michael and Robert P. Van Houweling. 2012. "Political pledges as credible commitments." Manuscript Stanford University.

Train, Kenneth. 2003. *Discrete Choice Methods with Simulation*. Cambridge: Cambridge University Press.

Tsebelis, George. 1995. "Decision making in political systems: Veto players in presidentialism, parliamentarism, multicameralism and multipartyism." *British Journal of Political Science* 25(3): 289–325.

Tsebelis, George. 2002. *Veto Players: How Political Institutions Work*. Princeton, NJ: Princeton University Press.

Tufte, Edward R. 1975. "Determinants of the outcomes of midterm congressional elections." *American Political Science Review* 69(03): 812–826.

Van Der Velden, Mariken, Gijs Schumacher and Barbara Vis. 2018. "Living in the past or living in the future? Analyzing parties' platform change in between elections, the Netherlands 1997–2014." *Political Communication* 35(3): 393–412.

Voeten, Erik. 2000. "Clashes in the assembly." *International Organization* 54(2): 185–215.

Volkens, Andrea et al. 2017. "The Manifesto Data Collection. Version 2017b.".

Wagner, Markus, Nick Vivyan, and Konstantin Glinitzer. 2019. "Costly signals: Voter responses to parliamentary dissent in Austria, Britain, and Germany." *Legislative Studies Quarterly* Forthcoming.

Wagner, Markus, Nick Vivyan and Konstantin Glinitzer. 2019. "Costly Signals: Voter responses to parliamentary dissent in austria, britain, and germany." *Legislative Studies Quarterly* Forthcoming.

Walter, Stefanie. 2016. "Crisis politics in Europe: Why austerity is easier to implement in some countries than in others." *Comparative Political Studies* 49(7): 841–873.

Warwick, Paul. 1979. "The durability of coalition governments in parliamentary democracies." *Comparative Political Studies* 11(4): 465–498.

Warwick, Paul V. 1996. "Coalition government membership in West European parliamentary democracies." *British Journal of Political Science* 26(4): 471–499.

Warwick, Paul V. and James N. Druckman. 2001. "Portfolio salience and the proportionality of payoffs in coalition governments." *British Journal of Political Science* 31(4): 627–649.

Weeks, Jessica L. 2012. "Strongmen and straw men: Authoritarian regimes and the initiation of international conflict." *American Political Science Review* 106(2): 326–347.

Weinstein, Neil D. 1980. "Unrealistic optimism about future life events." *Journal of Personality and Social Psychology* 39(5): 806.

Wells, Anthony. 2018. "Voting Intention since 2010." *UK Polling Report*.

Weschle, Simon. 2018. "Quantifying political relationships." *American Political Science Review* 112(4): 1090–1095.

Willumsen, David M., Christian Stecker and Klaus H. Goetz. 2018. "The electoral connection in staggered parliaments: Evidence from Australia, France, Germany and Japan." *European Journal of Political Research* 57(3): 759–780.

Woods, Richard. 2004. "Exploring the emotional territory for brands." *Journal of Consumer Behaviour: An International Research Review* 3(4): 388–403.

Zillmann, Dolf, Jennings Bryant and Barry S. Sapolsky. 1989. Enjoyment from Sports Spectatorship. In *Sports, Games, and Play: Social and Psychological Viewpoints*, ed. Jeffrey H. Goldstein. New York: Psychology Press pp. 248–285.

Zillmann, Dolf and Paul B. Paulus. 1993. *Spectators: Reactions to Sports Events and Effects on Athletic Performance*. New York: Macmillan, pp. 600–619.

Zuber, Richard A., Patrick Yiu, Reinhold P. Lamb and John M. Gandar. 2005. "Investor–fans? An examination of the performance of publicly traded English Premier League teams." *Applied Financial Economics* 15(5): 305–313.

Index

CPSIA information can be obtained
at www.ICGtesting.com
Printed in the USA
LVHW110411190821
695648LV00002B/156

9 781108 834803